D1402620

Selected
Works from

THE DAYTON ART INSTITUTE

Permanent Collection

THE DAYTON ART INSTITUTE

All rights reserved. No part of the book may be reproduced in any form or by any electronic or mechanical means without permission in writing from the publisher, except by a reviewer, who may quote brief passages in a review.

The production of this catalogue was supported in part by grants from the National Endowment for the Arts and by the James F. Dicke Family.

First Edition
Library of Congress Catalog Card Number 98-74397
ISBN 0-937809-18-7 (paperback)
ISBN 0-937809-19-5 (hard cover)

Copyright © 1999 The Dayton Art Institute
Published in 1999 by The Dayton Art Institute (Dayton, Ohio)

Typeset in BBodoni
Printed on 80 lb. Glen Eagle Dull Text and 120 lb. Cover
Printed by Brown & Kroger Printing Company

Printed in the United States of America

Staff Editors	Eileen E. Carr *Curator of Education, 1990-1997* Heather H. Galecka *Communications Manager* Sara W. Spidel *Director of Marketing and Communications*
Content Editors	James O. Caswell Charles Eldredge J. Patrice Marandel William and Elsie Peck Dorie Reents-Budet
Project Coordinators	Patricia Huls *Curatorial Assistant, 1990-1995* Lora Stowe *Curatorial Assistant*
Catalogue Design	Jennifer Perry *Art Director*
Color Corrections	Dan Mueller
Photography by	Bill Swartz, BBS Images ©1998, Christie's Images (pp. 37, 42) ©1998, Sotheby's, Inc. Images (pp. 257, 268, 274)

    NATIONAL ENDOWMENT FOR THE ARTS

COVER / INSIDE COVER: GASTON LA TOUCHE, (1854-1913) FRENCH. LE DINER AU CASINO (DINNER AT THE CASINO). OIL ON CANVAS, 39 x 37 5/8 INCHES (DETAIL). GIFT OF MRS. ROBERT SCHERMER, 1975.33.

This Catalogue is dedicated to

Helen L. Pinkney

for her numerous years of service and dedication to

THE DAYTON ART INSTITUTE

1999 BOARD OF TRUSTEES

James F. Dicke, II, President

Michael Adler
Tracy Bieser
Joyce M. Bowden
Esther Scott Carter
Allyson Danis
Rob Davis
Thomas DeLuca
Peter Dorsman
Dr. John F. Fleischauer
David M. Fogarty *
Patricia Francis
Cheryl Garrett
Reba E. Gaston
Debby Goldenberg
Anne Greene
John S. Haddick
John Herbert *
Kathy Hollingsworth
Major Jaruth Jefferson
Raymond W. Lane
Judy Lansaw
Albert W. Leland
Valerie Lemmie*
John W. Longstreth
Lou Mason
Robert C. Nevin
Vicki D. Pegg *
Valerie Quinn *
Thomas Roddy
Jenni Roer *
Christine Rose
Marshall D. Ruchman
R. Daniel Sadlier
Fred Schumm
Don Schweller
Jane Setzer
Robert Stan
William B. Ten Eyck
The Honorable Michael R. Turner *
Evan Valassiades*
Sam Warwar *
Dr. Karen Wells *
John Winch

* Denotes ex-officio

STAFF OF THE DAYTON ART INSTITUTE

Alexander Lee Nyerges, Director and CEO
Roberta Simon, Assistant to the Director

ARTTREK
Chris Saunders

CURATORIAL
Dominique H. Vasseur, *Barbara Siwecki*, Henry Bennett,
Todd Hall, Li Jian, Sally Kurtz, Helen Pinkney, Martin Pleiss,
Lora Stowe

DEVELOPMENT
Amy Farmer, Joy Georgakas, Hope Grandy, Lora Kraft,
Barbara Richardson, Julie Trull

EDUCATIONAL RESOURCES & SERVICES/LIBRARY
Helen Moss, *Norma Petkus*, Susan Anable, Erin Batty,
Pamela Houk, Gwen Kirkman, Alice Saidel, Denise Shoenberger,
Jamie Sharp, Kristina Sullivan, Emily Sykes

FACILITIES
Ed Zimmerman, Chuck Franz

FINANCE
Teri Hickey, Lisa Orr, Cindy Shellabarger

HUMAN RESOURCES
Kinceston Moore, Rachel Carr, Beulah Hopkins, Linda McComas

MARKETING & COMMUNICATIONS/ADMISSIONS
Sara Spidel, *Heather Galecka*, Anne Camery, Mary Lou Frantz,
Jennifer Perry, Diana Sprowl

THE MUSEUM STORE
Diane Haskell, *Kathy Daniszewski*, Amelia Bhatnagar, Jill Fox,
Christina Miller, Angela Simpson, Bonita Tamaki

SECURITY
Kinceston Moore, *Daryl Willis*, Prince Barrett, Joseph Bedwell,
Larry Brady Jr., Richard Dominick, Danny Estep, Michael Frye,
John Glass, Jesse Gonzalez, Iesha Hankins, Eloy Hernandez Jr.,
Karen Hutchins, Ericolis Kelley, Gary Marcum, Samuel Osburn,
Roy Parks, Evonne Randolph, Marsha Rice, Marvin Smith

SPECIAL EVENTS/CAFE MONET/MAINTENANCE
Terri Manley, *Deb Arzola*, *Barry Dozier*, Robert Arzola,
Jennifer Barber, James Blickensderfer, Dennis Cobaugh,
Carolyn Cochran, Mike Cordell, Clayton Eichelberger, Nicole Fiely,
Paula Grannan, Mary Alice Humphrey, Levi Lee, Jacob Manley,
Steve Poulton, Bonnie Robertson, Larry Schmid, Rhea Seals,
Cynthia Watson

* Bold type denotes department managers, italics denote managers

CONTENTS

ACKNOWLEDGEMENTS

This catalogue was written and selected under the guidance of the museum's former chief curator, Marianne Lorenz, and our current curatorial leader, Dominique H. Vasseur, who in 1999 will celebrate his 20th anniversary with The Dayton Art Institute. Each of the curators labored over the selection and the writing of the text for this publication. It is our hope not only to provide you with a wonderful overview of the museum's strong collections, but also to provide a modicum of art historical perspective for each work. The authors have considered the contextual settings for each work, including religious, political, historical, architectural, archaeological, and aesthetic influences. From this, we hope the reader will gain a new, or better, appreciation for these works of art and the people who created them.

This publication is the result of a true team effort. Our thanks go to Lora Stowe and Patricia Huls for their dedicated work on this momentous project. First Patti, then Lora coordinated the beautiful photography of, cataloguing of and historical information about each of the featured works. Lora also did an extraordinary job with editing, proofing, and ensuring the perfection of this publication. The design of this publication is the result of the hard work and talent of our art director, Jennifer Perry. The editing of this text has been a labor of love for Eileen Carr, Sara Spidel, Heather Galecka, Anne Camery, and our education staff.

Since this publication has been in process for more than five years, the team of writers includes both current and former curators. The one important constant, Senior Curator Dominique H. Vasseur, has been stalwart in his dedication. He is joined by colleagues Alex Nyerges, Marianne Lorenz, Li Jian, the late Clarence Kelley, Marianne Richter, Todd Smith, Roger Crum, and Priscilla Colt. Content editors have included art experts James O. Caswell, Charles Eldredge, J. Patrice Marandel, Dorie Reents-Budet and William and Elsie Peck.

Finally, we thank the National Endowment for the Arts and the James F. Dicke Family for their generous support of this catalogue.

INTRODUCTION

It is fitting to celebrate the 80th anniversary of The Dayton Art Institute with the publication of this catalogue highlighting the Permanent Collection. This is the largest publication ever produced focusing on the museum's holdings and the first overview of the museum's Collection to be compiled since 1969, when *Fifty Treasures* was published on the occasion of the museum's first 50 years.

It is equally appropriate to publish this catalogue in the year 1999. This is a perfect time to celebrate the dawn of a new millennium, applying late 20th century art historical perspective to eight decades of collecting as an institution. It is also providential in light of the museum's recent rebirth through the "Renaissance of a Dayton Masterpiece," the highly successful effort that provided more than $24 million toward building improvements, expansion, endowment enhancement, collection conservation and new programming. The museum's 1997 reopening after 18 months of construction gave rise to a renewed sense of importance for the growth and nurturing of the Collection. The Collection's "renaissance" has been bolstered by a number of targeted, successful collecting efforts and a considerable amount of good luck.

One of these efforts to improve the Collection has been the birth of the Medici Society. This select group is dedicated to the purchase of major works of art for the museum through annual contributions restricted to that purpose. This new program offers long-term benefits by providing essential funding for major art purchases, an effort not previously possible. Modeled after similar, successful programs at prominent art museums, the Medici Society will impact our galleries for years to come.

The rebirth of the museum's collecting focus could not be possible without the unprecedented support of major donors, such as the Dicke, Kettering and Berry families. Their generous support has helped to make this era in the history of The Dayton Art Institute one to be celebrated and recorded. Not since the days of Mrs. Julia Shaw Carnell in the 1930s, or the voracious collecting era of Tom Colt and his league of donors, has the museum witnessed such amazing growth in its Collection. The Kettering name, like that of Mrs. Carnell and The Honorable and Mrs. Jefferson Patterson, can be found throughout the galleries of the aptly named Patterson-Kettering Wing of Asian Art. Likewise, the generosity of the Berry Family is seen in the recent addition of the work by Bissolo and the early 19th century painting by Pierre-Nolasque Bergeret, both hanging in the Berry Wing of European Art.

Following in the tradition of these generous donors, we have the Dicke Family. The impact made by the Dicke Family, including Jim Sr. and Eilleen Dicke and Jim II and Janet Dicke, has been almost incalculable. The Dickes have not only been enormously generous in support of the Collection and the recent building campaign, but have lent their energies, ideas and enthusiasm to the betterment of the Art Institute. Collectively and individually, the Dickes have been generous beyond our expectations. Jim and Eilleen have been the motivating force behind the creation of the museum's soon-to-be-unveiled glass gallery, named in their honor. Their passion for glass is an inspiration. Jim II's love for collecting American art is surpassed only by his love for the history of art. A consummate collector and scholar, Jim II has also provided his leadership to the institution as President of the Board of Trustees, a role he assumed in 1998. The 1990s, and the years to come, will bear the indelible mark of the Dickes—scanning through this publication will bear ample proof of this fact.

This volume provides a snapshot of the museum's collections of paintings, sculpture and decorative art from around the globe. Some collections, such as works-on-paper—prints, drawings and photographs, which numerically comprise the vast majority of the museum's Collection—and the Oceanic Collection were not included for reasons of space. Future publications will be able to showcase these fabulous holdings. The selection of works was a difficult and arduous process, as the Collection holds such riches. However, the end-result is a stunning publication representing a Collection of great diversity and quality. I hope you celebrate this catalogue and the museum's 80th anniversary year by renewing your acquaintance with these brilliant works of art, viewing them in person as they should truly be seen.

ALEXANDER LEE NYERGES
Director and CEO

EVOLUTION OF A COLLECTION

A long-accepted adage in the world of art museums is the claim that the collection is the core of the institution, its heart and soul. The Dayton Art Institute's Collection stands not only as an aggregation of aesthetic objects representing the collective creativity of humankind throughout history, but also as a silent testimony to those who brought this Collection together. Every collection owes its allegiance first and foremost to collectors—the history of art collecting is as old as the creation of art itself. Dealers, curators, and directors comprise the other key ingredients to the formation of a collection. In the case of the Art Institute, the history of its Collection is a fascinating saga of dedication, foresight and generosity.

Mr. Louis J.P. Lott

Although it would be fitting to record a complete history of the Collection of The Dayton Art Institute, space does not permit that here. This more exhaustive effort should be, and perhaps will be, the result of a greatly needed publication on the history of the museum. Currently, the museum's extensive archives are being consolidated and catalogued through an archival program initiated through the museum's Art Reference Library/Louis J.P. Lott and Walter G. Schaffer Memorial Architecture Library. Once completed, the making of an historical tome on the art museum's colorful history should be the next logical step. But here, it is appropriate to reflect on some of the key players in this wonderful legacy and some of the works for which they were responsible in adding to the Collection.

THE EARLY YEARS

The first-recorded work of art in the Collection of the Art Institute was a gift, most appropriately, from the museum's founding force and leading patron benefactress, Julia Shaw Carnell. The widow of the late Frank Patterson, one of the founders of the National Cash Register Company, Mrs. Carnell set the tone for donors to the museum and created the institution as we know it. Her generosity and leadership resulted in the construction of the museum's 1930 National Historic Landmark building and in the early growth of the Collection. In 1919, shortly after the official founding of the museum, then known as the Dayton Museum of Fine Arts, Mrs. Carnell donated Harriet Frishmuth's *Joy of the Waters* (p. 76), which was then installed in the Art Institute's gardens. The 1920s saw the Collection grow slowly. With Japanese prints from Mrs. Anna and Helen Rogers, plus paintings by Willard Metcalf (p. 77), William Ritschel (p. 72) and Abbott Thayer donated by John Hayward, a Dayton attorney and member of the Board of Trustees, the Collection numbered only 263 works-of-art by decade's end.

John Christen Johansen, American. Mrs. Julia Shaw Carnell, 1940. Oil on canvas.

A New Temple for Art - 1930

Mr. John G. Lowe *Mr. Brainerd B. Thresher*

It was the opening of the grand Italian Renaissance-inspired structure designed by renowned museum architect Edward B. Green that spurred the first major growth of the Collection. Moving from the cramped quarters of its original home in a late 19th century mansion on Monument Avenue, the Art Institute took up residency in the spacious halls of the new building, with numerous, sparsely installed galleries. Director Siegfried Weng, who served from 1930 to 1950, oversaw the first significant growth of the Collection, despite the challenges of the Great Depression. A gift from the sculptor Lorado Taft, *Solitude of the Soul*, which again resides in the marble-colonnaded Sculpture Court—also known affectionately as the Great Hall—was accompanied by a number of other works that still maintain a prominent place in the museum's collections. Leon Kroll's painting of *Blanche Reading* was one of many gifts from John G. Lowe, a prominent Dayton businessman and also President of the Board of Trustees from 1925 to 1929. His other gifts include Ernest Blumenschein's *Canyon, Red and Black* (p. 87) and Matthias Stom's *Old Shepherd*.

During the 1930s, Mrs. Carnell traveled extensively and collected voraciously for the museum. Her gifts included a large group of Chinese ceramics, which now make up the core of the museum's outstanding Collection of Chinese art; the marvelous silver Tang dynasty *Vase* (p. 160); and a Japanese *Buddha* (p. 185). The Asian Collection was also the beneficiary of a large group of objects donated in 1942 by Brainerd B. Thresher. Thresher was one of the founding members of The Dayton Art Institute with a strong interest in art and collecting. In 1944, the Thomas Sully portrait of Elias Jonathan Dayton (p. 44), the son of our city's namesake Jonathan Dayton, was purchased by Thresher from the Spencer-Dayton Family. This was also the year Mrs. Carnell passed away, leaving more than 170 works to the Collection.

THE HONORABLE
JEFFERSON PATTERSON

The museum's Pre-Columbian Collection saw its beginning in 1947 with the gift of 39 Peruvian objects from The Honorable and Mrs. Jefferson Patterson. Jefferson Patterson was Mrs. Carnell's son and in his own right a very generous donor to the museum's Collection until his passing in 1978. Since that time, his widow, Mrs. Jefferson Patterson of Washington, D.C., has continued to be supportive of the Collection and the museum's recent capital efforts.

In 1950, the name of Kettering first graced the Collection's donor list with a gift of an important Shang dynasty *Ritual Vessel*. Since that initial gift, the Ketterings have been responsible for more than 1,200 gifts of art to the Collection, a truly extraordinary example of generosity and dedication to the Art Institute. Mrs. Kettering's gifts have included such fabulous works as the Eugene W. Kettering collection of Japanese sword fittings, a Ming dynasty gilt-bronze *Baby Buddha* (p. 169), a Western Han dynasty *Kneeling Woman* (p. 156) figure and a collection of 17th century Ming dynasty Huanghuali furniture.

MR. ROBERT BADENHOP

The early 1950s also brought the name of Robert Badenhop to the donor family. During the next decade, Badenhop, a New Jersey businessman with close ties to Dayton, donated paintings by Mary Cassatt (p. 58), William Adolphe Bouguereau (p. 267), Jean-Léon Gérôme (p. 260), and Jacob Grimmer, among many others. The Honorable and Mrs. Jefferson Patterson donated a large collection of Asian jade works, numbering more than 125 pieces, in 1951.

In 1952, Dayton's most important photographer of any generation, Jane Reece, donated her collection of more than 400 salon photographs and more than 9,000 glass plate negatives. This constitutes the largest body of her work anywhere and made possible Senior Curator Dominique H. Vasseur's splendid retrospective exhibition and equally marvelous publication that was part of the 1997 reopening schedule.

The following year, Joseph Rubin gave his prized *Waterlilies* (1903) by Claude Monet (p. 272) to the Art Institute, which today is arguably the most popular single work in the entire Collection. The Art Institute's director, Esther Seaver, persuaded New York businessman Rubin to donate this important work to a museum he had never visited. This type of amazing generosity is typical of the steady growth of Dayton's Collection, evident still today.

THE COLT YEARS

ARNOLD NEWMAN, AMERICAN.
MR. & MRS. THOMAS C.
COLT, JR., 1950. SILVER PRINT.

The name of Thomas C. Colt, Jr. graces the short list of people who have directed The Dayton Art Institute. During his tenure, from 1957 to 1975, the museum witnessed the most phenomenal growth of the Collection in terms of quality and quantity. Because of his foresight and the generosity of many, the Art Institute possesses some of the country's most brilliant Baroque paintings. His work with Mr. and Mrs. Elton MacDonald resulted in paintings by Canaletto, Hendrick TerBrugghen (p. 234), Mattia Preti (p. 240), Bartolomeo Manfredi (p. 228), and Ferdinand Bol (p. 238), Rembrandt's brightest and most successful student. The collections of Pre-Columbian art grew, as did the collection of Abstract Expressionist painting, with the addition of works by Ad Reinhardt, Joan Mitchell (p. 108; a work given by Max Pincus in honor of the MacDonalds), Mark Rothko (p. 117), Kenneth Noland (p. 110), and Mark Tobey.

Also under Colt's leadership, the Photography Collection improved with purchases of works by Ansel Adams and Edward Weston, as well as contemporary photographers of the 1960s and 1970s.

Upon the occasion of the Art Institute's 50th anniversary, several important acquisitions were made. The largest of these was a group of 17 Chinese, Japanese, and Korean ceramics from Mrs. Kettering. The impressive portrait of *Henry, Eighth Lord Arundell of Wardour* by Sir Joshua Reynolds (p. 253), the first president of the English Royal Academy, was given to the museum by Harry Price, Jr., the Board's president from 1967 to 1976.

In 1970, one of the museum's signature and most popular works, *High Noon* by Edward Hopper (p. 100), was contributed by Mr. and Mrs. Anthony Haswell. They had acquired the work 21 years previous from the Frank Rehn Gallery in New York City. The work is quintessentially Hopper and is among the most frequently requested works by museums around the world. It represents Hopper at his high point as a leader of mid-20th century painting in America.

The Photography Collection grew considerably again in the early 1970s under the careful guidance of Colt. A portfolio of works by Harry Callahan, 20 works by Walker Evans, and images by

SASCHA LAUTMAN, AMERICAN.   SASCHA LAUTMAN, AMERICAN.
MR. ELTON MacDONALD,   MRS. ELTON MacDONALD,
AROUND 1950. OIL ON CANVAS.   AROUND 1950. OIL ON CANVAS.

Emmet Gowin, who taught at the College of the Art Institute from 1967 to 1971, were added to strengthen the growing collection of American photography.

1970S ONWARD

In the middle of the 1970s, Mrs. Kettering made another significant mark on the Asian Collection. In 1974, she contributed a fabulous collection of Japanese *menuki* and other sword fittings, mentioned above. These elaborately carved sword fittings constitute one the largest collections of its kind in America. In 1976, she contributed a large group of Asian ceramics and sculpture, including Korean Koryo celadon ware, as well as a group of important 18th century English silver. Her purchase of a collection of Old Master prints that year was followed by her gift in 1978 of more than 100 works of Asian art and 30 more works in 1979.

ALEXANDER BROOK, AMERICAN. **MRS. VIRGINIA RIKE HASWELL**, *1946. OIL ON CANVAS.*

The estate of Virginia Rike Haswell brought with it riches in the form of significant paintings by Marsden Hartley (p. 93), Georgia O'Keeffe (p. 80) and Yasuo Kuniyoshi (p. 96), as well as highly desirable watercolors and prints by Edward Hopper to complement their earlier gift of Hopper's *High Noon* (p. 100).

The Associate Board's Art Ball continued to make significant contributions in the 1970s and 1980s. Among these new additions were Christopher Solari's *The Dead Christ* (p. 215), the 17th century Japanese work *The Poetess Lady Sagami* album leaf (p. 194), the massive Frank Stella painting *Wolfeboro II* (p. 116), the ever-popular 17th century Dutch painting *The Flea Hunt* by Gerrit van Honthorst (p. 235), the Jean-Baptiste Oudry *Still Life with Game in a Landscape* (p. 249), and a stunning 18th century Meissen platter. In 1979, funds from the Associate Board were matched with funds provided by Mr. and Mrs. Floyd L. Rietveld, National Cash Register (NCR) and Monsanto to acquire the magnificent trompe l'oeil *Still Life with Mug, Book, Smoking Materials and Crackers* by John Frederick Peto (p. 59).

In 1978, the Estate of the Honorable Jefferson Patterson specified his bequest of two important sculptures by American Paul Manship, *Wrestlers* and *Indian Hunter with His Dog* (p. 83), as well as a handsome pair of early 20th century Tiffany candlesticks.

During its early years, the National Endowment for the Arts (NEA) was a significant source of funding for the acquisition of art by contemporary artists. Grants to The Dayton Art Institute made possible major acquisitions, such as *Chantilly Desert* by Claes Oldenburg; the Fairfield Porter self-portrait; and the Charles Ginnever sculpture *Movin' Out for Jesse Owens*, located in Dave Hall Plaza downtown (NEA support combined with with funds from Jefferson Patterson and Armco). Unfortunately, these NEA funds evaporated in the 1980s, dealing a major blow to the acquisition programs of art museums across the country.

In 1987, the museum's largest purchase ever was engineered almost overnight by Director Bruce Evans. The Ponderosa Corporation, the national steakhouse franchiser, had been purchased and was relocating its headquarters. Its collection, amassed by Chairman and CEO Jerry Office, was among the assets to be sold. The procurement of a multi-million dollar bank loan, almost on-the-spot, was followed by a whirlwind fund-raising effort, culminating in the acquisition of a collection that included paintings by Robert Motherwell, Sam Francis, Helen Frankenthaler (p. 136), Willem de Kooning, Andy Warhol (p. 132), and Sam Gilliam (p. 120), as well as numerous photographs and prints including, Jasper Johns' *Color Number Series*, 1969.

In 1988, a brilliant work by John Twachtman, *View of the Brush House, Cos Cob Connecticut* (p. 66), was donated by Mr. and Mrs. William Patterson. In the same year, a series of gifts came once again from Mrs. Kettering: 30 Asian and European textiles; 40 Asian ceramics; and then 34 additional Asian works, including rare Chinese snuff bottles. Paintings by Camille Corot, Jean-François Millet, Sir Joshua Reynolds and two by Thomas Gainsborough were given to the Art Institute in 1991 by Mr. and Mrs. William Siebenthaler of Michigan, adding significantly to the European holdings.

MRS. VIRGINIA KETTERING

Earlier this decade, the estates of several artists donated works to the Collection. *Pamphili* (1971), a classic work by Philip Guston, was given by the estate of Musa Guston; *Quarry* (p. 106), a 1955 painting by Milton Avery, was contributed by the Milton Avery Trust; and the Edgerton Family Foundation gave a series of 17 photographs by the late Harold Edgerton.

The Associate Board's gifts to the museum through the Art Ball were renewed with great vigor in 1993, after a several-year hiatus. A marvelous Arts and Crafts cabinet from the Shop of the Crafters in Cincinnati was followed in 1994 by a suite of photographs by contemporary photographer Carrie Mae Weems. Then from 1995 to 1998, the Art Ball added to the Collection *Prehistory* by African-American Abstract Expressionist Norman Lewis (p. 102); the wonderful Barbizon School painting *Lake in the Woods at Dusk* by Charles-François Daubigny (p. 262); and a large, stunning painting by the late Ming dynasty artist Lan Ying entitled *Flying Snow on Myriad Peaks*.

During the 1980s and 1990s, the museum increased efforts toward deaccessioning (removal of works from a collection) in the interest of improving the Collection. Deaccessioned works—which because of quality, authenticity or condition are no longer part of the museum's overall collecting plan—are sold to make room and provide the financial means to support the purchase of new art works. Funds resulting from deaccessioning are strictly limited to new acquisitions, and in the 1980s, resulted in the purchase of two studies related to the painting by Gérôme; the Robert Duncanson *Mayan Ruins, Yucatan* (p. 48); *The Early Lovers* (p. 56) and the study for this painting by Eastman Johnson, photographs by Jerry Uelsmann; the De Scott Evans trompe l'oeil *Free Sample, Take One* (p. 62); as well as works from New Guinea, Africa and Japan.

In the early 1990s, the Board of Trustees adopted a comprehensive set of collection-management guidelines that outline the requirements for deaccessioning. These guidelines, used by the American Association of Museums, are given great attention on a continuing basis, as they guide the growth and improvement of the Collection. Since the adoption of the new guidelines, the museum has deaccessioned works that have provided funds for the purchase of several significant art works, including the Peter Frederick Rothermel painting *King Lear* (p. 50), the marvelous Hemba sculpture from Zaire, and the stunning Italian Renaissance painting by Pier Francesco Bissolo (p. 216).

THE DICKE ERA

The realization of this publishing project is the result of curatorial vision dating back more than a decade and a tremendous amount of research, writing and editing. It is also the result of financial support. The James F. Dicke Family has provided the support to make this collection catalogue possible. They have also been largely responsible for changing the face of the Collection. Although we did not know it at the time, 1994 proved to be the beginning of this family's tremendous generosity and exciting growth for the museum's collections.

MR. JAMES F. DICKE II

In 1994, the Dickes gave the Art Institute a portrait by Fairfield Porter and a work by Guy Pene DuBois. At the time, the Art Institute staff did not anticipate the wealth of gifts that was to follow from the Dicke Family. The list includes too many works to enumerate here, but the finest examples are: George Luks' masterful Ashcan School painting *The Bread Line* (p. 69); Cyrus Dallin's monumental bronze sculpture *Chief Massasoit*; the charming and magnetic still-life by Soren Emil Carlsen, *Iron Kettle with Onions* (p. 82); Stephen Hannock's *Mediterranean Nocturne*; Thomas Dewing's captivating painting *Lady with a Rose* (p. 74); *Adirondack Landscape* by Rockwell Kent (p.91); a quintessential Everett Shinn, *Tightrope Walker* (p. 79); the magnificent *Chippendale Side Chair* from the shop of Thomas Affleck (p. 37); the equally captivating Queen Anne slipper chair from Philadelphia; and the Ralph Earl portrait of Jacob Isaacs.

The Dickes have also been generous with gifts of art glass and have created a gallery dedicated to American and European glass, scheduled to open in 1999. Their gifts of glass have included Dale Chihuly's *Navaho Horseblanket Cylinder*, and works by Tiffany Studios, Daum, René Lalique, William Morris and others.

The Jim Dicke Family has also joined forces with the John Berry Family to purchase major works by Pierre-Nolasque Bergeret, *Marius Meditating on the Ruins of Carthage* (p. 256), and the 16th century Venetian masterpiece *The Holy Family with a Donor in a Landscape* by Pier Francesco Bissolo (p. 216). These works were spectacular additions to the Collection.

Most recently, Jim Dicke II's "discovery" of the magnificent, classic painting by Charles Sheeler deserves special mention. The work, *Stacks in Celebration* (p. 104), was found at Berry Hill Gallery in New York, where it had been sold nearly a decade earlier by none other than The Dayton Art Institute. The work had been deaccessioned and sold to help meet the funding needs for acquisition of the Ponderosa Collection—this sale was a move that was quickly regarded as a mistake. This painting is a quintessential work by one of the great masters of American Modernism and had been a gem in the museum's American 20th century Collection, serving as a wonderful counterpoint to the Hopper and other mid-century works. Lost from sight but not from memory, Jim II found the work on a trip to New York and immediately called the museum to inquire about an interest in reacquiring the painting. And, given the rare opportunity to correct a mistake from the past, the Art Institute eagerly affirmed its interest. Ironically, Mrs. Eloise Spaeth, a former Daytonian and long-time friend of the Art Institute, who contributed the Sheeler to the museum in 1969, passed away only weeks before Jim II rediscovered the painting.

Dayton Daily News

MR. ELMER WEBSTER

The end of the 20th century will also be noted for three other important collections entering the museum's holdings. The first was from the Estate of Elmer Webster and Robert Titsch. Webster, known to many both near and far, collected and dealt voraciously in 19th century American furniture and decorative arts. His special fondness for vernacular, folk and naïve art has left an indelible impression on the museum and its Collection. The Christian Shively *Cupboard* (p. 43) and more than 100 other exquisite examples of art, primarily from Ohio and the Midwest, were a significant addition to the American holdings. The funds realized from deaccessioning the other gifts made by this Estate have also leveraged Art Institute purchases in Webster's name, allowing his legacy of collecting to continue today.

The second is the collection of the late Jesse Philips. This important collection, which includes textbook Abstract Expressionist paintings by Jackson Pollock, Franz Kline, Mark Rothko, and Clyfford Still, is now owned by the Art Institute and will some day grace the museum galleries, thanks to the generosity of both Jesse and Caryl Philips.

The third, and even more significant major gift, has been from the collections of Mrs. Kettering. While the Ketterings have been very generous to the Art Institute over the years, the past few years have presented art contributions surpassing all expectations. From 1996 through 1998, Mrs. Kettering's gifts of Asian ceramics, furniture, jade, glass, textiles and works-on-paper have exceeded 335 objects, many of which filled important spaces in the Asian Collection. It is fitting, that Mrs. Kettering received The Dayton Art Institute's first-ever Presidential Distinguished Service Award, most appropriately presented to her by Jim Dicke II, her heir apparent as Patron Saint of the Art Institute.

It is the tradition of giving, as exemplified by the Kettering Family, Dicke Family and many others, which has made the Collection of The Dayton Art Institute so rich. Because of this wonderful legacy, this publication is already outdated, as new gifts continue to enter the Collection. It is this tradition of generosity that holds promise for an even brighter future.

ALEXANDER LEE NYERGES
Director and CEO

THE RENAISSANCE OF A DAYTON MASTERPIECE:

The Art Institute Building, 1928—1997

The architectural renaissance in 1997 of one of Dayton's most beloved landmarks began a new era in The Dayton Art Institute's history and future service to the community. But the past continues to speak through the original architecture—its grandeur, historic detail, and intimate links to Dayton's vision of itself as an industrial and cultural center. At the heart of the renovation and new construction project was the desire to foster the building's ongoing relationship with the neighborhood and establish architectural links to the original 1930 structure. The goal of the project was not to make a novel architectural statement but, rather, to renew and fulfill the architectural dreams the community held 70 years earlier. The architects looked upon this as an opportunity to design a structure that echoed the existing one, but that was also clearly identifiable as a late 20th century building. This was of particular importance due to the National Historic Landmark status of the 1930 museum.

We return time and again to the name of Julia Shaw Carnell when the subject of the original museum building is raised. She was responsible not only for funding the 1930 building project, but also for deciding what type of architectural statement it would make. Mrs. Carnell was born in 1863 into one of Dayton's most prominent families—the Shaws. She later married first into the Pattersons and then the Carnells—both equally affluent families in the city. Her first husband, Frank J. Patterson, brother of the founder of the National Cash Register Company, died in 1901 and in 1909, Mrs. Carnell married Harry G. Carnell, who passed away suddenly in 1931. Widely traveled and possessing the generous, philanthropic spirit typical of the wealthy during the period, Mrs. Carnell was beloved and revered throughout the community. She was known as the doer of many good deeds and "noble" undertakings.

She was also a woman of considerable strength and experience—and reportedly, a very shrewd and savvy businesswoman as well. Mrs. Carnell had been involved with the museum from its early days when it was located on the corner of Monument and St. Clair streets in downtown Dayton. By the late 1920s, the programs and collections had outgrown the museum's modest quarters and Mrs. Carnell offered to donate a new building on a spectacular site, recommended by the architect Edward B. Green, overlooking the Great Miami River. By all indications, the planning and design of the building itself were conceived solely by Mrs. Carnell, with little or no input, and committed to paper by the architect.

Dayton's architectural character in the late 1920s was richly Revivalist. Most of its major public and private buildings were inspired by the styles and surface ornament of previous eras and locales—classical Greece and Rome, Romanesque Italy, Germany or France, Renaissance Italy, English Tudor, etc. Many buildings mixed, in vigorous and egalitarian pastiche, the style and ornament of two or more of these periods. The richness and charm of Dayton's historic Revival architecture is now dimly perceived in a smattering of buildings that survived urban renewal or the need for more parking lots. But in the late 1920s, buildings such as the Rike-Kumler Building, Union Station, the E.J. Barney House, Steele High School and even the City Jail joined the survivors—the Victory Theatre, the Arcade, Memorial Hall, the YMCA, and the old Court House—to create a vital cityscape. The Masonic Temple, a building just a year or so older than the museum and with which the museum shares a commanding view of the Great Miami River, was done in a monumental, classical style with Greek columns adorning its imposing facade.

It would be inaccurate to imply that the seeming lack of "Modernist" architecture in Dayton reflects an unusually conservative or "backward" attitude on the part of the citizenry. In the first place, Revival architecture was common throughout the United States and Europe in large, sophisticated cities and small, out-of-the-way towns as well. Few of the museums built during the period reflected the new International Style architecture. However, several, such as the Joslyn Art Museum (Omaha, Nebraska) and the Colorado Springs Fine Art Center, were designed using the new Art Deco vocabulary.

Dayton was, in fact, an architecturally active city during the first part of the century. Dayton architect and Art Institute faculty member Louis Lott kept Daytonians informed of international Modernist trends through a series of lectures and newspaper articles that were not derogatory to Modernism. Calling the Victorian period an architectural "debacle," Lott praised "Revival" styles, but concluded that "in them we are expressing fashions of bygone ages, just as much as if we adopted their manner of dress" and "thus we are guilty of plagiarism."[1] Lott welcomed the advent of modern styles from Europe. However, he admitted that architects working in a revival vocabulary would be unlikely to work effectively with a new architectural language and that sufficient numbers of wealthy patrons did not yet exist in Dayton to make Modernism viable on a large scale. There were other opportunities for Daytonians to be exposed to Modernism as well. In September 1928, the Rike-Kumler Company had a display of modern furniture that included pieces by such innovative designers as Paul T. Frankl and Kem Weber. The choice of a traditional revivalist architecture for the museum then must then be viewed as a conscious choice—similar to the choices made by numerous other cities as they defined through architecture their relationship to art, culture, and civic development.

PEN AND INK EXTERIOR DESIGN AND MASSING SKETCHES (EXPANSION AND RENOVATION),
THE DAYTON ART INSTITUTE. LEVIN PORTER ASSOCIATES, INC. - ARCHITECTS.

EDWARD B. GREEN & SONS AND ALBERT H. HOPKINS, AMERICAN. THE DAYTON ART INSTITUTE, 1927. WATERCOLOR ON PAPER. 24 X 36 IN. GIFT OF MR. EDWARD B. GREEN, 1929.134A (DETAIL).

PEN AND MARKER SKETCH OF EARLY DESIGN CONCEPT DRAWING, INTERIOR OF SHAW GOTHIC CLOISTER, THE DAYTON ART INSTITUTE. LEVIN PORTER ASSOCIATES, INC. - ARCHITECTS.

The site chosen for the museum involved the demolition of one of Dayton's magnificent Victorian mansions, built by Calvin L. Hawes. Mrs. Carnell had taken an option on the Hawes property in 1923, and in 1926, announced the purchase. In 1927, excavation and demolition began. From the beginning, the decisions were in Carnell's hands. She chose the architectural firm of Edward B. Green and Sons of Buffalo, New York, who had previously completed the Albright-Knox Art Gallery in Buffalo and the Toledo Museum of Art, done in styles evoking Greco-Roman architecture. The decision to use an Italian Renaissance Revival style for the museum appears to have been the result of the joint enthusiasm of Mrs. Carnell, her son Jefferson Patterson, and Green's son, Edward B. Green, Jr. The latter had visited Italy several years previously and had been impressed by Italian Villas at Tivoli and Caprarola. The museum building was ultimately a conflation of the Villa Farnese and its Casino (garden house) at Caprarola by the 16th century Italian architect Giacomo da Vignola (1507–1573). The outside staircase that links the 1930 museum entrance to Riverview Avenue is an almost exact replica of the staircase at the Villa Farnese. The drive that runs between the staircase and the museum was done over Green's objections that it would ruin the continuous flow of architectural form, as well as vistor flow, from the bottom of the site to the museum doors.

The taste for Italian Renaissance architecture during the first half of the century is exemplified in Edith Wharton's 1904 paean to the style entitled *Italian Villas and Their Gardens*. Illustrated by Maxfield Parrish, this lush volume pays tribute not only to the aesthetic "magic" of Italian Renaissance villas and gardens but also to their ennobling, civilizing qualities. In speaking of the Villa Caprarola, Wharton conjures up images of Pico della Mirandola's Renaissance: ". . . within, one has a vision of noble ladies and their cavaliers sitting under rose arbors or strolling between espaliered lemon trees, discussing a Greek manuscript or a Roman bronze, or listening to the last sonnet of the cardinal's [Alexander Farnese, the cardinal who built the villa] court poet."[2] This association of Renaissance villa architecture with a vision of a learned, serene cultural utopia undoubtedly figured powerfully in the minds of architects and patrons at the time the museum was planned. Even the service building in the back, done in the style of an Italian farmhouse, harkened back to Italy.

For indeed, the ideal of the museum as a center for civic pride and cultural "enlightenment" for people of all walks of life was widespread among community leaders of the period. Museum architecture was designed with an eye to its effects on the morals, attitudes, and aspirations of the everyday citizen – not just the economic and educational elite. Thus, critic Frank Washburn-Freund, writing for Art News in 1927 on the opening of the new Detroit Institute of Arts, stated: "There is just a suggestion of the classic in form, spacing, and the happily sparse ornamentation, all indicating that this is a building dedicated to higher things, a place for people to come and, while forgetting their daily wants and troubles, live for a few hours in a clearer and healthier mental atmosphere."[3] Such thoughts correspond with those expressed during the opening ceremonies of the Dayton Art Institute in January 1930. The sculptor Loredo Taft stated: "This Art Institute will bring to

Dayton a love for nature; people will be more interested in the beauty of earth and sky after seeing this building . . . There has been a material opulence all over the world—we are here to take advantage of it. I always hark back to the 15th century for relaxation . . . This Art Institute will interest children. Genius here can flourish and there is great genius in America. There are souls that can be saved through the influence of beauty and it is our task to see that beauty flourishes."[4]

In the weeks before and after the opening of the museum, it was repeatedly referred to as a "temple of art." Again, such moral or religious connotations associated with art and the art museum were widely accepted. Dayton photographer Jane Reece effusively stated: "Mrs. Carnell is a saint! She is opening the door of heaven to many people of this city! . . . Think what she is doing for the children who will assemble here to learn how to fashion beautiful objects and to feed their hunger upon the lovely! This Art Institute is to mean more than some churches to this community. . . . The new Art Institute is a moral force."[5] Expectations were almost naively high: not only would the museum provide opportunities for aesthetic enjoyment, relaxation, and development of genius but be the smithy of moral and spiritual salvation as well.

It is interesting to note in this context that The Dayton Art Institute was built during a period that witnessed unprecedented building of museums. Museums proliferated in the early years of the Great Depression—the Columbus Museum of Art, the Nelson-Atkins Museum of Art (Kansas City, Missouri), the Detroit Institute of Arts, the Philadelphia Museum of Art, the Joslyn Art Museum, the Ringling Museum of Art (Sarasota, Florida), and many others opened within just a few years of The Dayton Art Institute. The grandeur of conception and execution of most of the new museums speaks to more than just the desire to properly house and display America's burgeoning public art collections. National pride was also at stake. Large numbers of Americans from all walks of life had experienced the wealth and magnificence of European museums and architecture during World War I. It now became imperative—if we were to keep up with or surpass European culture—to emulate these models. Art Institute Board President (1925–1929) John G. Lowe stated the aims clearly: "There seems to be no doubt that the average European, from the lowest to the highest class, has a keener art appreciation than the average American . . . Through [the] lapse of time Europeans have had the opportunity to embellish their cities and enrich their museums, buildings and parks. Since World War II, however, there has been a renaissance throughout the United States in art growth. New museums are springing up everywhere and city planning boards are improving the appearances of cities on all sides. This is a natural development, as the arts have always flourished in wealthy periods of nations. The greatest art work of Rome and Greece was developed while those countries were at the height of their power."[6] Cultural and artistic achievement were seen as necessary components in becoming a great nation to rival ancient and contemporary civilizations abroad.

In choosing E.B. Green, Mrs. Carnell had at her disposal a seasoned museum architect. Green's museums in Buffalo and Toledo had earned him international acclaim.[7] Green had designed Buffalo's Albright-Knox Art Gallery in 1905 in a Neoclassical-temple style based on an adaptation of the Erectheum on the Acropolis at Athens. The museum in Toledo is also done in a Neoclassical style. It was undoubtedly with these two institutions in mind that Mrs. Carnell chose E.B. Green and Sons as the architects for the Dayton Art Institute. Although the Dayton Art Institute is not done in a classical-temple style, it was nonetheless perceived as a temple—a high ground upon which the citizens of Dayton could gather and become educated, spiritually enlightened, and even socially liberated. Mr. Robert Patterson, in accepting the building from Mrs. Carnell on January 8, 1930 stated: "We know what joy has been yours, Mrs. Carnell, in the building of this magnificent temple of art." An

(Laura Leyes for) Levin Porter Associates, Inc. Proposed Facade for The Dayton Art Institute. Graphite and watercolor on paper. Signed and dated lower right "Laura Leyes '94". 14 1/4 x 36 1/2 inches. Museum purchase with funds provided by the "Renaissance of a Dayton Masterpiece" Campaign, 1994-1997, 1998.51.

19

illustration carried in the *Dayton Daily News* demonstrates the role that the museum was to play as high temple. In the lower portion of the illustration are industrial buildings and factories; atop these rest Greek and Roman temples, churches, and other world monuments; at the very top sits The Dayton Art Institute crowned with stars spelling out "Life Needs Art." *The New York Times*, in a March 9, 1930, article about The Dayton Art Institute, echoed the community's enthusiasms. Referring to its site as a "little acropolis," the article goes on to say that the building was "one of the most significant examples of Renaissance design in this country."

The collections of the museum in 1930 were quite small. Indeed, the majority of the spacious rooms were not used to house the permanent collection at all. The ground floor was given over almost entirely to offices and education classrooms. Later the library and a restaurant were placed on the ground floor as well. The South Wing of the upper galleries contained the Ming Temple and *Dragon Stone Reliefs* that Mrs. Carnell purchased shortly before the museum opened. The Permanent Collection contained a number of Japanese prints by Hiroshige, Hokusai, and others; a number of decorative clocks, cabinets, chairs; and paintings by Chauncey F. Ryder, Charles Hawthorne, Ivan Olinsky, Robert Whitmore, Eliot Clark, and Robert Eichelberger. Mrs. Carnell, in anticipation of the museum opening, donated several pieces of Italian 17th and 18th century furniture.

From its beginnings, The Dayton Art Institute was more than a museum—it was an art school as well. Originally, the Great Hall and Lower Court were home to large plaster-cast reproductions of the world's great sculptures that were routinely studied and copied by art students of the day. Students from local universities who desired art training came to The Dayton Art Institute for their classes. They executed the stenciling in the Italian Cloister, the restaurant, and other areas. By 1963, the school and the Permanent Collection had grown to the extent that a new building, donated by the Rike Family Foundation, was built to house the school's studio classrooms and administrative offices. The Rike Pavilion, dedicated in memory of Susanne Rike MacDonald, officially opened in 1965. The building design was inspired by an international style architectural vocabulary typical of school buildings of the period. A mere ten years later, the school was closed as the result of decreased enrollment as local universities built their own art faculties and studio facilities. When the school closed, museum offices, storage, and the art library moved into the Rike Pavilion and the 1930 facility was used only to display the museum's growing collections. In 1979, the entire lower-level North Wing was dedicated as the Patterson-Kettering Wing of Asian Art, reflecting the growth in the Asian Collection in large part through gifts from the Patterson and Kettering families. Wings were also devoted to American art, European art, and special exhibitions.

In 1979, the museum undertook a $3 million "New View" capital campaign that allowed the Art Institute to make much-needed roof repairs and create the Propylaeum, a new entrance providing public access from the parking lot to the 1930 building and the Rike Pavilion. The Propylaeum, designed by the local architectural firm of Levin Porter Associates, Inc., was one of the few outstanding examples of Postmodern architecture in Dayton. Typical of Postmodernism were its references to the museum's 1930 architecture: its bowed limestone wall was scaled and finished to emulate the original museum's stonework and a richly detailed portal of copper was a enlarged cross section of a stone cornice copied from the 1930 building. The Propylaeum was designed to serve as a physical link from the Rike Pavilion to the 1930 building and create an entrance to the museum off the parking lot. But access from the Propylaeum to the museum proved unsatisfactory as visitors were forced to pass through a series of confusing, underground corridors before reaching the main galleries.

The museum realized that an expansion and renovation program was necessary in order to present the Collection properly and accommodate future growth. Danis Industries volunteered the services of architect Mark Graeser to do a preliminary assessment. On the basis of this information in 1987, Levin Porter Associates, Inc. was contracted to do a long-range building plan for the museum. Working with museum Director Bruce Evans and the entire staff, this Facilities Master Plan examined all of the current space usage as well as future needs.

The 1987 Master Facilities Plan outlined a number of important institutional needs: new galleries for growing collections, additional art storage areas, entertainment spaces separate from the galleries, a new temporary exhibition wing, and improved flow for incoming and outgoing shipments of art. Expanded public amenities, such as The Museum Store and a restaurant, were also identified as major needs. Curiously, no action was taken on this plan until 1992 when the Board of Trustees and the new Director, Alex Nyerges, placed the facility at the top of the list of priorities for the museum. Levin Porter Associates, Inc. were engaged after a lengthy architectural selection process, with Tom Thickel as the design architect.

In initial design discussions, several plans that incorporated the Propylaeum were considered. In the end, it was decided that to retain the Propylaeum would be a costly, impractical, and unpopular option. Many Daytonians objected to this overtly Postmodern structure connected with the original architecture. It was decided to demolish the Propylaeum and build an entirely new entrance spacious enough to house the Museum Store and other visitor amenities as well as provide ground-floor access to the 1930 building.

DICKE WING OF AMERICAN ART - CONTEMPORARY GALLERY

PATTERSON-KETTERING WING OF ASIAN ART - AFRICAN GALLERY

The growth in the museum's collections and the need to provide a better display and storage environment necessitated the 1997 renovation and new construction project. While various scopes of work were considered, the main concern was to complete the original octagonal plan shown on Green's drawings and create an entrance hall befitting the museum's original architecture. New heating, ventilation, air conditioning, plumbing, and electrical systems were also installed throughout interestingly, Green thought that air conditioning was a passing fancy in 1928). In order to provide increased public and entertainment space, one of the two outdoor cloisters was covered by a skylight.

The siting of the 1930 building and the Rike Pavilion limited the potential shapes and orientation of the new General Motors Entrance Rotunda. A round structure was required to resolve the issues of the various axes created by the Rike Pavilion and the two new wings that completed Green's original octagonal plan. The Rotunda was built with future additions in mind that did not become part of the 1997 $17 million project. A Loggia along the existing Rike Pavilion was designed to complete the Rotunda and provide for a full-service restaurant, state-of-the-art storage areas for works of art, a small lecture hall, and other visitor amenities. Thus, a softening in the transition between the new Rotunda and the Rike Pavilion will be accomplished upon completion of this Loggia addition.

All materials used in the new construction were chosen with the quality and feel of the 1930 building in mind. Marble floors made with 24 x 24-inch panels, skim-coated plaster walls, brass accents, and limestone stairs echo those same details in the Great Hall. In order to achieve the utmost continuity between new and old, the museum ordered the exterior sandstone from the Briar Hill Quarry outside Cleveland that had supplied the sandstone for the 1930 structure. The quarry, which had previously closed but reopened in order to provide the stone for the new addition, was able to almost perfectly match the stone from the original museum building. All galleries, except that devoted to Contemporary art, were furnished with cork flooring, echoing the extensive use of this material by Green. Old grillwork that had been in storage for years was refinished and reused as return-air grills in the galleries. In the Contemporary gallery that had formerly been an open courtyard bordered by a brick wall with three semicircular open arches, wrought-iron grills purchased by Mrs. Carnell were restored and placed over glass windows looking out into the Italian Cloister. In this way, the sense of openness and spaciousness of the original architecture was maintained. This same concept was applied in the Shaw Gothic Cloister that opens onto the Medieval European galleries. Glass doors covered the three semicircular openings and the original stonework of the arches was restored. Thus, even in the new construction, details and feelings from the 1928 building were honored and capitalized upon.

Designing the Rotunda interior presented particular challenges as visitor services and amenities, such as a coatroom and The Museum Store, needed to be incorporated without intruding on the goal of offering visitors a grand and elegant ceremonial museum entrance. Luxurious materials, a classical design approach, and vigilance in minimizing visual clutter helped to achieve the goal of offering visitors a

Color Rendering of The Dayton Art Institute: Propylaeum. Levin Porter Smith, Inc. - Architect.

Tempera and Marker Rendering of Final Expansion Scheme, Phase I, expansion and Renovation, The Dayton Art Institute. Levin Porter Associates, Inc. - Architects.

pleasing, yet functional, entrance to the museum. The hand-forged steel handrails by Dayton artist Hamilton Dixon provide visual focus to the stairwell and make an immediate aesthetic statement. In planning the railing design with the artist, the museum stressed the need for a railing that carried some Neoclassical vocabulary to meld with similar allusions in the Rotunda architecture.

The reinstallation and reinterpretation of the Collection were among the major goals of the renovation. New galleries devoted to African, Oceanic, Pre-Columbian, Contemporary American, and Medieval European art allowed the museum to display these collections to their full advantage for the first time in the museum's history. The exhibition designer, Elroy Quenroe, worked to create environments for each work of art that spoke to the culture and aesthetic of artist and period. Works of art were arranged in a geographically and chronologically reasoned order for the first time in the museum's history and informative object labels were created so the novice visitor could better learn about and enjoy the collections. The entire project was planned and completed with the Collection in our hearts and with the community in our minds. We hope Mrs. Carnell would approve.

MARIANNE LORENZ
Assistant Director for Collections and Programs, 1989-1998

GENERAL MOTORS ENTRANCE ROTUNDA STAIRCASE

SHAW GOTHIC CLOISTER

GENERAL MOTORS ENTRANCE ROTUNDA

ENDNOTES:

1. *Dayton Journal.* October 19, 1929.

2. Wharton, Edith. *Italian Villas and Their Gardens.* 1904: p. 128.

3. Washburn-Freund, Frank. *Art News.* 1927, p. 1.

4. *Dayton Daily News.* January 8, 1930.

5. *Dayton Journal.* June 2, 1929.

6. *Dayton Journal.* June 2, 1929.

7. Claude Brewer, Cecil. *Journal of the British Institute of British Architects.* March 29, 1919: p. 83ff.

Collection

CATALOGUE ENTRIES

*Aurthors
in alphabetical order:*

Priscilla Colt (PC)
Consultant on Contemporary Art, 1967-1972

Roger J. Crum (RJC)
Assistant Professor of Art History, The University of Dayton

Clarence W. Kelley (CWK)
Curator of Asian Art, 1981-1994

Li Jian (LJ)
Curator of Asian Art, 1995-present

Marianne Lorenz (MAL)
Assistant Director for Collections and Programs, 1990-1998

Alexander Lee Nyerges (ALN)
Director and CEO, 1992-present

Marianne Richter (MAR)
Curator of American Art, 1991-1995

Todd D. Smith (TDS)
Curator of American Art, 1995-1997

Dominique H. Vasseur (DHV)
Senior Curator/Curator of European Art, 1979-present

Selected
Works from

AFRICAN ART

The Dayton Art

Institute Permanent

Collection

Africa

Jenne style, Mali

KNEELING FEMALE FIGURE, *11th -16th century*

Terra-cotta

H: 10 1/4 inches

Museum purchase, 1981.9

This small figure, made of fired clay, is one of dozens of similar figural works unearthed since the 1930s from habitation mounds that cluster in the Inland Niger Delta of Mali. They date from the period that saw the rise and fall of the Mali and Songhai empires and development of complex urban centers of learning and commerce. Jenne, the city that gives the style its name, was a major port during the ancient trans-Saharan trade with North Africa and the Near East. It is the oldest city in West Africa and the site of a famous mosque and many adobe buildings of great architectural distinction.

The woman kneels in a position of respect and obeisance. Her numerous bracelets and anklets and the large amulet of her necklace are probably indications of high social status. The temple scarifications are thought to identify her as belonging to Kagora Soninke, a group that is believed to have migrated in the 15th century to the Bandiagara escarpment where it could have influenced the culture of the Dogon people.

The figure was hand-and-tool-formed from a solid mass of clay, tempered (mixed) with pulverized bits of pottery and organic matter to insure its integrity during firing. The details were incised, or appliquéd. It was covered with a thin coat of colored slip (a mixture of clay and water) and fired in an open pit at a relatively low temperature.

What the figure's function was and what the distinctive gestures signify remain unknown. In some African societies, hands on the head signify grief and mourning; or it is possible that the gestures indicate a source of pain and the sculpture was made as a surrogate to appeal to the spiritual beings in a healing ritual such as has been documented among the Dogon people in this century.

PC

SUGGESTED READINGS:

de Grunne, Bernard. **Terres Cuites Anciennes de l'Quest Africain.** Louvain-la-Neuve: Institute superieur d'archeologie et d'histoire de l'art, College Erasme, 1980 (text in English and French).

McIntosh, Susan, and Roderick McIntosh. "Finding West Africa's Oldest City." **National Geographic** (Volume 162, No. 3, 1982).

Africa
Republic of Zaire, Kuba people

FEMALE MASK (NGADY MWAASH), *19th century*

Wood, cowrie shells, glass beads, paint, raffia cloth, trade cloth
H: 10 5/8 inches (face only)
Museum purchase with funds provided by the Anne E. Charch Bequest, 1991.1

This elaborate image of a beautiful woman is a Kuba mask, a type originating with the Northern Kete and used by a number of peoples of the ancient Kuba federation in Southern Zaire. It is one of three mask types that have varying roles in a repertoire of masquerades that play a large part in shaping and giving order to Kuba societies. They appear in initiation rituals, royal celebrations at the Kingdom's capital, and funerals. *Ngady Mwaash* (a female mask) is the sister of *Woot* (Creator God) and wife of *Mwaash a Mbooy*, the founding hero and king of the *Bushoong* (his brother), the antihero who represents the commoners and competes for the favors of *Ngady Mwaash*.

The female mask's headdress is a diviner (priestess) and symbolizes another facet of its persona. As such, she is closely associated with the nature spirits that have a powerful and persistent influence in daily lives of the Kuba peoples. The diagonal lines extending from the lower eyelid to the jaw line represent tears that this, and other masks of Central Africa, shed when they take part in the funeral ritual of an initiated member of their clan. The meaning of the fabric band that covers her lips is not reported.

Ngady Mwaash also performs as Kalyengal ("mother of initiation") in ceremonies that celebrate the young initiate's rebirth and prepare him to enter adulthood. This crucial change of status is symbolized by his passage through the spread out legs of the female masquerade.

Formally, the mask combines the Kuba artist's affection for animated surface pattern and his/her respect for underlying sculptural form and anatomy. The ovoid shape of the head and the broad, yet nuanced, planes of the face contrast strikingly with the lively geometry of the surface. In addition to the beads, cowries and fiber balls lend scale and color to the larger forms. These well-orchestrated details find analogous patterns in the sounds and movement of the accompanying music and dance.

PC

SUGGESTED READINGS:

Koloss, Hans-Joachim. **Art of Central Africa: Masterpieces from the Berlin Museum für Volkerkunde**. *Exhibition catalogue. New York: The Metropolitan Museum of Art, 1990.*

Preston, George N. **Sets, Series and Ensembles in African Art**. *Exhibition catalogue. New York: Center for African Art, 1985.*

Africa
Republic of Zaire, Lobala people
SLIT DRUM IN THE FORM OF A BUFFALO, *20th century*
Wood
L: 8 feet, 8 1/2 inches
Museum purchase with funds provided by the Thomas C. Colt, Jr., Memorial Fund,
1985.39

A slit drum (also called a slit gong) is essentially a hollowed-out log or block of wood that, when struck, makes a pleasant and resonant sound. It has long been used in Central Africa to transmit messages over some distance and also accompany dance. Often depicting the forest buffalo, at times it reached imposing size and stood for the power and prestige of the chief, enhancing his ability to lead and protect his village.

Once the drum's outside perimeter was established, it was carefully hollowed out to leave a thick and thin lip on either side of the slit. This produced higher (female) and lower (male) sounds, approximating those of the tonal language characteristic of the Bantu language family. The skilled drummer, using variations in accent and rhythms, could make the drum "talk" in an abridgement of the spoken language. It was most sonorous in the late evening or early morning and could be heard over distances of four to 12 miles.

The Art Institute's drum belongs to a stylistically cohesive group made in the Ubangi River village of Dongo. Of these, it is the largest and formally the sparest. The buffalo's torso (the sound chamber) and legs (the supports) echo the shapes of the original log's cylinder; against these are played the delicately proportioned head, neck, and tail. A long, flat plane, reaching from the tail through the head, contributes to its unity and dramatic impact. The civilized act of the highly skilled artist-craftsman has metaphorically brought the untamed force of the forest under control and transferred its power to the chief and the village.

In 1905, the British carried out a punitive expedition against a village of northern Zaire and the officer in charge reported:

> The [village] drum was an object of great reverence; we saw several . . . but none so big. Apparently the size was relative to each "sultan's" importance. That we carried away the drum was of great effect in assuring the people that Yambio [the chief] was really done for.

Reports from the Congo, dating as early as 1942, attest to the rise of new technologies and the gradual silencing of the drums.

PC

SUGGESTED READINGS:

Brandel, Rose. **The Music of Central Africa: an Ethnomusicological Study**. *The Hague: M. Nijhoff, 1961.*

Carrington, J.F. **Talking Drums of Africa**. *London: Carey Kingsgate Press, 1946.*

Africa
Republic of Zaire, Yombe people
MALE RITUAL FIGURE (NKISI), *late 19th - early 20th century*
Wood, glass, iron, kaolin
H: 7 1/2 inches
Museum purchase, 1978.111

This is a power figure (*nkisi*), which means that its owner ritually added to it ingredients such as millet flour and animal blood for their protective and/or curative powers. In this instance, the material has been added to the crown of the head. The Yombe are a subgroup of the Kongo, a powerful kingdom with a long history rich in wood, stone, and metal sculpture making that functioned to enhance the secular and religious powers of its leaders. Cultural and commercial contacts with Europeans dating back to the 15th century may have influenced Kongo art in the direction of stylized naturalism or perhaps this was an indigenous tendency. In any case, it is integral to this figure as evidenced by the ease with which the kneeling pose and gem-like carving of detail are executed.

The figure is as rich in meaning as it is in form. The kneeling pose is a convention meant to convey respect or to indicate that the kneeler wishes to intervene in an discussion. He chews on a stalk of a plant (*mukhuisa*) believed to be useful in driving out evil spirits. The iron band encircling it gives the appearance of a ceremonial object. In his left hand he holds a horn, perhaps a drinking cup which signifies status. A close look at this reveals an intriguing and unexplained detail: the abnormal crook or upturn of the last joint of the little finger, also seen on a *nkisi* in the collection of the Berlin Museum für Volkerkunde.

Comparisons of this figure with a kneeling figure in The Metropolitan Museum of Art and early photos of power figures collected in the region before 1874 reveal a broad stylistic range within the general type. The Art Institute's figure falls somewhere between the full and striking naturalism of the former and the conventional treatment of the latter. Further research may reveal whether the differences reflect a change over time, localized variations, or the effect of outside influences.

PC

SUGGESTED READINGS:

Koloss, Hans-Joachim. **Art of Central Africa: Masterpieces from the Berlin Museum für Volkerkunde**. *Exhibition catalogue. New York: The Metropolitan Museum of Art, 1990.*

MacGaffey, Wayne, and Michael Harris. **Astonishment and Power: Kongo Minkisi and the Art of Renee Stout**. *Exhibition catalogue. Washington, D.C.: National Museum of African Art, 1993.*

Africa
Republic of Zaire, Lulua people

STANDING FEMALE FIGURE (LUPINGA LUA LUIMPE)

second half, 19th century
Wood, camwood powder, palm oil
H: 21 1/2 inches
Museum purchase with funds provided by the Associate Board's 1972 Art Ball and
other sources, 1971.149

This compact and richly elaborated figure was made to bring beauty and good fortune to the Lulua newborn according to scholarly reports from the field. Inhabited by the spirits of the ancestors, it was placed near the child upon its birth to ensure that the spirits' protective powers and wisdom would be perpetuated. Visual images served both practical and spiritual needs in African societies by transmitting through the generations the values that gave order to their collective and personal lives. It was believed that beauty and perfection of form made them effective.

The sculpture's clearly articulated volumes reveal a firm grasp of anatomical structure. The counterthrusts of head, shoulders, and belly (with its prominent navel that was believed to emphasize the link between mother and child) are sensitively balanced and then stabilized by the large feet. Details of an intricate headdress, overall scarification, and costume cover the surface in low relief. The surface was further enriched with a complex mix of red earth (or camwood powder), kaolin, and palm oil, added by the mother in ritual applications. Baby, mother, and sculpture were coated in these materials and then bathed in rainwater (preferred for purity over lake or stream water). The cup in the figure's left hand was filled with symbolic ingredients.

It is likely that the figure predates 1880 to 1885, the height of the rule of the Mukenga Kalamba, who, during his supremacy, purged traditional institutions, destroyed sculptures, and forbade representations of scarifications as well as scarification itself. Given its age, it is difficult to reconstruct with certainty its full meaning, but field information has been taken as a starting point. According to experts, the figure's attributes belong to the ceremonial garb of a chief, notable, or hunter/warrior. These accessories date from an epoch at least a century or more ago.

PC

SUGGESTED READINGS:

Cahill, Jane van Nuis. "A Rare Bena Lulua Sculpture." **Bulletin of The Dayton Art Institute** (Vol. 31, 1): 1-4.

Timmermans, Paul. "Essai de Typologie la Sculpture des Bena Luluwa de Kasai." **African Tervuren** (Vol. 12): 12-27.

Africa

Nigeria, Yoruba people

SHEATH AND CROWN FOR RITUAL STAFF, *20th century*

Beads, cotton fabric, leather

H: 60 inches

Gift of Mr. and Mrs. Vincent Bolling, Jr., 1975.61

This splendid beaded sheath (*ewu*) clothed a ritual sword—the symbol of the powers of *Orisha Oko*, a Yoruba female deity of agriculture and fertility. Attached are a cap (to protect the sword's handle), arms, a quadruped, four "flaps", and two "pockets" at the lower end. On its surface, a face and a long dagger are depicted. The attached arms are very unusual among documented sheaths.

The face, the zigzags, and the interlaces figured on the sheath also appear on crowns and other royal Yoruba beadwork. According to one scholar, the face represents ancestral power, while the zigzag and the interlace signify supernatural command. Thus, the sword and the sheath together embody universal Yoruba values: fertility, wealth, respect for ancestor and divinity, generosity, and social order.

Five layers of cotton fabric form the foundation for the sheath's beadwork. The beads are strung on cotton thread and sewn in tightly spaced rows. A printed, cotton lining covers the exposed stitchery on the reverse side, and the combination of cloth layers and beads forms a semi-rigid plane. Eyes, nose, and mouth are modeled in low relief, while other components (arms, bird, and quadruped) are separately formed in the round and attached. It seems better to call the technique bead construction, rather than beadwork or embroidery, since the beads act as integral structured units in an interplay of form, color, and texture.

The iron sword itself was believed to have multiple powers; it was a guardian of the farm and its produce, a symbol of fertility for the barren female devotee, and an accessory to judicial authority in trials of witchcraft. Differing legends relate its origins. One tells of a barren woman who was unfairly accused of witchcraft. When she was tried and proved innocent, blacksmiths were called upon to forge a shining sword from her hoes, after which she bore children and became a rich and powerful figure.

PC

SUGGESTED READINGS:

Fagg, William, and John Pemberton. **Yoruba Beadwork**. *New York: Pace Editions, 1980.*

Thompson, Robert Farris. **Black Gods and Kings: Yoruba Art at the University of California**. *Bloomington: Indiana University Press, 1976.*

Selected

Works from

AMERICAN ART

The Dayton Art

Institute Permanent

Collection

American (Massachusetts)
SLANT–TOP DESK, *around 1770*
Mahogany, eastern white pine, and basswood
H: 45 x W: 41 1/4 x D: 20 1/2 inches
Gift of Mrs. Charles F. Dickson, 1964.23

This Chippendale-style desk, made for Sarah Wilson Bullock of Williamstown, Massachusetts, probably has a Massachusetts origin. The "oxbow" shape of the desk front, the carved shell drop on the skirt, and the highly articulated talons on the ball-and-claw feet were all popular among Massachusetts furniture makers. The slant-top opens to reveal seven small drawers that alternate with open file compartments featuring scalloped dividers. An inlaid sunburst design is featured on the locked center compartment, an unusual decorative element in a period in which carving and japanning (lacquering) were preferred to inlay. The butterfly brasses, most likely imported from England, are original to the piece. The primary wood is imported, fine-grain mahogany, prized by both furniture makers and patrons for its rich color, pattern, durability, and grain. The presence of inlay and use of mahogany, a luxury wood, indicate that this desk was intended for a person of affluence.

The English Chippendale style was popularized by the 1754 publication of Thomas Chippendale's design book, *The Gentleman and Cabinet-Maker's Director*, although elements of this new aesthetic were already fashionable during the 1740s. The Chippendale style differs from the preceding Queen Anne style in its new emphasis on curvilinearity, asymmetry, and ornate decoration based on Chinese, Gothic, and French design sources. In America, the Chippendale style was popular from the 1750s until the 1790s. Colonial furniture makers adapted the style to suit Americans' taste for substantial, plain pieces, and thus American pieces, especially those made in Puritan New England centers, are less ornate than their European counterparts. Additionally, the new forms and decorative motifs were often used in combination with older elements such as the ball-and-claw foot. As a result of such modifications, American Chippendale pieces have their own distinctive quality, as seen in this robust, slant-top desk.

MAR

SUGGESTED READINGS:

Hecksher, Morris H., and Leslie Greene Bowman. **American Rococo, 1750-1775: Elegance in Ornament**. New York: The Metropolitan Museum of Art and Los Angeles County Museum of Art, 1992.

Jobe, Brock, and Myrna Kaye. **New England Furniture: Queen Anne and Chippendale**. Boston: Houghton Mifflin Company, 1984.

Attributed to Thomas Affleck (1740-1795)

American (Philadelphia), 18th century

CHIPPENDALE SIDE CHAIR, *around 1772*

Mahogany with modern upholstery

H: 38 inches

Museum purchase with funds provided by the James F. Dicke Family, 1998.9

In the second half of the 18th century, Philadelphia was the largest and wealthiest city in America. In these pre-Revolutionary times, Philadelphia's close ties to England resulted in Philadelphians' keen appreciation for the latest in English taste and fashion. Among these in furniture was the introduction of the Chippendale style, named for the important English cabinetmaker Thomas Chippendale (1718?-1779). American furniture makers were particularly influenced by Chippendale's 1762 publication entitled *The Gentleman and Cabinet-Maker's Director.* This book of engraved designs by Chippendale was one of the most important examples of English Rococo—an elegant and exuberant style originating in France earlier in the century.

In 1763, Scottish-born Thomas Affleck arrived in Philadelphia where he joined cabinetmaker Joshua Fisher and sons. In 1772, Sarah Logan married into the Fisher family and it is probably for this occasion that Sarah's father William ordered a number of pieces of furniture for the new bride and groom. It is thought that this side chair and five other identical ones were part of the Logan-Fisher commission. Incidentally, Affleck worked with the Fisher establishment through the beginning of the American Revolution. However, the Logan-Fishers and Affleck were forced to leave Philadelphia on account of their sympathies to the Quakers and Royalist England.

While Philadelphia furniture makers most often adapted Chippendale's designs to suit their own purposes, Affleck, with only minor modifications, virtually copied the design from plate X in *The Gentleman and Cabinet-Maker's Director.* Indeed, of Philadelphia chairs by any number of cabinetmakers, this one seems to follow Chippendale's original intent most closely. Fortunately, of the other five chairs thought to be in this set, three others are in the following collections: the Philadelphia Museum of Art, The Metropolitan Museum of Art, and the Winterthur Museum (Winterthur, Delaware). One other is in a private collection and the sixth one has yet to be located.

DHV

Suggested Readings:

Hecksher, Morrison. **American Furniture in The Metropolitan Museum of Art**. *New York: Random House, 1985, p. 99, fig. 53.*

Hummel, Charles. **A Winterthur Guide to American Chippendale Furniture**. *New York: Crown Publishing Co., 1976, p. 75, fig. 69.*

Philadelphia: Three Centuries of Philadelphia Furniture. *Philadelphia, 1976, p. 98.*

John Trumbull
(1756-1843) American

ROMANTIC LANDSCAPE, *around 1783*

Oil on wood panel

12 x 18 inches

Gift of Mr. I. Austin Kelly III, in memory of his great-great-grandfather,
Ironton Austin Kelly, founder of Ironton, Ohio, 1971.264

John Trumbull studied painting in England with fellow American artist Benjamin West, who had him copy the Old Masters as well as learn contemporary styles. Indeed, *Romantic Landscape* shows Trumbull's familiarity with the work of earlier landscape artists, such as the French 17th century painter Claude Lorrain, and the contemporary English school of landscape painting. The painting's composition is carefully arranged to create a picturesque view in which varied topographical features form a pleasing whole. For example, shadowed rock formations in the left foreground contrast with the sparkling river in the middle ground. The copse in which a castle is visible, tower on the hill in the background, and swirling clouds at right add to the landscape's studied charm. The tranquil scene is bathed in golden light, a device Trumbull likely derived from the influential example of Lorrain.

This work is one of Trumbull's earliest landscape paintings, probably made soon after his return from his first trip to England in 1780. Trumbull, writing in 1841, recalled painting this landscape before his trip. More recently, scholars have attributed *Romantic Landscape* to about 1783, based on the painting's great similarities to Trumbull's works of 1783 and 1784. The early date of this painting is noteworthy, for most of Trumbull's landscapes were created more than 20 years later, between 1804 and 1808.

Trumbull is best remembered today for his paintings of historical events such as *The Declaration of Independence*—one version of which hangs in the United States Capitol. Like many artists of his time, he viewed history painting as the highest form of the pictorial arts and devoted much of his career to its pursuit. Remarkably, his works were achieved under a considerable handicap: a childhood accident left Trumbull blind in one eye.

MAR

SUGGESTED READINGS:

Copper, Helen A. **John Trumbull: The Hand and Spirit of a Painter**. *Patricia Mullen Burnham, Martin Price, Jules David Prown, Oswaldo Rodriguez Roque, Egon Verheyen and Bryan Wolf essays. Exhibition catalogue. New Haven: Yale University Art Gallery, 1982.*

Jaffe, Irma B. **John Trumbull: Patriot Artist of the American Revolution**. *Boston: New York Graphic Society, 1975.*

Sizer, Theodore. **The Works of Colonel John Trumbull**. *Rev. ed. New Haven and London: Yale University Press, 1967.*

American (Pennsylvania)

18th century

PAINTED CHEST, *1790*

Poplar wood, painted, with brass pulls

H: 26 1/2 x W: 50 1/2 x D: 20 1/2 inches

Gift of the Estate of Mr. Elmer R. Webster and Mr. Robert A. Titsch, 1995.52

Painted wooden chests, such as this handsome example, play an important role in the furniture tradition of southeastern Pennsylvania, a land settled by German immigrants. Largely farmers, these hard-working people brought with them the cultural traditions, among them work, thrift, and their faith. The conservative German settlers found in this rich region fertile soil to till and abundant raw materials from which to create the necessities for their neat and tidy homes.

At the time of her wedding, a young woman would bring a dowry to her husband, hence these were sometimes referred to as dowry chests. Like this one bearing the name "Darina Kleinin," a chest would have been an important piece of furniture to a young bride especially in a time before closets and built-in storage. As part of a long tradition of European painted peasant furniture, chests were a necessary place to store clothing, blankets, and valuables. Since they were portable, they also could be used as trunks during travels. Their painted decoration was pleasing to the eye and added to the home's decor. The artisans who decorated them used a variety of motifs: birds, flowers, foliate forms, people, and fanciful animals and creatures; they often included the name of the owner and the date of production.

DHV

Suggested Reading:

Lichten, Frances. **The Art of Rural Pennsylvania**. *New York: Charles Scribner's Sons, 1946.*

Benjamin West
(1738-1820) American

ADONIS, around 1800-1805

Oil on canvas

20 1/8 x 14 1/8 inches

Museum purchase with funds provided by the Honorable Jefferson Patterson, 1982.3

Adonis, a late painting by Benjamin West, reflects the artist's lifelong interest in classical subject matter. It also shows his relatively new awareness of the expressive qualities of color. West depicts Venus' paramour, a hunter, seated by his hounds. Adonis' occupation and connection to Venus are alluded to by the presence of cherubs (a symbol of Venus) carrying a torch and hunting horn. West's knowledge of the great Venetian colorist, Titian (around 1487-1576), is apparent in the rich, appealing colors. The red cloak, blue sky, and the dark hair and eyes provide dramatic contrasts to the soft pinks, grays, and fleshtones. Paintings and sculpture from the Classical and the Renaissance periods may have inspired Adonis' turned pose, which is combined with the sinuous, elongated lines that are characteristic of West's figures.

The child of Pennsylvania Quakers, West went abroad in 1760 and never returned to America. He traveled first to Italy, where he was strongly influenced by Anton Raphael Mengs (1728-1779), one of the pioneers of the Neoclassical style (in which the artist emulates works from classical antiquity). What was to be a short visit to London in 1763 became the colonist's permanent home. West met with great success, eventually serving as the Royal Academy's second president and as historical painter to George III. Although an expatriate, he was an important teacher of many aspiring American painters, including Gilbert Stuart (1755-1828), Charles Willson Peale (1741-1827), and John Trumbull (1756-1843), all of whom traveled to London to study with him.

MAR

SUGGESTED READINGS:

von Erffa, Helmut, and Allen Staley. **The Paintings of Benjamin West**. Exhibition catalogue. New Haven and London: Yale University Press, 1986.

Staley, Allen. **Benjamin West: American Painter at the English Court**. Exhibition catalogue. Baltimore: Baltimore Museum of Art, 1989.

American

19th century

SIDEBOARD, *around 1810*

Mahogany and walnut

H: 4 feet, 1 inch x W: 6 feet, 5 inches x D: 22 1/4 inches

Gift of Mr. Frederick Beck Patterson, 1966.56

The simple lines of this sideboard are characteristic of furniture produced during the American Federal period (1790-1815). The Federal style was the American interpretation of English and French Neoclassicism, a style inspired by excavations at two ancient Roman sites, Pompeii (1748) and Herculaneum (1738). In America, the Neoclassical style, with its clean lines, delicacy, and simple ornamentation, was called "Federal," because it coincided with the rise of the new republic. Americans embraced the Federal style as a departure from the heavier look of the preceding Chippendale style, and because of its associations with the Roman republic, on which American democracy was modeled.

The sideboard, a form new to Federal period dining rooms, was used to store tableware and wine bottles and serve food on its broad surface. Unlike Chippendale furniture, in which ornate carving had been prevalent, Federal pieces relied on inlay and rich veneers in contrasting woods to create strong decorative statements. In this sideboard, veneers of mahogany, a favorite wood of the period, and walnut burl exemplify the new taste. The popularity of classical motifs is apparent in the inclusion of the central swag.

American furniture makers became acquainted with the Neoclassical style from the work of such talented immigrants as Duncan Phyfe and Charles-Honoré Lannuier, as well as from furniture imported from England and the continent, and from two influential design books: George Hepplewhite's *The Cabinet-Makers' and Upholsterers' Guide* (1788) and Thomas Sheraton's *The Cabinet-Maker and Upholsterer's Drawing Book* (1791-1794). Although regional differences occurred in Federal pieces, common design sources and easier transportation between cities made for a greater exchange of ideas between areas.

MAR

SUGGESTED READINGS:

Cooper, Wendy. **Classical Taste in America**. *New York: Abbeville Press, 1993.*

Montgomery, Charles F. **American Furniture: The Federal Period in the Henry Francis du Pont Winterthur Museum**. *New York: Bonanza Books, 1966.*

American (New York City)

Early 19th century

CLASSICAL PIER TABLE, *around 1810-1820*

Wood with mahogany veneer, marble top, alabaster columns, gilt bronze fittings,
mirror, and gilt

H: 36 3/4 x W: 42 1/2 x D: 19 inches

Museum purchase with funds provided by the James F. Dicke Family, 1998.8

Just as American cabinetmakers adapted the European Rococo style by basing their designs on Thomas Chippendale, they also emulated the Neoclassical style that had originated in France in the early part of the 19th century. Neoclassicism came about as the result of several factors; one of the most important of these was the discovery in the mid-18th century of the Roman cities of Pompeii and Herculaneum, which had been buried by volcanic eruptions during the 1st century. The excavations of these cities offered Europeans a first-hand glimpse of how Romans lived, what their furniture looked like, and how their homes were decorated. The French Revolution in 1789 also contributed to the demise of the Rococo in favor of the more elegantly simple Neoclassical style known by several names: Louis XVI, Directoire, and after 1804, Empire, so-named for French Emperor Napoleon I.

Prominent Americans like Benjamin Franklin and Thomas Jefferson had visited Paris during the 1770s and 1780s and had seen the fashionable Neoclassical style. Later, following the French Revolution, many French nobles emigrated to the United States bringing with them their Neoclassical furniture. To a successful young Republic like the United States, the style well suited its purposes, since Neoclassicism called to mind the power and grandeur of the ancient Roman Republic. Furniture, like this pier table, placed against a wall between two windows or doors (i.e. a pier), displays the clean rectilinear, or graceful, curving line characteristic of Roman furniture. Likewise, elements like the columns, acanthus-paw feet, and gilt, low-relief decoration add historical detail that are unmistakably classical in intent.

DHV

Suggested Readings:

Davidson, Marshall B. **The American Heritage History of American Antiques from the Revolution to the Civil War***. New York: The American Heritage Publishing Co., 1968.*

Winchester, Alice, ed. **The Antiques Book***. New York: A.A. Wyn, 1950.*

Attributed to Christian Shively, Jr.
(1770-1836) American

CUPBOARD, *around 1810-1820*
Cherry, walnut, and maple woods
H: 8 feet x W: 5 feet, 2 inches x D: 21 inches
Gift of the Estate of Mr. Elmer R. Webster and Mr. Robert A. Titsch, 1995.48

Christian Shively, Jr., moved with his family from Huntingdon County, Pennsylvania, to the Wolf Creek settlement, west of Dayton, Ohio, in 1805. By virtue of his great strength, Shively was an important addition to the settlement especially during log rollings and barn raisings. Known as a "jack of all trades," Shively had many talents, including physician, bone setter, community undertaker, and cabinetmaker. Although he and his wife, Susan Gripe Shively, are documented as living in a log cabin, business was good for Shively. In 1811, he contracted David Baker of Dayton, Ohio, to build him a two-story stone house, a symbol of his financial success.

The issue of identifying early 19th century Ohio furniture is difficult, as cabinetmakers rarely marked or signed their finished works. Cabinets by Christian Shively, Jr. are no exception; therefore, one must rely on construction materials, visual comparanda, as well as provenance, and local history. The use of walnut and cherry woods is an important feature in identifying Shively's work since a number of walnut and cherry Shively cupboards were located within ten miles of his Wolf Creek home. In 1943, this cabinet belonging to Noah Shively, a grandson of Christian, Jr., appeared on the antiques market and was acquired by the donors. In the years following, other similar cabinets logically thought to be the work of Christian, Jr., were identified from his descendants' households.

This piece is typical of Shively's work in its use of 1 1/8-inch thick walnut and cherry wood. Stylistically, the cupboard bridges the contemporary elegant style of the East Coast and the more no-nonsense style typical of the Northwest Territory. It is, nevertheless, a handsomely proportioned piece, distinguished by an elaborate crown molding, glazed doors, and scrolled side panels.

DHV

Suggested Readings:

Hageman, Jane Sikes. **Ohio Furniture Makers**. Vol. 1. Cincinnati: J.S. Hageman, 1984.

Muller, Charles R. **Made in Ohio: Furniture 1788-1888**. Exhibition catalogue. Columbus, OH: Columbus Museum of Art, 1984: 13-14. Cat. No. 2: 20.

Thomas Sully
(1783-1872) American

PORTRAIT OF ELIAS JONATHAN DAYTON, 1813

Oil on canvas
35 1/4 x 28 1/2 inches
Museum fund for purchase from the Spencer-Dayton Family, 1944.87.1

Thomas Sully's portrait of Dayton was painted three years after the artist's first stay in England. He had studied with American-born portraitist and history painter Benjamin West and the fashionable portraitist Sir Thomas Lawrence. Sully's specialty was portraiture, and he was a prolific artist who painted more than 2,600 works during his long career. In *Portrait of Elias Jonathan Dayton*, the free brushwork and rich coloring reflect the aesthetic sensibility of the Romantic period. Sully later turned from this painterly style to a highly idealized style in which brushwork and color are very controlled.

The sitter in this work, Elias Jonathan Dayton, was the son of General Jonathan Dayton, for whom the city of Dayton, Ohio, was named. The General was one of the original four purchasers of land between the Mad and Great Miami rivers. Although the elder Dayton never visited the area, his son traveled here in 1824 on business for his father. The trip was ill-fated; Elias Dayton died on the return trip to his family home in New Jersey. Shown here at age 33, he is the epitome of the fashionable gentleman of the early Romantic period.

MAR

SUGGESTED READINGS:

Biddle, Edward and Mantle Fielding. **The Life and Works of Thomas Sully (1783-1872)**. New York: Da Capo Press, 1970.

Fabian, Monroe H. **Mr. Sully, Portrait Painter: The Works of Thomas Sully (1783-1872)**. Exhibition catalogue, National Portrait Gallery. Washington, D.C.: Smithsonian Institution Press, 1983.

American
LAFAYETTE COMMEMORATIVE COVERLET, 1824

Wool and cotton, double weave

7 feet, 11 inches x 9 feet, 2 inches

Inscribed "Agriculture & Manufacturers are the Foundation of Our Independence,
July 4, 1824. Gnrl. Lafayette, Tamma Sacket"

Gift of Mr. Elmer R. Webster and Mr. Robert A. Titsch, 1989.70

As one of the last surviving heroes of the American Revolution, General Lafayette received great public acclaim during his famous 1824 "Farewell Tour" of the United States. Americans considered Lafayette to be a link to George Washington, with whom the Frenchman had been so close that he considered the President to be his adopted father. Lafayette's visit also inspired a host of artists and craftsmen to create a number of commemorative paintings, ceramics, and prints, among other things. The Art Institute's coverlet, made for Tamma Sacket, is such a piece. Formerly attributed to John Alexander, the coverlet is now thought to have been made in Ulster County, New York, by one of a group of Scottish-immigrant weavers who shared a common pattern.

Coverlets, used as bed coverings, became common in America in the early 19th century when a number of so-called "fancy weavers" came to America from the British Isles and Germany. In the 1820s, figured patterns, such as that seen in this example, replaced geometric patterns as new technology made complicated designs less costly to produce. The blue and white color scheme was favored among coverlet-makers because indigo was one of few available colorfast dyes.

The Masonic symbols in this coverlet, such as the pillars and square and compass, suggest that the maker or the recipient's family was familiar with the Fraternity of Freemasons. The Freemason movement was very prominent in the early years of the American republic. Many of the founding fathers, including Washington, were Masons. Lafayette, in emulation of his hero, had likewise become a Mason and during his Farewell Tour, Masonic orders organized celebrations in his honor. Because the fraternity had ties to medieval stonemason guilds, Freemasons were concerned with and supported building projects. In the coverlet, that interest is reflected in the inclusion of a building, which may represent Independence Hall, newly renovated for Lafayette's visit.

MAR

SUGGESTED READINGS:

Goody, Rabbit. *"Will the Real James Alexander Coverlets Please Stand Up."* **The Clarion** *(No. 17, 1, Spring 1992): 52-58.*

Homespun to Factory Made: Woolen Textiles in America, *1776-1876. North Andover: Merrimack Valley Textile Museum, 1977.*

Idzerda, Stanley J., Anne C. Loveland, and Marc H. Miller. **Lafayette, Hero of Two Worlds: The Art and Pageantry of His Farewell Tour of America, 1824-1825**. *Exhibition catalogue, The Queens Museum. Distributed by University Press of New England, 1989.*

Attributed to Elizabeth Rheinthaller

American (Montgomery County, Ohio), 19th century

WHIG ROSE QUILT, 1840-1880

Cotton appliqué with stuffed work, red, green, yellow calicos on white ground

with red binding

81 x 80 1/2 inches

Gift of Mr. Elmer R. Webster and Mr. Robert A. Titsch, 1987.267

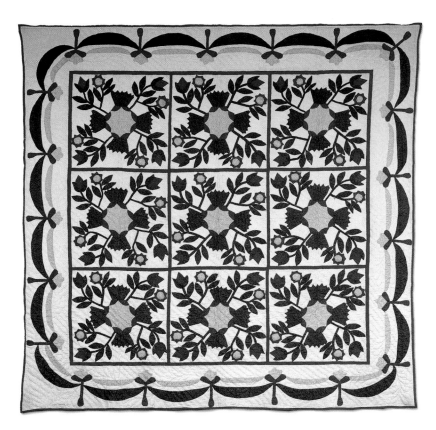

Red and green floral appliqué quilts were very popular throughout Ohio from 1840 until the end of the 1870s, particularly among German immigrants and first-generation German-Americans. A style that originated in the East, the quilt might owe its popularity to the mid-19th century vogue for large, floral designs and red and green color schemes in interior decorating. The Whig Rose pattern of this quilt is named for the 19th century political party and was one of many rose designs favored by quilters. Like most floral appliqué quilts, this one has a repeating design in several blocks framed by a swag border. Secondary colors of pink, yellow (as here), and orange were sometimes used as accents in red and green floral appliqué quilts.

Because appliqué quilts, such as this one, used more material than pieced quilts, they were not intended for daily use. Consequently, a large number of them have survived in relatively good condition. Appliquéd quilts were created by cutting fabric into basic shapes and then sewing the pieces onto a larger cloth into a predetermined pattern. Unlike pieced quilts, in which a straight edge is necessary in order to sew the pieces together, the quilter can use curved pieces in appliqué. As a result of this freedom, curvilinear designs were favored, making floral subjects ideal for appliqué quilts. A filling, called batting, was sandwiched between the top, ornamental layer and a bottom layer that was typically plain muslin. Quilting, which kept the batting in place, was done last. In the case of this quilt, stuffing was added to the center of the flowers before the maker quilted the piece. The quilting in this example is plain, consisting of straight diagonal rows across the quilt.

MAR

SUGGESTED READINGS:

America's Glorious Quilts. Dennis Duke and Deborah Harding, eds. New York: Hugh Lauter Levin Associates, Inc., 1987.

Brackman, Barbara. **Clues in the Calico: A Guide to Identifying and Dating Antique Quilts**. McLean, VA: EPM Publications, 1989.

Clark, Ricky, George W. Knepper, and Ellice Ronsheim. **Quilts in Community: Ohio's Traditions**. Nashville, TN: Rutledge Hill Press, 1991.

Hiram Powers
(1805-1873) American
EVE DISCONSOLATE, *after 1841*
Marble
H: 22 inches
Gift of The Toledo Museum of Art, 1938.48

While the sculptor Hiram Powers was a noted portraitist, his true interest lay in creating full-size "ideal" pieces in which a noble sentiment or idea was expressed. In these works, as he expressed in a letter to Elizabeth Barrett Browning, Powers wished to convey a sense of the figure's soul. His first full-size ideal work was a statue of Eve, begun in 1838; Eve continued to be one of his favorite subjects for many years. The Art Institute's bust was probably made after the large-scale work gained popularity and critical acclaim. Powers ideal pieces, which included the immensely popular and acclaimed *Greek Slave*, were important for elevating Americans' taste in sculpture beyond portraiture.

After early study in Cincinnati, Powers moved to Florence in 1837, where he remained until his death. He gained an international reputation as a sculptor working in the Neoclassical style. Technically, he was an innovator who was much admired by Europeans as well as Americans. In the mid-19th century, most sculptors created clay models from which assistants made plaster casts that remained on display for potential patrons. Upon receiving an order, workmen duplicated a cast in marble using the mechanical pointing process. Powers discovered a way to remain more directly involved in the process, inventing a technique for modeling and carving right into the plaster. Thus, assistants were not needed until the cast was ready to copy in marble.

Powers prided himself on his attention to detail, and he was especially admired for his skill at finishing marble. By using special tools, he made marble surfaces suggest the actual texture of flesh. *Eve Disconsolate* does, indeed, have a convincingly life-like surface texture, which, along with the figure's highly idealized features, was much admired in the 19th century.

MAR

SUGGESTED READINGS:

Crane, Sylvia E. **White Silence: Greenough, Powers and Crawford, American Sculptors in Nineteenth-century Italy**. Coral Gables, FL: University of Miami Press, 1972.

Craven, Wayne. **Sculpture in America: From the Colonial Period to the Present**. New York: Thomas Crowell Company, 1968.

Hiram Powers' Paradise Lost. April Kingsley, curator. Exhibition catalogue. Yonkers: The Hudson River Museum, 1985.

Wunder, Richard P. **Hiram Powers: Vermont Sculptor, 1805-1873**. (2 Volumes). Newark: University of Delaware Press, 1991.

Robert Scott Duncanson
(1821-1872) American

MAYAN RUINS, YUCATAN, 1848

Oil on canvas

14 x 20 inches

Museum purchase with funds provided by the Daniel Blau Endowment, 1984.105

In the 1840s, when the maturing African-American portraitist, still-life, and landscape artist Robert Scott Duncanson lived in and around Cincinnati, the city was a hotbed for discussions on slavery and emancipation. The year 1841, the year Duncanson moved to Mount Healthy, 15 miles north of Cincinnati, also saw the city's notorious race riot. Throughout the decade, Cincinnati negotiated its position as a safe place for freed slaves while keeping its strong economic ties to the South. It is in this context that Duncanson created works such as *Mayan Ruins, Yucatan*, which although it does not directly address, may suggest the contemporary social and political climate of the day. Ostensibly, this painting falls within a type of exotic landscape practiced by such landscape greats as Thomas Cole, Frederick Church, or Martin Johnson Heade. As did many painters of this time, Duncanson turned to illustrations from books and periodicals to find the inspiration for his paintings. The 1840s, an important formative time in Duncanson's career, saw pioneering explorations of Central America by two Englishmen, John Stevens and Frederick Catherwood. Their travels were published in 1843 as *Incidents of Travel in the Yucatan* and, not surprisingly (since Duncanson never traveled to South or Central America), an engraved illustration of the primary building at Kabah (vol. I, plate 15) seems to have provided the inspiration for Duncanson's fantastic picture.

Letters show that the light-skinned Duncanson was well aware of his minority status in a world of predominantly white male artists. The largely self-taught artist relied heavily upon commissions from wealthy Cincinnatians and abolitionists, especially Nicholas Longworth for whom he painted landscape murals in the Longworth home (now the Taft Museum). Patrons like Longworth felt at ease with Duncanson's Hudson River School-derived landscapes and specifically enjoyed the lack of overt attention to racial issues within his works. Nevertheless, works such as this one may indirectly point to another heated racial debate of the time, that of the origin of the Maya, the indigenous people of Mexico, Central and South America. As such, this work may show Duncanson's knowledge of the contemporary interest in the Maya who had been "rediscovered" in 1839 as well as an acknowledgement of questions regarding race and personal identity.

TDS and DHV

SUGGESTED READINGS:

Hartigan, Lynda Roscoe. **Sharing Traditions: Five Black Artists in Nineteenth-Century America**. Exhibition catalogue. Washington, D.C.: National Museum of American Art, 1985.

Ketner, Joseph D. **The Emergence of the African-American Artist: Robert S. Duncanson 1821-1872**. Columbia and London: University of Missouri Press, 1993.

Manthorne, Katherine. **Tropical Renaissance: North American Artists Exploring Latin America, 1839-1879**. Washington, D.C.: Smithsonian, 1989.

McElroy, Guy. **Robert S. Duncanson: A Centennial Exhibition**. Exhibition catalogue. Cincinnati: Cincinnati Art Museum, 1972.

Junius Brutus Stearns
(1810-1885) American

WASHINGTON ON HIS DEATHBED, *1851*

Oil on canvas

37 x 54 1/8 inches

Gift of Mr. Robert Badenhop, 1954.16

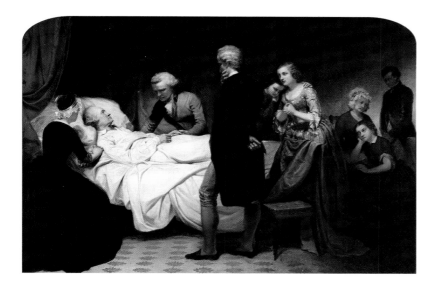

In the 19th century, historical events were considered the noblest type of subject. Although not so well known today, Junius Brutus Stearns was one of the most acclaimed American painters to specialize in history painting. He began painting historical subjects in 1840 and is best known for his series of four canvases depicting the life of George Washington, of which *Washington on his Deathbed* is the last. The other three chronicle Washington's marriage and his farming and military careers. Stearns commenced this series in 1849, the 50th anniversary of Washington's death and a time when Americans were especially interested in their first President.

Stearns' depiction of Washington's death attests to his thorough research, which included talking to Washington's step-grandson and reading eyewitness accounts of the event. Martha Washington is shown standing by her husband's side, while the President's superintendent, Tobias Lear, holds his hand. Washington's friend and doctor, James Craik, is at the foot of the bed. The figures at the right are the five servants who were present at the President's death.

Washington displays a calm, stoical attitude toward death. In control of his emotions, the hero steadfastly confronts his end. Although this is one combat he cannot win, Washington's unemotional acceptance makes him nonetheless triumphant over death. His companions are equally subdued, grieving in a quiet, seemly manner. In the 19th century, such a display of self-control embodied the ideal Christian attitude toward death, which held that only through calm acceptance could one be said to be victorious. Stearns thus uses the historical event to create a paradigm of Christian virtue.

MAR

Suggested Reading:

Thistlethwaite, Mark. "Picturing the Past: Junius Brutus Stearns' Paintings of George Washington." **Arts in Virginia** *(Vol. 25, No. 2-3, 1985): 12-23.*

Peter Frederick Rothermel
(1812-1895) American

KING LEAR, *1858*

Oil on canvas

125 x 87 1/4 inches

Museum purchase with funds provided in part by the James F. Dicke Family, 1996.272

ALN

SUGGESTED READINGS:

Thistlethwaite, Mark. **Painting in the Grand Manner: The Art of Peter Frederick Rothermel (1812-1895).** *Chadds Ford, PA: Brandywine River Museum, 1995.*

Following in the footsteps of young America's great history painters such as John Trumbull and Benjamin West, Peter Frederick Rothermel became the torchbearer for this tradition until the torch slowly flickered and was extinguished by the end of the 19th century. In his day, Rothermel was one of the most respected and highly paid painters. In 1849, he was described as belonging "to the very foremost rank of living history painters in this country, and in the opinion of many of those able to form a correct judgment, takes the lead of all." A history of Philadelphia, written in 1884, recorded that at mid-century, "No Philadelphia artist is more widely known than Peter F. Rothermel." At the time of his death in 1895, he was largely forgotten. One obituary said of him, "with him passes away the veteran of that sturdy style of historical painting now neglected and out of vogue."

Born in 1817, in Nescopeck, Pennsylvania, Rothermel began his adult life as a surveyor and sign painter. He studied with painters John R. Smith and Otis Bass and then at the Pennsylvania Academy of the Fine Arts, where he would later serve nearly a decade as a board member. Beginning as a portrait painter, his first known portrait dates from 1838. He turned to history painting as a profession, one at which he excelled. History painting in the early 19th century was often regarded as the highest form of painting to which an artist could aspire, a notion in which Rothermel passionately believed. In the new nation, it was popular for its appeal to patriotism and the growing national identity. Rothermel's most widely regarded and popular works were his 1851 depiction of Patrick Henry's legendary speech against the British Stamp Act and his 1867 mural-like work of Pickett's Charge from the Battle of Gettysburg. The painting measures 16 by 32 feet, for which he was paid a commission of $25,000, a sum that rivaled the commissions of leading landscape painters such as Albert Bierstadt and Frederick Church.

In 1856, Rothermel traveled to Europe and then settled in Rome where he joined dozens of American artists including Sanford Gifford and Worthington Whittredge. While abroad, he became acquainted with work of Peter Paul Rubens and Eugène Delacroix, whose work he greatly admired. In 1858, while still in Rome, he created this work. He returned to the United States in 1859 to continue his history painting. He is thought to have been a mentor and friend to another Philadelphia painter, Thomas Eakins, whose brother-in-law married Rothermel's daughter.

This work, *King Lear*, depicts Act 4, Scene 6 from Shakespeare's play, a source he used often for inspiration. This is one of three paintings he executed from the play, including a smaller version of this work, which is now in a private collection. The work was commissioned for the private art gallery in the Rittenhouse Square mansion of noted Philadelphia collector Joseph Harrison, Jr., for a price of $3,000.

Edward Edmondson
(1830-1884) American

THE TEMPERANCE LECTURE, *1861*

Oil on canvas

24 x 20 inches

Gift of the Dayton Public Library, 1953.31

The moral tone of Edward Edmondson's *The Temperance Lecture*, common to many paintings of everyday life (genre painting) in the Victorian era, reflects an artistic tradition derived from such 18th century English painters as William Hogarth and realized throughout 19th century American art and culture. Children, who symbolized innocence, were often an integral part of these works, serving to heighten the message's impact. Here, the weeping boy's silent reproach causes the older man (presumably his father), clearly affected by this mute "lecture," to hang his head in shame. The figures' rags and homeless state reflect their poverty, an evil associated with excessive drinking. Edmondson's attention to the details of their decaying surroundings underscores their disgrace. Edmondson's choice of subject matter reflects Americans' concern over the problem of alcoholism in the mid-19th century, a time that saw the rise of temperance groups such as the Order of Good Templars. Because of the great need for sober, able-bodied men in 1861, the year in which the Civil War began, Edmondson's depiction of the evils attached to drink was especially timely.

The Temperance Lecture is the only known genre painting made by Edmondson, one of Dayton's most accomplished painters of the 19th century. It seems to have been popular locally, for 24 years after its completion, it was reproduced as a chromolithograph by a Cincinnati firm; the Art Institute also owns an impression of this print. In addition to this sole genre painting, Edmondson painted many portraits, landscapes, and still-lifes. Although some contemporary accounts claim that he received only one formal art lesson, the true extent of his training is unknown. However, it is likely that Edmondson's education was furthered by his friendship with the photographer Thomas Walker Cridland, who had been part of the New York art scene before moving to Dayton in 1852. Cridland's son, Thomas Harper Cridland, served as the model for the figure of the boy in *The Temperance Lecture*. Edmondson later moved his studio to Cridland's home. In the 1880s, Edmondson moved his family to California, where the artist died in 1884.

MAR

Suggested Readings:

Evans, Bruce H. **The Paintings of Edward Edmondson (1830-1884)**. *Exhibition catalogue. Dayton, OH: The Dayton Art Institute, 1972.*

Hills, Patricia. **The Painter's America: Rural and Urban Life, 1810-1910**. *New York and Washington, D.C.: Praeger Publishers in association with the Whitney Museum of American Art, 1974.*

Sanford R. Gifford
(1823-1880) American
SCRIBNER'S PASTURE IN THE CATSKILLS, *around 1863*
Oil on canvas
8 x 18 1/2 inches
Gift of Mr. I. Austin Kelly III, in memory of his great-great-grandfather,
Ironton Austin Kelly, founder of Ironton, Ohio, 1978.179

Sanford Gifford's landscape paintings present tranquil views of the natural world, such as that seen in *Scribner's Pasture in the Catskills*. The field depicted in this scene belonged to Scribner's Boarding House, a well-known tourist stop located near Kaaterskill Falls. The brushy application of paint and the rich golden tones of the trees and earth are hallmarks of Gifford's style. Especially fascinated by light and atmosphere, his landscapes were often varnished several times to create a hazy, veiled effect. Unlike the wilderness often depicted by Thomas Cole or Frederick Church, Gifford's scenes usually convey a more pastoral, bucolic vision of nature. Thus, in this painting, Gifford does not condemn the fact that the wilderness has been cleared; instead the central figures of man and dog are an integral part of this harmonious painting.

Gifford, who grew up in Hudson, New York, across the river from Thomas Cole's home, had decided by his early twenties to specialize in landscape painting. Although he admired Cole's work, Gifford's own intimate views of nature were more akin to the paintings of Asher B. Durand, the other great, first-generation Hudson River School artist. After the mid-1850s, Gifford's interest in the properties of light and in atmospheric effect was evident in such works as *Scribner's Pasture in the Catskills*. While he sketched outdoors regularly, Gifford's final works, made in his studio, were based more on a combination of specific views and his imagination. Sometimes criticized for exaggerating atmospheric effects to the point of blurry indistinctness, at their best, Gifford's "air-paintings" were remarkably true to nature.

MAR

Suggested Readings:

American Paradise: The World of the Hudson River School. *Exhibition catalogue. New York: Metropolitan Museum of Art, 1987.*

Cikovsky, Jr., Nikolai. **Sanford Robinson Gifford**. *Exhibition catalogue. Austin: University of Texas Press, 1970.*

Myers, Kenneth. **The Catskills: Painters, Writers, and Tourists in the Mountains, 1820-1895**. *Exhibition catalogue. Yonkers: The Hudson River Museum of Westchester, 1987.*

Weiss, Ida. **Sanford Robinson Gifford**. *New York: Garland Series, 1977.*

Charles Soule, Jr.
(1835-1897) American
CIVIL WAR WIDOW, around 1865
24 1/2 x 20 inches
Gift of Mrs. Helen Soule Boehm, 1961.18

The image of the role of women during the Civil War that Americans currently carry has derived from Hollywood spectacles of the event. However, as historians are beginning to rediscover, the place of women during the war was as central as in later wars. Ranging from maintaining the home front and the business sector to organizing large fund-raising activities, such as the Sanitary Fairs, to support the efforts, women were as important to the sustaining of the culture as their fighting fathers, brothers, or husbands.

Instead of focusing on the positive accomplishments of these women in *Civil War Widow*, Charles Soule, Jr. illustrates another truth of the *war between the states*. For subjects like Soule's, the aftermath of the war meant a different place within a patriarchal society. Widows often became wards of their families or of the state, and significantly, following the war, the very men they had aided usually forced these women out of the businesses they had helped to maintain. What fate awaits this widow remains uncertain. Grieving and mourning found their place among American visual representation during the latter part of the 19th century, often appearing as mass-produced prints, book illustrations, and images in gift books and other moralistic texts.

The son of the Dayton portraitist Charles Soule, Sr., Charles Jr. began his career like others as a carriage and sign painter and by 1858 was listed in the Dayton business directory as a portrait painter. He, like his father, traveled throughout the region as an itinerant artist. While the emotional impetus for the painting is not yet known, its visual prototype is known. Soule based this painting on a work titled *Evangeline* by the Scottish artist, Thomas Faed. *Evangeline* derives from Henry Wadsworth Longfellow's 1847 poem of the same title. Set in Acadie (present-day Nova Scotia), Longfellow's eponymous heroine spent her life searching for her lover Gabriel who was seized and deported by the British during their colonization. As a standard image for mourning and female loss Faed's work was widely distributed in the United States through prints, photographs, and postcards. It is, no doubt, through one of these examples that Soule saw and later copied (with only the slightest rearranging) the image.

TDS

Suggested Readings:

Maher, KAthleen, **Heroes of the Home Front: Life North of the Battlefield**, *exhibition catalogue, The Lockwood-Mathews Mansion Museum, Norwalk, CT., 1995.*

Albert Bierstadt
(1830-1902) American

SCENE IN YOSEMITE VALLEY, *around 1864-1874*

Oil on canvas
20 7/8 x 29 inches
Museum purchase with funds provided by the Daniel Blau Endowment, 1976.58

SUGGESTED READINGS:

Anderson, Nancy K. and Linda S. Ferber. **Albert Bierstadt: Art and Enterprise**. *Exhibition catalogue, New York: The Brooklyn Museum in association with Hudson Hills Press, 1991.*

Hendricks, Gorden. **Albert Bierstadt: Painter of the American West**. *Exhibition catalogue, New York: Harry N. Abrams, Inc., in association with the Amon Carter Museum of Western Art, 1973.*

By the early 1860s, the thirst for knowledge of the American West had reached a fevered pitch. The Western landscape that was imbued with competing national, sectional, religious, and philosophical meanings became the chosen subject matter for many painters, photographers, novelists, essayists, ministers, and social commentators. In particular, the region of Yosemite in California received a significant amount of this attention. Various photographic views of Yosemite were mass-produced and circulated in the early 1860s. For example, New Yorkers had been able to see Carleton Watkins' photographs of Yosemite and the so-called Big Trees in 1862. *Boston Transcript* readers had lived the California experience through the stories and published epistles of their own native son and preacher, Thomas Starr King. It was against such a backdrop that Albert Bierstadt, along with writer Fitz Hugh Ludlow, set off in May 1863 to observe, capture, and convey the majesties and the power of the Far West.

By August 1863, Bierstadt, Ludlow, and their entourage were on their way from San Francisco to Mariposa, and then on into the heart of Yosemite. Writing of his experiences some seven years after the trip, Ludlow remarked on the artistic dimension of the trip:

> I will assert that during their seven weeks' camp in the Valley, they [the artists] learned more and gained greater material for future triumphs than they had gotten in all their lives before at the feet of the greatest masters.

In fact, when safely ensconced in his New York studio, Bierstadt converted his plain-air work into some of the most eagerly anticipated canvases of the decade.

Bierstadt's work reveled in the beauty and majesty of the natural wonders. In 1864, probably as a result of Bierstadt's presentation of the new Eden, President Lincoln set aside Yosemite Valley and Mariposa Redwoods as a public park. This action, combined with the 1869 completion of the Transcontinental Railroad, contributed to the great influx of tourists to Yosemite. Such an increase led Bierstadt, upon his return to the region in 1872, to decry, somewhat nostalgically, the lost untouched wilderness.

Bierstadt's *Scene in Yosemite Valley* combines drawings and elements from his on-the-spot sketches and functions within the religious and sectionalist rhetoric of the Civil War. During the war, in fact, the Western landscape with its sweeping, untouched fertility and beauty was regarded as the necessary antidote to the destruction leveled on eastern and southern lands. For some of Bierstadt's audience, particularly those steeped in the war discourses, the West symbolized a new beginning, a new Eden full of hope and peace, ready to take the place of the war-damaged lands of the East.

TDS

John F. Kensett
(1816-1872) American

SUNSET LANDSCAPE, *around 1870*
Oil on paperboard
9 1/4 x 12 1/4 inches
Gift of Mrs. R. Warren White, 1964.8

T his oil sketch by John Kensett—one of his many coastal scenes—was probably made on a sketching expedition late in the artist's life. One of the younger, "second generation" Hudson River School artists, Kensett reflected in his paintings this movement's belief in nature as the visible manifestation of God. His lyrical interpretation of nature is apparent in *Sunset Landscape*; sky and water dominate the work's composition, while the emphasis on horizontal and vertical lines imbues it with a feeling of stillness and calm. The vivid, intense colors of *Sunset Landscape* attest to Kensett's lifelong interest in recording light and atmospheric effects. The presence of an underlayer of red paint and the simple composition (typical of his later works) make it likely that this undated work was created near the end of Kensett's life.

A Connecticut native, Kensett worked as an engraver at several publishing houses in New Haven and New York for many years before he was finally able to support himself from his paintings. Like many Hudson River School artists, he spent summers sketching in the New England and New York countrysides and winters making large-scale oil paintings from his sketches. During his lifetime, critics and the public alike favored his work, and Kensett became a prominent member of New York's artistic and social circles.

MAR

Suggested Readings:

Driscoll, John Paul, and John K. Howat. **John Frederick Kensett: An American Master.** *Exhibition catalogue, Worcester Art Museum. New York and London, W.W. Norton & Company, 1985.*

Howat, John K. **American Paradise: The World of the Hudson River School.** *Exhibition catalogue. New York: The Metropolitan Museum of Art, 1987.*

Howat, John K. **John Frederick Kensett 1816-1872.** *Exhibition catalogue. New York: The American Federation of Arts, 1968.*

Eastman Johnson
(1824-1906) American

THE EARLY LOVERS, *1870s*

Oil on academy board

22 x 27 1/2 inches

Museum purchase with funds provided by the 1985 Associate Board, 1984.106

STUDY FOR THE EARLY LOVERS, *1870s*

Oil on canvas

12 1/2 x 14 3/4 inches

Museum purchase with funds provided by the 1985 Associate Board, 1984.107

Eastman Johnson's paintings of country life, such as *The Early Lovers*, appealed to 19th century patrons who were nostalgic for their rural roots. Frequently sentimental, his genre images (paintings of everyday life) followed in the tradition of earlier American painters of this subject matter, but without the moralizing tone often found in such work. In the Art Institute's painting, the perennially popular theme of young lovers is given fresh treatment through Johnson's use of natural poses for the pair whose physical distance and psychological closeness underscores the couple's desire to be together.

Trained at the Royal Academy in Düsseldorf, Germany, which was known as a genre school, Johnson was one of the most technically proficient American artists working in the 1860s and 1870s. As with many of his genre paintings, *The Early Lovers* is based on a sketch he painted on location, probably in the woods of Maine. With the study as a reference, the artist then returned to his studio where models posed for the two central characters. Johnson is known to have preferred his sketches to the finished paintings and frequently kept the studies after selling the larger versions. He did this with *The Early Lovers*; the sketch in the Art Institute's Collection is one of many studies visible in a photograph of his studio taken shortly before his death.

MAR

Suggested Readings:

Baur, John J.H. **Eastman Johnson: An American Genre Painter**. *Exhibition catalogue. Brooklyn: The Brooklyn Museum, 1940.*

Hills, Patricia. **Eastman Johnson**. *Exhibition catalogue, The Whitney Museum of American Art. New York: Clarkson N. Potter, Inc., 1972.*

Hills, Patricia. **The Genre Painting of Eastman Johnson: The Sources and Development of His Style and Themes**. *Ph.D. diss., New York University, 1973. New York and London: Garland Publishing, 1977.*

Alexander Helwig Wyant

(1836-1892) American

DERBYSHIRE LANDSCAPE, *1871*

Oil on canvas

22 x 36 inches

Museum purchase with funds provided in part by Mr. and Mrs. Floyd Rietveld, the NCR Corporation, and Monsanto Research Corporation, 1985.6

Alexander Wyant became acquainted with the work of English painters such as John Constable during an 1865 visit to England, and, for several years afterwards, Wyant's style was indebted to the English landscape school. *Derbyshire Landscape*, with its English town framed by a pastoral landscape, is a prime example of the artist's work from the period following this trip abroad. The path at the left and the rolling landscape lead the eye to the small Derbyshire town and picturesque ruins. The painting dates to an important transitional period in Wyant's style. As a result, *Derbyshire Landscape* combines elements of the artist's earlier, meticulously detailed paintings, with his later, highly fluid technique. In the foreground, the rendering of vegetation is precise, while Wyant's treatment of the sky and the distant village is hazier, creating atmospheric perspective. The approaching storm adds a melancholy, foreboding quality that is often found in Wyant's landscapes after 1870.

An Ohio native, Wyant was greatly impressed by the works of the young George Inness (1825-1894) and, in 1859, traveled to New York where he met the artist and sought his advice. Wyant subsequently studied art in New York and with the Düsseldorf-school artist Hans Friedrich Gude in Germany. It was after Wyant's brief stay in Germany in 1865 that he visited England and Ireland. Wyant's style gradually changed in later years to one marked by heavy impasto and de-emphasis on detail. This new style became more pronounced after Wyant suffered a stroke in 1874; forced to use his left hand, Wyant's paintings almost solely focused on atmosphere and light.

MAR

Suggested Readings:

Bermingham, Peter. **American Art in the Barbizon Mood**. *Exhibition catalogue, National Collection of Fine Arts. Washington, D.C.: Smithsonian Institution Press, 1975.*

Clark, Eliot Candee. **Alexander Wyant**. *New York: Privately printed, 1916.*

Olpin, Robert S. **Alexander Helwig Wyant 1836-1892**. *Exhibition catalogue. Salt Lake City: The University of Utah, Museum of Fine Arts, 1968.*

Mary Cassatt

(1844-1926) American

PORTRAIT OF A WOMAN, 1872

Oil on canvas

23 1/4 x 19 3/4 inches

Gift of Mr. Robert Badenhop, 1955.67

Mary Cassatt painted *Portrait of a Woman* in 1872, during an eight-month stay in Parma, Italy. The painting is dedicated to Carlo Raimondi, a teacher at the Parma Academy from whom Cassatt rented studio space and probably had lessons in printmaking. It was during this, her third trip abroad, that Cassatt decided to settle in Europe permanently.

Painted several years before Cassatt espoused Impressionism, this portrait shows the influence of Italian Baroque painting, especially in its golden light, classical drapery, and, above all, in the figure's monumental proportions. *Portrait of a Woman* is one of several paintings the artist made of monumental, costumed women during her studies in Parma. Its sense of three-dimensionality differs from Cassatt's later work, in which space is flattened. Throughout her artistic career, Cassatt frequently used women and children as subject matter and depicted them with an unusual degree of understanding and sympathy. Like Edgar Degas, Cassatt was more interested in the everyday subject matter and gesture espoused by the Impressionists than she was concerned with theories about light and brushwork technique. She had a remarkable gift for suggesting emotional connections or states; in this painting, the woman's pensive expression has a poignancy that reveals that this talent developed early.

MAR

SUGGESTED READINGS:

Breeskin, Adelyn Dohme. **Mary Cassatt: A Catalogue Raisonné of the Oils, Pastels, Watercolors and Drawings**. *Washington, D.C.: Smithsonian Institution Press, 1970.*

Mathews, Nancy Mowll. **Mary Cassatt**. *New York: Harry N. Ambrams, Inc. in association with The National Museum of American Art.*

John Frederick Peto

(1854-1907) American

STILL LIFE WITH MUG, BOOK, SMOKING MATERIALS
AND CRACKERS, *around 1880-1890*

Oil on canvas

14 x 17 inches

Museum purchase with funds provided by Mr. and Mrs. Floyd L. Rietveld, the NCR
Corporation, Monsanto Research Corporation, and the 1986 Associate Board, 1986.59

SUGGESTED READINGS:

Gerdts, William H. **Painters of the Humble Truth: Masterpieces of American Still Life, 1801-1937.**
Columbia: University of Missouri Press, 1981.

Wilmerding, John. **Important Information Inside: The Art of John F. Peto and the Idea of Still-Life**
Painting in Nineteenth-Century America. Washington, D.C.: National Gallery of Art, 1983.

By the final decades of the 19th century, a vogue for a certain style of still-life painting can be noted. Unlike earlier instances of such paintings, the still-lifes produced during the 1870s, 1880s, and 1890s indicate a change in attitude toward the genre and toward the types of objects depicted. Whereas in earlier American still-lifes (such as those by Raphaelle Peale and Severin Roesen) lush, luxuriant items were captured in sumptuous settings, later examples show objects notable for their crude appearance, utilitarian nature, and lack of newness. These items often stand in direct contrast to the highly polished, manufactured objects available to consumers in the period.

A factor in the stylistic change, and the accompanying popularity of images such as John Frederick Peto's, was the increased role which the economic marketplace played in shaping production and consumption, a place formerly occupied by the art academy and its ranking of painting types. Prior to the late 19th century, still-life painting had been relegated to the lowest position within this hierarchy. It held that the rote copying of objects and slavish mimetic realism of such an enterprise demonstrated the least amount of creativity on behalf of the artist. However, by the last decades of the century, the force of the marketplace and the emergence of an entire class of entrepreneurial patrons who desired a style of painting that betokened an earlier, less hectic way of life afforded still-life painting a higher status. In the quickly emerging world of big business during the late part of the century, these works celebrated a certain past—one that was both a near past as well as a manufactured one, worked to shore-up concerns about the flux and uncertainty of the urban environment, and provided pictorial refuge. This nostalgic yearning permeated many aspects of American culture including music, art, literature, and theater and resulted in the aesthetic of Peto's painting. Through its celebration of the object as commodity, Peto's painting and other still-lifes from this period draw attention to the growing regard for painting as a commodity itself.

What Peto presents are "manly" objects, or more precisely objects which signify the masculine sphere for the late 19th century viewer: a well-worn book, an older ceramic mug, a tobacco box, a pipe carefully perched on the edge of the table, matches, and three crackers. This composition typifies Peto's style and palette, and owes some recognition to his mentor William Harnett. Unlike Harnett however, whose works have a crystal-clear surface treatment (a treatment which itself attempts to deny the presence of the artist) and thus can be truly called "trompe l'oeil," Peto's aesthetic does not strive for such a precise picture plane. Rather, his surfaces have a tactile, rough finish, a finish slightly more in line with the objects shown. This distinction was lost on historians of the early 20th century who often collapsed the work of Peto into that of Harnett, consigning Peto to a position of the unknown for many decades.

Albert Robert Valentien for Rookwood Pottery
(1882-1925) American

LARGE "ORIENTAL" JAR DECORATED WITH FROGS, 1882

Red clay
H: 10 1/2 inches
Gift of the Alma C. Brunner Trust, 1991.10

Founded in 1880 by Maria Longworth Nichols Storer, the Rookwood Pottery created early ceramics, such as this large jar, that demonstrate an interest in Japanese art. The whimsical frogs and use of line, rather than shading, to model the frogs and lily pads are hallmarks of a Japanese-influenced decorative style. Also typical to ware produced in the pottery's early years is the liberal use of gilding, either applied with a sponge, as in this case, or by brush.

Rookwood Pottery played a leading part in the midwestern Art Pottery movement of the late 19th century. Like other art potteries, Rookwood Pottery emphasized the aesthetic component over functionality and relied on hand decoration. Although some art potteries followed the example of the English Arts and Crafts movement, which stressed completely hand-crafted pieces, Rookwood Pottery used standardized, prefabricated forms. The company concentrated instead on surface decoration.

A code on the bottom of Rookwood pieces identifies the form number, color of clay (in this case, red clay), and the decorator. Albert Valentien, who designed this piece, joined the Rookwood Pottery in 1881 as its first full-time professional designer. He had studied at the School of Design at the University of Cincinnati and later, in 1905, left the pottery to return to painting, concentrating on wildflowers. This "oriental" jar, one of Valentien's earlier efforts, is from a less-polished phase of the designer's work and of Rookwood Pottery itself. Although the depictions of the frogs and the slightly raised forms are executed more crudely than Valentien's later works, this rare piece has the charming, expressive qualities of early Rookwood ceramics.

MAR

SUGGESTED READINGS:

Ellis, Anita J. **Rookwood Pottery: The Glorious Gamble**. *Exhibition catalogue. Cincinnati: Cincinnati Art Museum, Cincinnati, 1993.*

Nelson, Marion John. **Art Pottery of the Midwest**. *Exhibition catalogue, University Art Museum, Minneapolis: University of Minnesota, 1988.*

Samuel Richards
(1853-1893) American
BLISSFUL HOURS, 1885
Oil on canvas
39 1/2 x 57 1/4 inches
Gift of Mrs. Frank A. Brown, 1953.16

A mong the American paintings exhibited at the 1893 Chicago World's Columbian Exposition was Samuel Richards' *Blissful Hours*. The world's fair, celebrating the anniversary of Columbus' discovery of the New World, was notable for showcasing the arts. Works by leading contemporary American artists and sculptors were displayed in temporary structures designed by prominent American architects of the day. As a part of this monumental exhibition, *Blissful Hours* has historical interest beyond its artistic merits.

A native of Indiana, Richards painted this work in Munich, Germany, where he studied from 1880 to 1891, when he returned to America to be the director of the Denver Art League. The Munich academy's strong influence on his work is especially apparent in his attention to detail and use of backlighting. Richards described the painting's sentimental subject matter, typical of many late Victorian works, in a letter to its purchaser, David Gebhart:

> It represents a village maiden musing over her approaching wedding, busy with the last touches upon her bridal dress; You can see by the fresh made tea placed upon the table, and the chair placed near, that she is waiting for her lover who will come now any moment. . . . she is too happy to be serious, yet is lost to all but her thoughts, the wedding tomorrow, a future home of her own, all the future she pictures in rosy hues. One can think how life has disappointed so many as hopeful as she, and yet it can be that she will be even happier than she dreams.

Richards worked directly from nature, a fact he noted later in the same letter. He took pride in his fidelity to detail and his handling of the soft light which suffuses the scene.

MAR

Suggested Readings:

Gerdts, William H. **Art Across America: Two Centuries of Regional Painting, 1710-1920**, Volume II. New York: Abbeville Press, 1990.

Peat, Wilbur D. **Pioneer Painters of Indiana**. Indianapolis: Art Association of Indianapolis, 1954.

De Scott Evans
(1847-1898) American

FREE SAMPLE, TAKE ONE, 1891

Oil on canvas
12 1/4 x 10 inches
Museum purchase with funds provided by the 1985 Associate Board, 1984.108

I n the late 19th century, illusionistic (or "trompe l'oeil") still-lifes became popular with a number of American artists and audiences, if not with critics. Trompe l'oeil painting was not a new artistic tradition; in Europe and America, such still-lifes had been commonplace in the late 18th and early 19th centuries. Incorporating humor, meticulous brushwork, and the vertical format preferred by many trompe l'oeil artists, De Scott Evans' *Free Sample, Take One* is an excellent example of the style. The painting's format, paralleling the canvas plane, creates a shallow space from which the peanuts seem to project into the viewer's space, making the still-life appear real. A slip of paper, inviting observers to sample the nuts, offers the possibility of an unexpected and humorous discovery of Evans' illusionism. The textures of the painted wood grain, glass, and nuts are vividly recreated; the saw marks on the left edge of the wood are especially convincing.

Evans himself remains an enigma, for the trompe l'oeil still-lifes attributed to him are signed in various manners: S. S. David (as with the Art Institute's work), Scott David, Stanley S. David, or De Scott Evans. His reasons for using pseudonyms on some still-life paintings will probably never be discovered. Born David Scott Evans, he was best known in his own time as a portraitist and genre painter. Evans, who originally went by "D. Scott Evans," began signing his portraits and genre paintings "De Scott Evans" upon his return from studying with William Adolphe Bougereau in Paris, presumably in an attempt to reflect his new cosmopolitan outlook. Like other works of the type and despite their popularity with the public, art critics of his day would likely have deemed Evans' trompe l'oeil paintings trivial, but today still-lifes such as *Free Sample, Take One* are considered his most important work.

MAR

Suggested Readings:

Gerdts, William H., and Russell Blake. **American Still Life Painting**. *New York, Washington, and London: Praeger Publishers, 1971.*

Maciejunes, Nannette V. **A New Variety, Try One: De Scott Evans or S.S. David**. *Exhibition catalogue. Columbus: Columbus Museum of Art, 1985.*

William Ordway Partridge
(1861-1930) American

MADONNA IN HER MATURITY, 1892

Marble

H: 25 inches

Gift of Mrs. Charles Harries Simms, 1942.30

William Ordway Partridge's wife served as the model for this bust, which falls somewhere between two popular American sculpture traditions, naturalistic portraits and idealistic figures. Partridge's interest in representing the Madonna in middle-age shows a concern with representing a specific—rather than idealized—state of being. Thus, the Madonna's features have a greater degree of individuality (seen in the puffiness under the eyes, the furrowed brow, and the long nose) than those found in Neoclassical sculptures. Partridge did not intend, however, to create a wholly naturalistic conception of the mature Virgin Mary, as is apparent from the extremely smooth treatment of the skin (except the forehead), the figure's calm and reserved expression, and the simplified treatment of drapery. As a result, the figure appears to be a real, sympathetic person but also removed from everyday existence, a balance that befits the Virgin Mary.

Born in Paris to wealthy parents, Partridge was a man of many talents: lecturer, poet, critic, actor, and sculptor. After studying sculpture in Florence, Rome, and Paris, he established a studio in Milton, Massachusetts. *Madonna in Her Maturity* was exhibited at the 1892 Paris Salon and was subsequently purchased by Ferdinand Peck, a prominent Chicagoan. In 1893, a plaster copy of *Madonna in Her Maturity* was displayed at the Chicago World's Columbian Exposition under the title *Mary*. Partridge returned to this subject in 1897, creating a second version in marble that has since disappeared. His later work became less idealized, as he sought a more expressive sculptural style.

MAR

SUGGESTED READINGS:

Craven, Wayne. **Sculpture in America: From the Colonial Period to the Present**. *New York: Thomas Crowell Company, 1968.*

William O. Partridge, American Sculptor. *Exhibition catalogue. Plattsburgh, NY: State University College Plattsburgh, 1974.*

Childe Hassam
(1859-1935) American
EARLY MORNING CALM, 1901
Oil on canvas
25 x 30 inches
Gift of Mrs. Harrie G. Carnell, 1942.3

Early Morning Calm reflects Childe Hassam's commitment to Impressionist painting techniques. Hassam had become acquainted with Impressionism during his 1886 to 1889 stay in Paris, when he attended classes at the popular Académie Julian. In this work, his preference for pastel tones and colors applied next to each other without blending resulted in a glowing, brilliant painting. Impressionists, whether French or American, also favored roughly textured canvases, feeling that raised areas of pigment would better reflect light. Here, areas in which the canvas surface is still visible make a dramatic contrast with areas of thickly applied pigment.

Hassam traveled widely in search of subjects; from the mid-1880s to 1916, he often visited the Isles of Shoals, a group of islands ten miles off the New Hampshire coast, near Portsmouth. *Early Morning Calm* depicts the Atlantic Ocean as seen from the largest island, Appledore. Hassam's interest in the lush vegetation of the island, partially inspired by his friendship with island poet and gardener Celia Laighton Thaxter (1835-1894), is evident here in the abundance of the beautiful wildflowers.

The solidity of the cliffs in this painting is characteristic of many works by American Impressionists, which often have a greater sense of underlying form than that of their French counterparts. Claude Monet had advocated ignoring the specific objects in scenes so that the overall impression could be captured, advice Americans generally did not follow. Indeed, Hassam's *Early Morning Calm* has a strong sense of place, revealing an artist as much committed to recreating the beauties of a specific locale as he was to capturing an impression.

MAR

Suggested Readings:

Curry, David Park. **Childe Hassam: An Island Garden Revisited**. Exhibition catalogue, Denver Art Museum. New York: W.W. Norton & Company, 1990.

Gerdts, William H. **American Impressionism**. New York: Abbeville Press, 1984.

Hiesinger, Ulrich W. **Childe Hassam: American Impressionist**. Munich: Prestel, 1994.

John Henry Twachtman
(1853-1902) American

VIEW OF THE BRUSH HOUSE, COS COB,
CONNECTICUT, around 1901

Oil on canvas

30 x 30 inches

Gift of Mr. William P. Patterson, 1988.66

The countryside around Greenwich, Connecticut, was the inspiration for some of John Henry Twachtman's finest landscapes. Twachtman created this painting during one of his teaching sessions in Cos Cob. Just visible, beneath the horizon line of this painting, is the mill pond behind the Brush House, one of the oldest buildings in Cos Cob and a popular subject among artists. An Impressionist work, *View of the Brush House, Cos Cob, Connecticut* has a spontaneous, sketchlike quality that is created by Twachtman's use of long, loose brushstrokes and unpainted areas of canvas. The insubstantial forms of the lilac bushes and the central position of the tree obscure the Brush House, depicted in the right background. Twachtman was known in his time for his preference for soft pastel tones such as the pale greens and golds present in this work. An artist whose paintings reflect his subjective response to particular times of day and seasons, this early spring landscape is characteristic of Twachtman's "intuitive" style.

Born in Cincinnati, Twachtman spent a part of the 1870s studying in Munich, an established destination for many American art students. His work of that period was created in the dark, painterly "Munich" style popularized among Americans by Frank Duveneck. Twachtman's second trip to Europe in 1883, to study at the Académie Julian in Paris, resulted in a lightening of his palette and greater attention to draftsmanship. He also began selecting colors that would create a specific mood, much like the style of his compatriot James Abbott McNeill Whistler. In the 1890s, after his move to Connecticut, Impressionism increasingly influenced Twachtman's style. He was a popular art teacher in Cos Cob, which in the 1890s became a thriving artists' colony that attracted such important American Impressionists as J. Alden Weir and Theodore Robinson. After 1897, Twachtman exhibited with The Ten, a New England-based group that formed in protest of the Society of American Artists. Although Twachtman was not as well-known to the public as some of the others in the group (which included Weir and Childe Hassam), his subtle, evocative landscapes were greatly admired by his peers.

MAR

Suggested Readings:

Boyle, Richard J. **John Twachtman**. *New York: Watson-Guptill, 1979.*

Chotner, Deborah, Lisa N. Peters, and Kathleen A. Pyne. **John Twachtman: Connecticut Landscapes**. *Exhibition catalogue. Washington, D.C.: National Gallery of Art, 1989.*

Twachtman in Gloucester: His Last Years, 1900-1902. *New York: Universe/Ira Spanierman Gallery, distributed by St. Martin's Press, 1987.*

Jacques Sicard for Weller Pottery
American (Zanesville, Ohio)
VASE, 1902-1907
Ceramic with metallic luster glaze
17 3/4 x 5 1/4 inches
Gift of Mr. Stephen Fales, 1983.47

With its beginnings in England after that country's poor showing at the Crystal Palace Exhibition of 1851, the Art Pottery movement spread to America during the 1880s. To be more precise, the Centennial Exhibition of 1876 in Philadelphia galvanized American artists and businessmen into creating and marketing pottery that was of the highest quality and affordable. In addition, untapped economic opportunities in home decor attracted numerous entrepreneurs to the business. Operating within an irresolvable ideological and practical tension between art and profitability, the industry of art pottery experienced unprecedented growth from the 1880s to the beginning of World War I. One of the most significant and pioneering of these new potteries was Rookwood Pottery, based in Cincinnati. For more than 30 years, this pottery company set the standard for quality of design and execution. Rookwood also established a working environment that not only included women but gave them an opportunity to create within a respectable public space. Specifically, this industry, by drawing upon the accepted tradition of china painting by women, was able to employ women in a job that, according to contemporary sentiment, suited their temperament.

Just as Rookwood was setting the standard of excellence, other potteries in Ohio appeared on the scene. Founded in Fultomham, Ohio, in 1872 and later moved to Zanesville, Weller Pottery started producing flowerpots and crocks, but it soon became the most well-known and largest company to mass produce low-priced art pottery. For most of its history, Weller looked to Rookwood for designs and inspirations. The notable exception to this general pattern occurred when Weller hired Sicard, a noted French potter. Employed from 1901 to 1907, Sicard produced a line of vessels, eponymously named Sicardo, that are characterized by the use of metallic lusters on iridescent ground. The vase in this collection typifies Sicardo ware's reliance on natural forms for subject matter.

TDS

Suggested Readings:

*Evans, Paul, **Art Pottery of the United States**, New York: Feingold & Lewis, 1987.*

Clara Driscoll for Tiffany Studios
American
DRAGONFLY LAMP, *after 1902*
Base: bronze, with reddish patina; Shade: blued leaded glass
Marked: "TIFFANY STUDIOS/NEW YORK/366" on base, "TIFFANY STUDIOS NEW YORK" on shade
H: 25 1/2 inches
Gift of The Alma C. Brunner Trust, 1991.4

Designer Louis Comfort Tiffany's work with glass, which was enormously popular in the late 19th and early 20th centuries, took many directions, including stained-glass windows, vases, and, after the late 1890s, lamps with leaded shades. Lamps appealed to Tiffany because they combined light with color and glass; indeed, his leaded glass lamps can be seen as miniature stained-glass windows. In addition to his glasswork, Tiffany also created important works using bronze and other metals, ceramics, and enamels. He relied on his talented studio to design and make many Tiffany pieces in order to meet public demand.

The "Dragonfly" lamp was one of the studio's finest and most successful works. Its design, which was conceived by Clara Driscoll in 1900, won a prize at the Paris International Exposition of that year. The Art Institute's lamp was one of many made by the studio, in this case probably after 1902, when the company's stamp changed from "Tiffany Glass and Decorating Co." to "Tiffany Studios, New York." The number 366 is also stamped into the base and refers to the lamp's model number. It is not known how many lamps of each design the studio created.

Driscoll, a gifted designer, began working for Tiffany in 1887, and by 1904 was one of the highest paid women workers in America. The "Dragonfly" lamp is probably her best-known design. Tiffany always gave Driscoll full credit for her work, although he undoubtedly maintained some executive supervision over this piece, as he did with everything the studios produced.

The beautiful dragonfly lamp shows Driscoll's adherence to Tiffany's Art Nouveau aesthetic of simplified forms, harmonious colors, and the beauties of commonplace nature. Tendrils twine around the bronze pole while the rounded base has a stylized leaf design. The dragonflies flank the bottom of the shade and are offset by cabochon glass pieces. The female employees who worked on the leading selected the shade's blue-green and gold glass pieces. Thus, as a result of their liberty to choose, the same lamp might be made in more than one color scheme.

MAR

Suggested Readings:

Koch, Robert. **Louis C. Tiffany's Glass-Bronzes-Lamps: A Complete Collector's Guide.** *New York: Crown Publishers, Inc., 1971.*

Koch, Robert. **Louis C. Tiffany, Rebel in Glass.** *New York: Crown Publishers, 1964.*

McKean, Hugh F. **The "Lost" Treasures of Louis Comfort Tiffany.** *Garden City, NY: Doubleday & Company, 1980.*

George Benjamin Luks
(1866-1933) American

THE BREAD LINE, *1905-1925*

Oil on panel

17 x 21 inches

Museum purchase with funds provided by the James F. Dicke Family, 1997.18

The Bread Line is typical of George Luks' subject matter in the first two decades of the 20th century. The urban poor—their plight as well as their innate dignity—intrigued Luks and other artist friends such as Everett Shinn, John Sloan, and William Glackens. Within this group, sometimes known as The Ashcan School, Luks was known for his bombastic personality and acute empathy with humanity.

The Bread Line also demonstrates Luks' vibrant, highly saturated palette and quick, excited brush strokes. The latter are Luks' debt to European Modernism, as well as to Dutch 17th century master Frans Hals. Luks had seen these influences on trips abroad in 1889, 1892, 1902, and 1904. Luks neither condemns nor pities his subjects, but rather presents them as an integral aspect of urban life.

Public reception to works by Luks, Robert Henri, Sloan, and other members of the Ashcan School was generally negative. Following an exhibition of their work in 1908 at the MacBeth Gallery in New York, one reviewer wrote: "Vulgarity smites one in the face at this exhibition." By challenging public perceptions about how and what to paint, the Ashcan School artists forged new territory in bringing American art in line with its more progressive European counterparts.

Luks was born into a genteel family in Williamsport, Pennsylvania. He studied at the Pennsylvania Academy for the Fine Arts and, in 1889, went to Düsseldorf, Germany, to study. He also worked as a newspaper artist in Philadelphia. Luks' hard-drinking and boisterous habits were widely known. He died following a fight in a New York speakeasy.

MAL

Suggested Readings:

George Luks: An American Artist. *Exhibition catalogue, Sordoni Art Gallery, Wilkes-Barre: Wilkes College, 1987.*

Zurier, Rebecca, Robert W. Snyder, and Virginia M. Mecklenburg. **Metropolitan Lives: The Ashcan Artists and Their New York**. *Washington, D.C.: National Museum of American Art, 1995.*

John Sloan

(1871-1951) American

THE COBURN PLAYERS, *1910*

Oil on canvas

26 1/8 x 32 inches

Museum purchase with funds provided by the Junior League of Dayton, Ohio, Inc. and

Mrs. Susanne Rike McConnaughey, 1961.6

At the turn of the 20th century, a group of young artists was interested in depicting scenes of everyday city life, such as seen in John Sloan's *The Coburn Players*. As one of the most talented of the circle of urban realists, frequently referred to as the Ashcan School, John Sloan painted urban scenes in a loose, expressive style until the 1920s. Sloan wished to describe his environs in an unsentimental, evocative manner. Grays and browns, the prevalent colors of urban life, dominate in his paintings; in *The Coburn Players*, they reflect the evening atmosphere. Lighter highlights draw our attention—like that of the audience—to the performance. The specific play being enacted is not important; instead, through an emphasis on the actors' gestures, the darkened audience, and the glow created by the stage lights, Sloan captured the effect of the overall scene. The artist commented about this painting:

> This is an impression of a beautiful occasion, an out door performance on the campus of Columbia University. Many details are omitted—among them I note the absence of the mosquitos. These small pests attended to our ankles while the Coburns kept our minds amused.

Sloan's interest in depicting the life around him had two important sources of inspiration. From his work as a newspaper sketch artist, he learned to make rapid sketches and developed a strong visual memory. Additionally, his friendship with artist and teacher Robert Henri, whom he met in 1892, had great impact on his career. Henri inspired Sloan and others through informal lectures about the importance of establishing artistic freedom and of depicting everyday life in a candid manner. In 1908, Sloan's belief in autonomy and democracy led him to join seven other artists in exhibiting independently of the then-powerful National Academy of Design. As a member of The Eight, Sloan forged a path for artistic freedom by asserting artists' rights to individual expression.

MAR

SUGGESTED READINGS:

Elzea, Rowland, and Elizabeth Hawkes. **John Sloan: Spectator of Life**. *Exhibition catalogue. Wilmington, DE: Delaware Art Museum, 1988.*

John Sloan 1871-1951: His Life and Paintings and Graphics. *Exhibition catalogue. Washington, D.C: National Gallery of Art, 1971.*

John Sloan's Oil Paintings: A Catalogue Raisonné. *Rowland Elzea, compiler. Newark, DE: University of Delaware Press, 1991.*

Sloan, John. **Gist of Art**. *New York: American Artists Group, 1944.*

Florine Stettheimer
(1871-1944) American

FLOWERS NUMBER 6, *around 1910*

Oil on canvas

30 x 36 inches

Gift of the Estate of Ettie Stettheimer, 1965.133

There is a mystique that surrounds the persona and work of Florine Stettheimer. This mystique is a result of actions by the artist and the art community. Having been trained in an academic manner, studying with Kenyon Cox at the Art Students League, Stettheimer quickly developed a style far removed from the academic traditions of proportion and representation and the emerging abstract aesthetic. Stettheimer instead constructed images that bespeak her own insulated and self-referential world. This world consisted of elegant salons convened at her family's New York City apartment by her mother, Rosetta, her sisters, Carrie and Ettie, herself, and by the likes of Marcel Duchamp, Marsden Hartley, Elie Nadelman, Carl van Vechten, and Sherwood Anderson.

Possibly as a result of the poor critical reception of her first (and only) one-person show in 1916, Stettheimer refused gallery representation, this despite the numerous attempts by established dealers like Alfred Stieglitz. So concerned with her image, the artist left specific instructions in her will that her work be destroyed at the time of her death. Her executor and her family disobeyed these wishes, and in 1946, Marcel Duchamp organized a posthumous exhibition of her works at the Museum of Modern Art in New York. This exhibition, set against the backdrop of the postwar industrial boom of the time, was doomed from the start. Stettheimer's frothy canvases and their accompanying artificiality were no match for the overdetermined masculine ethos of the moment. All of this is not to argue that Stettheimer was without her supporters; in fact, she was an integral part, vital force, and significant influence on 20th century American art.

Probably from the 1910s, *Flowers Number 6* captures a bit of the mood of Stettheimer's entire oeuvre. The two pots of flowers, each with its distinctive character, are offset by the lithe figure caught in sculpture, possibly drawn from the work of Elie Nadelman. This figure might provide us a clue to the intended owner of the work, as Stettheimer often created portraits out of cryptic and not-so-cryptic references to her friends. In addition, she had a tendency to present figures whose gender was meant to be ambiguous.

TDS

SUGGESTED READINGS:

Bloemink, Barbara S. **The Life & Art of Florine Stettheimer**. *New Haven: Yale University Press, 1995.*

Tyler, Parker. **Florine Stettheimer: A Life in Art**. *New York: Farrar, Straust Co., 1963.*

William Ritschel
(1864-1949) American

MONTEREY COAST, *after 1911*

Oil on canvas

37 x 48 inches

Gift of Mr. John B. Hayward, 1929.2

One of the most prominent of the artists who moved to the Monterey Peninsula in the early 20th century, Ritschel was noted for coastal scenes such as *Monterey Coast*. Ritschel's style was inspired by some of the more decorative aspects of Impressionism. In the Art Institute's painting, harmonious shades of blue and blue-green predominate. The short brush-strokes and the heavy impasto (particularly in the swirling waters in the foreground) are also an Impressionist technique to create a textured painting surface. Unlike the work of some French artists such as Monet and Pissarro, however, the rock forms have substance and are not subsidiary to the effects of light.

Born in Bavaria, Ritschel's interest in both art and the sea seems to have developed at an early age. After brief service at sea, he studied at the Royal Academy of Munich. When he was 30, the artist moved to New York. The seascapes and coastal scenes for which Ritschel is best remembered were made after his move in 1911 to Carmel, California, then a burgeoning art colony. There, Ritschel must have been something of a local eccentric, for he frequently dressed in sarongs and designed a medieval home (known simply as "the Castle") overlooking the cliffs. From this vantage point, Ritschel was ideally situated to create paintings, like *Monterey Coast*, that were evocative of the area's scenic beauty.

MAR

SUGGESTED READING:

Gerdts, William H. **Art Across America: Two Centuries of Regional Painting, 1710-1920.** *New York: Abbeville Press, 1990.*

Cecilia Beaux
(1855-1942) American

THE VELIE BOYS, *1913*

Oil on canvas

77 1/4 x 47 1/4 inches

Museum purchase with funds provided by the James F. Dicke Family, 1998.1

Cecilia Beaux's portrait of the two sons of Stephen Velie of Kansas City, Missouri, continues the grand portrait tradition in the style of John Singer Sargent and James Abbott McNeill Whistler. Pictured at the Glouster, Massachusetts, seaside the two boys, are the very picture of fresh-faced youth. Dressed identically in blue sailor suits, the boys are idealized and have a grown-up, sophisticated air about them. The leisured poses, impeccable dress, and lovely seaside resort set the social and economic standing of the subjects.

Beaux was one of America's most sought-after portrait painters around the turn of the century. Theodore Roosevelt, Henry James, and Georges Clemenceau all sat for portraits by Beaux. Her wealthy and sophisticated clientele were often depicted in luxurious settings and dressed in expensive ball gowns or dress suits. Beaux, who was born in Philadelphia, studied painting at the Pennsylvania Academy and took private painting lessons with William Sartain. In 1888, Beaux, like many other Americans of the period, traveled to Paris to study at the Académie Julian and Colorossi. By 1900, she wintered in New York and spent her summers in a studio in Glouster, Massachusetts, where the Art Institute's painting was done.

MAL

SUGGESTED READINGS:

Beaux, Cecilia. **Background with Figures**. Boston: Houghton Mifflin Company, 1930.

Tappert, Tara Leigh. **Cecilia Beaux and the Art of Portraiture**. Washington, D.C.: Smithsonian Institution, 1995.

Thomas Wilmer Dewing
(1851-1938) American

LADY WITH A ROSE, around 1915-1924

Oil on canvas

24 x 20 inches

Museum purchase with funds provided by the James F. Dicke Family, 1998.2

M uch as French Impressionist Edgar Degas painted ballet dancers and bathing women in a seemingly obsessive manner, Thomas Wilmer Dewing spent most of his long career exploring the theme of the beautiful woman. Although their artistic styles are markedly different, the comparison between Dewing and Degas is not altogether inappropriate. Both artists were deeply interested in Renaissance painters and the "Old Masters." Degas was reportedly misanthropic and difficult, as was, Dewing, perhaps to a lesser degree. And yet, Dewing's women are from an entirely different world than those of Degas. Where Degas preferred to paint laundresses, shopkeepers, and even prostitutes, Dewing's women are elegant, refined, and reserved to the point of detachment.

Dewing, like many post-Civil War American artists, studied in Paris where he was the first American to enroll in the Académie Julian. There he received a basic training grounded in the Academic tradition. After returning to the United States in 1880, Dewing began to espouse the more fashionable philosophy of "art for art's sake" as promoted by James Abbott McNeill Whistler, the English Pre-Raphaelites, and the French Symbolists. Showing his distaste for the prosaic and realistic, Dewing stated "the purpose of the artist is to see beautifully." Around 1890, Dewing began to define the subject of painting that was to occupy him for the rest of his career-depictions of a beautiful woman standing or seated in a garden or a sparsely appointed room. This painting is thought to be a late work or one that Dewing reworked, as was his habit in later life.

Dewing detested the sentimental and this is immediately apparent in his works' lack of narrative or anecdotal subject. Dewing's subjects, like this seated woman holding a rose, exist in ambiguous spaces that evoke feelings of reverie or melancholy, spaces incidentally where no men intrude. It was said that Dewing's women were free from sensuality, and perhaps this accounts for their ethereal, even somewhat spiritual quality. Although Dewing enjoyed a relatively high level of success during his career and was afforded the patronage of collectors like Stanford White and Charles Lang Freer, the arrival of "modern" art in New York in 1913 marked the beginning of a new era in American art as well as a period of increased dissatisfaction and isolation for the aging Dewing.

DHV

SUGGESTED READING:

Hobbs, Susan A. *The Art of Thomas Wilmer Dewing: Beauty Reconfigured.* Exhibition catalogue, Brooklyn Museum. Washington, D.C.: Smithsonian Institution Press, 1996.

John Henry Bradley Storrs
(1885-1956) American

THREE BATHERS, *around 1916-1919*

Plaster

H: 14 1/8 inches

Museum purchase with funds provided by the Associate Board's 1995 Art Ball, 1995.10

During the last years of the 1910s, John Storrs explored numerous stylistic avenues within his sculpture, and as such might be seen as symbolizing the emerging possibilities for American artists. Trained in the *atelier* (studio) of Auguste Rodin beginning in 1912, Storrs started his career with representational and figural compositions. By 1916, the artist had turned his attention to the aesthetic philosophies of Cubism, Vorticism, and Italian Futurism. The last of these appeared after Storrs' visit to the Panama-Pacific Exhibition in San Francisco in 1914. These international art movements had been introduced to the American public in 1913 with the Armory Show and by 1916, most patrons, collectors, and the art public were familiar with the tenets of broken planes and frenetic energy that characterized these aesthetic viewpoints. What resulted from these competing tendencies of representation and abstraction can be seen in *Three Bathers*—from the work's inability to abandon fully the form, yet it desires to present a selective picture of the form.

In his first one-man show in 1920 at the Folsom Galleries in New York, Storrs exhibited a bronze version of *Three Bathers* (location unknown) along with earlier Rodinesque examples and, more significantly, a series of woodcuts. The latter group owed a great aesthetic debt to the German Expressionists, particularly Emil Nolde and Ludwig Kirchner, in their use of the medium in bold, inventive ways. The heaviness of the lines and the strength of the incision within these woodcuts can be seen on the surface of *Three Bathers*.

Finally, of particular regional note, Storrs was commissioned in 1920 by the Aero Club of France to create a commemorative piece in honor of Wilbur Wright's flights in Europe. The monument with a winged figure was erected in 1922 in Le Mans. By 1923, Storrs was heavily involved in the international avant-garde, enjoyed numerous exhibitions, and witnessed his poetry published by the leading avant-garde publications of the day.

TDS

SUGGESTED READINGS:

Dinin, Kenneth. "John Storrs: Organic Functionalism in a Modern Idiom." *The Journal of Decorative and Propaganda Arts 1875-1945* (Fall 1987): 48-73.

Frackman, Nicole. *John Storrs*. New York: Whitney Museum of American Art, 1986.

John Storrs: Rhythm of Line. Exhibition catalogue. New York: Hirschl & Adler Galleries, 1993.

Shapiro, Michael Edward. "Twentieth-Century American Sculpture." *The Saint Louis Art Museum 1986 Winter Bulletin* (Winter 1986): 15.

Harriet Whitney Frishmuth
(1880-1980) American

JOY OF THE WATERS, *1917*

Bronze
H: 63 1/2 inches
Gift of Mrs. Harrie G. Carnell, 1919.1

One of Harriet Frishmuth's first and most popular garden fountains, *Joy of the Waters* depicts, in dancelike movement, the figure's reaction to having her toes splashed with cold water. Frishmuth's skillful rendering of the female physique is especially evident in the subtle definition of the figure's muscles and ribs. The girl's springing, energetic step, joyful expression, and animated hair create an exuberant mood and suggest that she may be a water sprite.

Frishmuth made two versions of *Joy of the Waters*: the 63 1/2-inch size, of which there were more than 60 bronze castings, including the Art Institute's, and a smaller, 46-inch fountain, created in 1920, of which there were more than 40 castings. The model for this 1917 bronze was a Belgian girl named Janette Ransome. When Frishmuth made the second version of the subject, she used her favorite model, the dancer Desha Delteil. Both bronzes were among Frishmuth's most popular works, especially during the 1920s, a period of heightened vogue in America for garden sculpture and fountains.

The beginning of the 20th century saw a number of women (among them Frishmuth, Anna Hyatt Huntington, and Gertrude Vanderbilt Whitney) successfully pursue careers as sculptors, a field that had traditionally been considered masculine. Born in Philadelphia, Frishmuth briefly studied with Rodin in Paris around 1900 from whom she said she learned two important things:

> First, always look at the silhouette of a subject and be guided by it; second, remember that movement is the transition from one attitude to another. It is a bit of what was and a bit of what is to be.

Frishmuth later studied at the Art Students League in New York before setting up her own studio about 1908. Throughout her career, she was especially interested in depicting stylized movement, especially of the female figure, as exemplified by *Joy of the Waters*.

MAR

SUGGESTED READINGS:

Conner, Janis, and Joel Rosenkrantz. **Rediscoveries in American Sculpture: Studio Works 1893-1939**. *Austin: University of Texas Press, 1989.*

Fort, Ilene Susan. **The Figure in American Sculpture: A Question of Modernity**. *Los Angeles: Los Angeles County Museum in association with University of Washington Press, 1995.*

"Harriet Whitney Frishmuth, American Sculptor." **Courier** (October 1971, Vol. 9, No. 1): 21-35.

Sculpture by Harriet Whitney Frishmuth. *Brookgreen, South Carolina: Brookgreen Gardens, 1937.*

Willard Metcalf
(1858-1925) American

VALLEY IN SPRING, 1920

Oil on canvas

35 7/8 x 36 inches

Gift of Mr. John B. Hayward, 1929.3

The pastel palette, feathery brushwork, and soft light of *Valley in Spring* are characteristic of Willard Metcalf's Impressionist paintings. In his later years, Metcalf was especially drawn to the New England countryside, seeking to convey its distinctive qualities through the use of the Impressionist techniques of broken brushwork, high-keyed colors, and dissolution of form. His ability to evoke the atmosphere, light, and subtle coloration of New England terrain is apparent in *Valley in Spring*. The painting's tranquil mood and delicate, airy landscape make it easy to understand why Metcalf was called the "poet laureate" of New England.

Born in Lowell, Massachusetts, Metcalf studied at the school of the Museum of Fine Arts in Boston and at the Académie Julian in Paris. In 1898, he and nine other primarily American Impressionist painters seceded from the Society of American Artists to form an independent exhibiting group known as The Ten. Although Metcalf was friendly with a number of Impressionists and had summered in Giverny from 1886 to 1888, it was not until 1904, during his self-described "renaissance," that he became seriously interested in Impressionism. These late works met with much praise from critics who, overlooking his French training, singled Metcalf out as a truly "American" painter.

MAR

SUGGESTED READINGS:

Gerdts, William H. **American Impressionism**. New York: Abberville Press, 1981.

de Veer, Elizabeth, and Richard J. Boyle. **Sunlight and Shadow: The Life and Art of Willard L. Metcalf**. New York: Abbeville Press, 1987.

Williard Leroy Metcalf: A Retrospective. Exhibition catalogue. Springfield, MA: Museum of Fine Arts, 1976.

Arthur Wesley Dow
(1857-1922) American

UNTITLED LANDSCAPE (SUNSET ON SNOW), *undated*

Oil on canvas

18 x 32 inches

Museum purchase with funds provided by the James F. Dicke Family, 1998.4

The setting of this landscape is the Blue Dragon waterway and marshes near Arthur Wesley Dow's native Ipswich, Massachusetts. The artist's Bayberry Hill studio overlooked this scene and Dow painted it repeatedly. In this version of the subject, Dow has rendered the landscape in a sketchy, impressionistic fashion. Dow's use of pinks, blues, and white creates the aura of a late afternoon sunset on the snowy marshland. The lack of specific detail and the ethereal quality of the setting and colors conjure up the feeling the artist had in looking upon the scene, rather than a precise description of it. Evoking the transcendental, mysterious aspects of the landscape was central to much of Dow's work.

Dow was trained as a painter in a Boston studio followed by study in Paris and trips to Pont-Aven in Brittany where he was exposed to a variety of ideas including the Post Impressionism of Paul Gauguin and Maurice Denis. At Pont-Aven, he had sketched the landscape repeatedly at sunset, with particular attention to the shifting colors created by the low light. Yet it was his discovery of Japanese prints in 1891 that formed the nucleus of Dow's theories and practice of art. Dow appreciated the simplicity and flat forms of Japanese art and stated that one of its main strengths is that "it is concerned solely with the beautiful and is not obfuscated by concerns of truth, accuracy, sincerity or conscientiousness." Dow was also a great admirer of James Abbott McNeill Whistler—the muted, limited palette of *Untitled Landscape* may be in response to the greys and browns favored by that painter.

Dow is perhaps better known as the teacher of Georgia O'Keeffe than he is as a painter in his own right. The summer art school he ran in Ipswich, as well as his teaching posts at Pratt, and later his job as the head of the fine arts department at Columbia University, all were opportunities for Dow to pass on his ideas about "correct drawing" and the "decorative" or "flat" treatment of form. Dow also published a textbook, *Composition*, that was widely read and used in art curricula.

MAL

Suggested Reading:

Moffatt, Frederick C. **Arthur Wesley Dow**. *Exhibition catalogue, National Collection of Fine Arts. Washington, D.C.: Smithsonian Institution Press, 1977.*

Everett Shinn
(1876-1953) American

TIGHTROPE WALKER, 1924

Oil on canvas
23 1/2 x 18 inches
Museum purchase with funds provided by the James F. Dicke Family and the
E. Jeanette Myers Fund, 1998.7

The magic and drama of the circus fascinated the artist Everett Shinn throughout his life. Here, the spotlighted performer's body and the glittering crystal chandelier above it are the focus of Shinn's attention. The faces of the crowd and even the face of the tightrope walker are only dimly hinted. Instead, Shinn renders the atmosphere of the theater and puts the viewer at almost eye level with the performer so that we share his experience. The dramatic effects of the shimmering light and the unusual viewpoint are not uncommon in the work of Shinn, but here he has exercised them to create an almost mystical atmosphere.

In the early part of the century, Shinn was a part of the groups known as The Eight and the The Ashcan School. They chose as subject matter everyday life in the city. All members of the group lived in New York City and documented the environment, labors, and pastimes of the middle and lower classes. Scenes of movie theaters, fruit stands, ferryboat shoppers, and parks predominate in the work of The Eight. Some critics have called Shinn "an American Degas" because of his unusual vantage points and interest in the theater. In fact, Shinn traveled to Paris in 1900 and had seen the work of Degas, Toulouse-Lautrec, and other European moderns.

Of all the members of the Ashcan School, Shinn was the most successful during his lifetime. He was a well-known illustrator for magazines, did a number of mural commissions (including those in the bar at the Plaza Hotel), did movie set designs for Goldwyn Pictures and William Randolph Hearst, and usually found a market for his paintings and pastels. He also produced and acted in plays he wrote himself. His fascination with acrobats and the circus began when he was a very young child and continued until his death.

MAL

SUGGESTED READINGS:

de Shazo, Edith. **Everett Shinn: A Figure in His Time**. New York: Clarkson N. Potter, Inc.,1974.

Zurier, Rebecca, Robert W. Snyder, and Virginia M. Mecklenburg. **Metropolitan Lives: The Ashcan Artists and Their New York**. Washington D.C.: National Museum of American Art, 1995.

Georgia O'Keeffe
(1887-1986) American
PURPLE LEAVES, 1922
Oil on canvas on board
12 x 9 inches
Bequest of Virginia Rike Haswell, 1977.60

Paintings such as *Purple Leaves* reveal Georgia O'Keeffe's distinctive combinations of representation and abstraction. She frequently isolated and magnified natural objects, enabling viewers to observe the world around them in new ways. In this painting, the leaves are presented frontally and enlarged for careful examination. Color functions as an independent formal element; the unusual tint of the leaves adds to the painting's overall abstraction. While O'Keeffe painted the leaves in a characteristically simple manner without extraneous detail, her emphasis on their curvilinear forms creates a distinct sensuous rhythm.

During her career, O'Keeffe alternated her style between great abstraction and clear representation. She often treated a theme in a series of works, examining the objects with varying degrees of abstraction. *Purple Leaves* is one of many paintings of leaves the artist did in the early 1920s at Lake George, New York, the vacation home of her spouse, Alfred Stieglitz. A related painting, *Autumn Leaves–Lake George, N.Y.* (1924) is in the collection of the Columbus Museum of Art.

O'Keeffe was a prominent member of the New York avant-garde, united with the early Modernists Marsden Hartley, Arthur Dove, John Marin, and photographer Paul Strand in the circle around Stieglitz. Like Hartley and Dove, O'Keeffe's approach was both abstract and emotive. For most people, she is also closely identified with northern New Mexico, where she painted often from 1929 onward and lived year-round after the late 1940s. Her landscapes and paintings of bones and buildings capture the desert's stark beauty in numerous and various guises.

MAR

Suggested Readings:

Cowat, Jack, Juan Hamilton and Sarah Greenough. **Georgia O'Keeffe: Art and Letters**. Exhibition catalogue. Washington and New York: National Gallery of Art and New York Graphic Society Books, 1987.

Eldredge, Charles Child. **Georgia O'Keeffe**. New York: Harry N. Abrams, Inc., 1991.

Goodrich, Lloyd and Doris Bry. **Georgia O'Keeffe**. Exhibition catalogue. New York: The Whitney Museum of American Art, 1970.

Lisle, Laurie. **Portrait of An Artist: A Biography of Georgia O'Keeffe**. Albuquerque: University of New Mexico Press, 1986.

Eliot Candee Clark
(1883-1980) American

SAVANNAH HARBOR AT TWILIGHT, *around 1924-1925*

Oil on canvas

31 3/4 x 42 inches

Gift of the Artist, 1929.1

S avannah Harbor at Twilight dates to the mid-1920s, when Eliot Clark was featured in two exhibitions at Savannah's Telfair Academy and taught classes for the Savannah Art Club. In this work, Clark explored Tonalism, a style that had become popular among American artists in the late 19th century. In Tonalist works, artists seek to create mood and atmosphere by keying their palette to gradations of one or two colors, most often silvery grays or golden browns. Evening scenes are especially effective subjects for such paintings. James Abbott McNeill Whistler was a great influence on Tonalist painters, particularly in his use of expressive, rather than descriptive, color. Like Whistler's London and Valpariso nocturnes, Clark's painting explores the atmospheric effects of dusk and still, watery surfaces. The blue-gray palette of *Savannah Harbor at Twilight* evokes the tranquility and the heavy, still air frequently associated with this time of day, particularly in the South. Clark emphasizes the mood with his uniformly horizontal brushstroke, a technique that adds to the feeling of repose that permeates this scene.

Clark's principal teacher was his father, Walter, a landscape painter whose friends included many prominent artists: John Twachtman, George Inness, Frank Duveneck, and Edward Potthast. In addition to following his father's example in painting landscapes, the younger Clark also wrote books and articles about art and several monographs on American artists. Later in his life, he served as president of the National Academy of Design. In his paintings, Clark alternately worked in Tonalist, Realist, Pointillist, and Impressionist styles. Although these styles were no longer radical by the 1920s, the date of the Art Institute's painting, they remained popular with more conservative artists.

MAR

SUGGESTED READINGS:

Clark, Eliot. "Notes from My Memory." **American Artist** (Summer 1957, Vol. 21): 72, 87-88.

Eliot Clark-American Impressionist. Exhibition catalogue. New York: Hammer Galleries, 1981.

Lawall, David B. **Eliot Clark, N.A., Retrospective Exhibition**. Exhibition catalogue. Charlottesville: The University of Virginia Art Museum, 1975.

Walter Clark (1848-1917) and Eliot Clark (1883-1980), A Tradition in American Painting. Exhibition catalogue, Manitowoc, Wisconsin: Rohr-West Museum, 1980.

Sören Emil Carlsen

(1853-1932) American

IRON KETTLE WITH ONIONS, *around 1925*

Oil on board

12 1/4 x 13 3/4 inches

Museum purchase with funds provided by the James F. Dicke Family, 1997.21

Sören Emil Carlsen is known to many art historians as the American Chardin. This designation is the result of Carlsen's fascination with the carefully arranged, humble still-lifes of the 18th century French master Jean-Baptiste-Simeon Chardin. It was in Paris that Carlsen began his study of Chardin, and his interest in Chardin's harmonious composition and limited palette lasted throughout his life.

Iron Kettle with Onions exemplifies Carlsen's still-life work in the manner of Chardin. The simple kettle and small onions are rendered with the utmost economy that does not diminish but rather enhances them. Carlsen's goal was not to create an illusionistic effect. His interest was in an atmospheric rendering that captures the effects of light and shadow. The careful arrangement of the subject and a muted palette of grays, whites, and greens create a rich visual harmony within the very limited means set by the artist.

Carlsen was born in Denmark and came to America in 1872. In 1875, he went to Paris, where his interest in Chardin was sparked. He returned to America and became well-known in Boston and New York circles as a still-life painter. In 1887, he became the director of San Francisco's School of Design. He went on to direct the Art Students League and enjoyed considerable success as a portraitist as well.

MAL

SUGGESTED READING:

Gerdts, William H. **Art Across America: 3 Centuries of Regional Painting**. Vol. 3. New York: Abbeville Press, 1990.

Paul Manship
(1885-1967) American
INDIAN HUNTER WITH HIS DOG, 1926
Bronze on marble base
H: 23 3/4 inches
Bequest of the Honorable Jefferson Patterson, 1979.96

One of Paul Manship's most popular bronzes, *Indian Hunter with His Dog* is a scale reduction of an outdoor sculpture that is located in Manship's hometown, St. Paul, Minnesota. It is thought that 12 small bronzes of the large-scale piece were made. Manship said on several different occasions that *Indian Hunter with His Dog* was his favorite piece, for it reminded him of boyhood summers spent duck hunting and fishing at Bald Eagle Lake, Minnesota.

The sculptor began receiving honors and prizes early in his career, perhaps most notably the American *Prix de Rome*, which enabled him to study in Rome between 1909 and 1913. There he became especially interested in archaic Greek art, Greek vase-painting, and Roman bronze statuary, all of which influenced his own art. Like preclassical Greek sculpture, *Indian Hunter with His Dog* is conceived and viewed in plane or from one vantage point. Although Manship's interest in naturalism is evident, the simplification of detail and sleek, highly polished surface lend an abstract quality to the piece. In many ways, Manship can be seen as bridging the gulf between the academic tradition and Modernism; for while his subjects were drawn from traditional sources such as classical mythology, his streamlined forms reflected a modern outlook. He was one of two American sculptors whose work was included in the 1925 Paris *Exposition Internationale des Arts Décoratifs et Industriels Modernes*, from which derives the term Art Deco. Although he did not consider himself part of the Art Deco movement, Manship's sleek, simplified style, which often emphasized speed or rhythmic movement, had many Art Deco characteristics.

TDS

SUGGESTED READINGS:

Manship, John. **Paul Manship**. New York: Abbeville Press, 1989.

Paul Manship: Changing Taste in America. Exhibition catalogue. St. Paul: Minnesota Museum of Art, 1985.

Rand, Harry. **Paul Manship**. Exhibition catalogue, National Museum of American Art. Washington and London: Smithsonian Institution Press, 1989.

Rather, Susan. **Archaism, Modernism, and the Art of Paul Manship**. Austin: University of Texas Press, 1993.

Ernest Lawson

(1883-1939) Canadian-American

THROUGH THE ASPENS, *around 1927-1930*

Oil on canvas

20 1/4 x 24 1/4 inches

Gift of Mrs. Harrie G. Carnell, 1944.149

Painted while Ernest Lawson was an instructor at the Broadmoor Academy in Colorado Springs, Colorado, *Through the Aspens* dates to the artist's late period when his paintings became increasingly expressionistic in style. Lawson applied the vivid shades of blue, green, and brown with a palette knife, a technique common to many of his later works. The resulting thick impasto creates rich surface texture. Lawson's landscape paintings (his only subject matter) often centered on the relationship between civilization and the natural world. In *Through the Aspens,* for example, the animation of the trees in the foreground contrasts with the smoothly painted house and cultivated land in the background.

American Impressionism was of great influence in developing Lawson's style. The Canadian-born artist studied with John Twachtman at the Art Students League in New York and with Twachtman and J. Alden Weir during summers in Cos Cob, Connecticut. While attending the traditionalist Académie Julian in Paris, Lawson independently studied French Impressionist paintings as well and made the acquaintance of Alfred Sisley. Like the Impressionists, Lawson painted from nature and was interested in capturing the effects of light and shadow using layers of broken color. However, Lawson's paintings were not an attempt to render the natural world objectively, but rather his personal response to the subject. Perhaps because his emotions were such an important part of the painting process, Lawson did not ordinarily make preliminary drawings, choosing instead to work directly on the canvas.

Lawson's greatest acclaim came in the years before World War I. A member of The Eight, part of the Ashcan School and the group of American artists who exhibited together at the MacBeth Gallery in 1908, Lawson also maintained relationships in more conservative artistic circles. As a result, he was the only member of The Eight who continued to be included in National Academy of Design exhibitions. His later years were marked by financial and personal problems, from which his stay in Colorado brought brief respite.

MAR

Suggested Readings:

Broder, Patricia Jones. **The American West: The Modern Vision.** Boston: Little, Brown and Company, 1984.

Karpiscak, Adeline Lee. **Ernest Lawson:** 1873-1939. Exhibition catalogue. Tucson: The University of Arizona Museum of Art, 1979.

Milroy, Elizabeth. **Painters of a New Century: The Eight & American Art.** Exhibition catalogue. Milwaukee: Milwaukee Art Museum, 1991.

Alfred Henry Maurer
(1868-1932) American
STILL LIFE, around 1928
Oil on composition board
18 1/2 x 21 3/4 inches
Gift of Mr. and Mrs. Hudson D. Walker in memory of Mr. Otto Spaeth, 1967.84

In Alfred Henry Maurer's still-lifes from the late 1920s and early 1930s, the artist emphasized geometric relationships and intense, subjective colors—the outcome, expressive, innovative paintings. *Still Life* is characteristic of these late works. The striped pitcher sits at the center of a more abstract surrounding composition. The fact that Maurer did not wish to create the illusion of depth is apparent from the vertically tilted tabletop and tablecloth—both treated as simplified shapes—and flattened space. The thickly applied color creates a dynamic surface that adds to the painting's energetic colors and lines.

Maurer's career was profoundly affected by two stays in Paris, particularly his long second sojourn (1902-1914) when he became acquainted with many avant-garde artists and frequented the salon of Gertrude Stein. The new movements of Cubism and Fauvism had especial impact on his work; in *Still Life*, this influence is visible in his interest in abstract spatial relationships and his use of intense, unusual colors, respectively.

While Maurer's earlier paintings, which showed the influence of Robert Henri and William Merritt Chase, had met with much critical favor in America, his Modernist works did not. When he was forced to return to the United States after the outbreak of war in Europe, he became frustrated over his lack of recognition. Unable to support himself, Maurer lived in New York with his dictatorial father, Louis, a former Currier and Ives artist who constantly disparaged his son's work. Despite the younger Maurer's increasing unhappiness (which led to his eventual suicide two weeks after Louis Maurer's death), his late work is considered to be among his finest.

MAR

SUGGESTED READINGS:

Breeskin, Adelyn D. *Alfred H. Maurer 1868-1932*. Exhibition catalogue, National Collection of Fine Arts. Washington, D.C.: Smithsonian Institution Press, 1973.

McCausland, Elizabeth. *A.H. Maurer*. New York: Published for Walker Art Center by A.A. Wyn, 1951.

Arthur B. Davies
(1862-1928) American

SILENCE, WATERFALL AND FOREST, *undated*

Oil on canvas
29 3/4 x 17 1/2 inches
Gift of Mr. C. N. Bliss, 1943.2

This painting is a fine example of Arthur B. Davies' work, which typically presents female figures set in an idyllic scene. *Silence, Waterfall and Forest* depicts a classically dressed woman standing beside a deer in a California redwood forest; she cups her ear to listen, perhaps to the waterfall, perhaps to something else unseen. Her elongated form seems to be one with the tall tree behind her, suggesting the equivalence of woman and nature. As with many of Davies' paintings, she is a mysterious presence who exists outside of everyday life. The softened forms, especially of the woman's face, help to create a still and poetic mood that is typical of Davies' work.

Davies was a member of a group of artists who were known as The Eight, a sub-group of the Ashcan School movement. Although Davies' style differed greatly from most of the group, who painted descriptive scenes of urban life, he shared with them a commitment to finding artistic freedom outside of the powerful National Academy of Design. Davies' commitment to this principle was demonstrated in the major role he played, as president of the Association of American Painters and Sculptors, in staging the 1913 Armory Show. This landmark exhibition introduced Americans to major works from the contemporary avant-garde movements of Europe and had enormous impact on artists, critics, and the U.S. public. For a time after the Armory Show, Davies worked in a decorative style that was inspired by Cubism before returning to the lyric style seen in *Silence, Waterfall and Forest*.

MAR

SUGGESTED READINGS:

Arthur B. Davies: Essays on the Man and His Art. *Cambridge, MA: The Riverside Press, 1924.*

Czestochowski, Joseph S. **The Works of Arthur B. Davies**. *Chicago: University of Chicago Press, 1980.*

Ernest Leonard Blumenschein
(1874-1960) American

CANYON, RED AND BLACK, *1934*

Oil on canvas

40 x 45 inches

Gift of Mr. John G. Lowe, 1935.14

The simple, geometric composition of Ernest Blumenschein's *Canyon, Red and Black* heightens the strong impact of the painting's Southwestern subject. Large boulders in the foreground frame the scene, which is composed of three major triangular areas: the foreground slope, which is shown in shadow; the second triangular rock formation in the middle ground; and a triangle of background rocks, which bridges the gap between the two nearer cliffs. Further balance is created from the repetition of shapes (for example, the boulder in the right foreground is mirrored by the rock above it), and by the interplay of sunlight and shadow. As in many of his late paintings, Blumenschein emphasized rich, red tones. The rocks' strong shapes are enhanced by the broadly painted, flat colors. Blumenschein's treatment gives the landscape an immutable, timeless appearance, despite the fact that, as we can see by the landslide of rocks in the middle ground, movement and change continue to redefine the terrain.

One of Blumenschein's intentions in painting was to recreate his initial reaction to his subject. In *Canyon, Red and Black*, the low vantage point adds emotional impact by making viewers feel as if they are actually standing in the canyon. This low point of view, coupled with the high horizon line in the distance, heightens the enormity of the rock structure.

Blumenschein, who grew up in Dayton, was one of the most famous members of the Taos Society of Artists. Formed in 1912, the Society served as an exhibiting organization for some of the first artists to be drawn to the people and scenery of Taos, New Mexico. Blumenschein's own interest in the Southwest began in the 1890s, during his studies at the Académie Julien in Paris. There he met Joseph Henry Sharp, an artist who had already visited the Taos region and extolled its beauties. Blumenschein first visited Taos in 1898, but did not move there permanently until 1919. Among his Taos colleagues, Blumenschein was considered to be the most accomplished.

MAR

Suggested Readings:

Eldredge, Charles, Julie Schimmel and William H. Truettner. **Art in New Mexico, 1900-1945: Paths to Taos and Sante Fe**. *Exhibition catalogue, National Museum of American Art. Washington, D.C.: Abbeville Press, 1986.*

Henning, Jr., William T. **Ernest L. Blumenschein Retrospective**. *Exhibition catalogue. Colorado Springs: Colorado Springs Fine Arts Center, 1978.*

Stuart Davis
(1894-1964) American

LANDSCAPE WITH BROKEN MACHINE, *1935*

Gouache on paper
15 1/4 x 22 1/8 inches
Bequest of Virginia Rike Haswell, 1977.39

In 1935, Stuart Davis was serving as president of the Artist Union and executing covers for its magazine *Art Front*, a publication for which Davis also served as editor. These two duties were just a sample of Davis' political and social commitments. During the 1930s, Davis, an avowed Marxist, was attempting to persuade the public that artists should be considered like other workers, and as such should be entitled to the same privileges of unions and collective action.

This political and social activism was complemented by Davis' whole-hearted dedication to abstract aesthetics. By the middle of the 1930s, he was positing that the real subject matter of art was not the object, figure, or scene depicted but rather the formal elements. Line became a primary agent for expression within his work. This disavowal of representation can be interpreted as a direct attack on the "sentimental" (as Davis named it) and the traditional aesthetic of the American Scene painters Thomas Hart Benton, Grant Wood, and John Curry. Moreover, Davis' indefatigable support of Modernism can be seen as a rebuke of the desire by Soviet Communists for art that, by its very purpose as propaganda, must be representational.

Looking at *Landscape with Broken Machine*, most viewers would be hard pressed to detect or experience a political message, despite the fact that by 1935 Davis was strongly connected with the major leftist international political movements. The inability to recognize Socialist symbols within the painting does not, however, preclude a political reading of the work. For Davis, Modernism (and its accompanying abstracted aesthetic) could serve the cause of revolution in greater leagues than representational art, for the former emerged out of a struggle against the traditions of "bourgeois academic traditions." And such a struggle, at least in the years of the Popular Front, found a larger home in the international Marxist political movement.

TDS

Suggested Readings:

Arnason, H.H. **Stuart Davis Memorial Exhibition**. *Washington, D.C.: National Collection of Fine Arts, 1965.*

Sims, Lowrey Stokes, et al. **Stuart Davis: American Painter**. *Exhibition catalogue. New York: The Metropolitan Museum of Art and Harry N. Abrams, Inc., 1991.*

Wilkin, Karen. **Stuart Davis**. *New York: Abbeville Press, 1987.*

Dwinell Grant
(1912-1992) American

RED CIRCLE, *1938*

Oil on canvas

30 x 40 1/4 inches

Gift of Dwinell Grant, 1939.39

Painter and filmmaker Dwinell Grant was born in Springfield, Ohio, and educated at The Dayton Art Institute. In 1936, he founded the art department at Wittenberg University. *Red Circle* is an example of Grant's interest in the non-objective art pioneered by artists working in Europe such as Wassily Kandinsky and Kasimir Malevich. Using the pure vocabulary of circles, lines, and rectangles, Grant worked intuitively to create a painting that has no association with a story or recognizable object. Like Kandinsky, Grant was interested in an art whose inspiration, like music, came from emotions or intellect rather than the outside world. While Grant's work is based on intuition, he adhered to general rules of composition and color harmony that he derived from his own studies, as well as the writings of Kandinksy and Gestalt theory. The result is a work that is mysterious and visually satisfying. The circle, which according to Kandinksy was the most concise, yet opulent, of forms, is used here in a variety of sizes and colors. The large red circle anchors the work. Other shapes, such as the triangle and rectangle, are used to balance the composition and produce a sense of movement and vitality.

Grant probably discovered the work of Kandinsky in the mid-1930s through the publications and exhibition catalogues published by Hilla Rebay, then curator of the Museum of Non-Objective Painting (now the Solomon R. Guggenheim Museum in New York). In 1938, he was given his first exhibition, which included *Red Circle*, at The Dayton Art Institute. While such painting was not particularly radical for its day, it was considered by some to be "un-American" due to its similarity to the work of Kandinsky and other artists working in Germany. Wittenberg presented Grant with an ultimatum: quit painting and teaching non-objective art or be fired. Grant left Wittenberg and went to New York where he became Rebay's personal assistant from 1940 to 1942. There he continued to paint and make non-objective films and the Guggenheim Museum now holds nine of his paintings.

MAL

Suggested Readings:

Levin, Gail, and Marianne Lorenz. **Theme and Improvisation: Kandinsky and the American Avant-Garde, 1912-1950**. *Exhibition catalogue, The Dayton Art Institute. Boston: Bulfinch Press, 1992.*

Mecklenburg, Virginia. **The Patricia and Phillip Frost Collection**. *Exhibition catalogue, National Museum of American Art. Washington, D.C.: Smithsonian Institution Press, 1989.*

Milton Avery
(1885-1965) American

THE TREE, VERMONT, *1940*

Oil on canvas
27 1/2 x 35 1/2 inches
Gift of Mr. Roy R. Neuberger, 1949.3

In preparation for his landscape paintings, Milton Avery typically made sketches of local Vermont scenery from which he created several watercolors of the same subject. Eventually, he selected a watercolor to use as the basis for a painting; like many of his oils, Avery may have painted *The Tree, Vermont* several months, or even years, after he first sketched the subject. The painting's expressive brushwork is augmented by Avery's use of the brush end to create energetic lines along the bowed branches. The abbreviated depictions of the undergrowth and the animated lines of the tree at the right imbue the painting with a sketchlike quality typical of his work from the 1930s and 1940s.

The summers that Avery spent in Vermont during the 1930s brought about a return to landscape painting, subject matter the artist had not explored since the mid-1920s. While the naturalistic space, painterly brushwork, and somewhat amorphous shapes in *The Tree, Vermont* differ stylistically from the clearly defined shapes, broad areas of color, flat space, and thin brushwork of the artist's best work, this painting is representative of the landscapes the artist painted in Vermont. The 1930s and early 1940s were times of stylistic experimentation for Avery, and works such as *The Tree, Vermont* were created alongside paintings that explored abstract relationships to a greater degree. Yet, Avery's work, no matter how abstract it might seem, was always rooted in the natural, observed world.

Throughout his life, he was committed to exploring aesthetic issues, especially the formal and expressive qualities of color. In this regard, Avery can be seen as a successor to such European modernists as Henri Matisse (1869-1954) and Wassily Kandinsky (1866-1944) and as an important and influential precursor to the Color-Field artists Helen Frankenthaler, Morris Louis, and Kenneth Noland.

MAR

SUGGESTED READINGS:

Breeskin, Adelyn D. **Milton Avery**. *Exhibition catalogue, The National Collection of Fine Arts. Washington, D.C.: Smithsonian Institution, 1969.*

Haskell, Barbara. **Milton Avery**. *Exhibition catalogue, Whitney Museum of American Art. New York: Harper & Row Publishers, 1982.*

Hobbs, Robert. **Milton Avery**. *New York: Hudson Hills Press, 1990.*

Rockwell Kent

(1882-1971) American

ADIRONDACK LANDSCAPE, *around 1940*

Oil on canvas

34 x 44 inches

Museum purchase with funds provided by the James F. Dicke Family, 1998.6

In 1928, Rockwell Kent moved with his second wife, Frances Lee, to the Adirondacks and established a farm that he called Asgaard, the Norse word for "home of the gods." Kent found the landscape around the farm inspirational and his Adirondack landscapes comprise a major part of his repretoire. Kent is known primarily for his often awe-inspiring depictions of northern landscapes and the Art Institute's painting reflects Kent's ability to imbue the land with a spiritual or otherworldly quality. Kent himself said that his was "to paint the rhythm of eternity." *Adirondack Landscape*, with its simplified forms, rich colors, and abstract shapes, evokes the power, harmony, and beauty of the Adirondack Mountains. Kent's skill as a painter to create volume using broad, lively brush strokes can be noted in the powerful depiction of clouds in *Adirondack Landscape*.

Kent was a vigorous man who spent much of his life on painting expeditions to subpolar regions such as Newfoundland, Alaska, and Greenland. Like the Canadian artist Lawren Harris, Kent sought out mountains, glaciers, icy water, and icebergs and painted their awe-inspiring mystery. Kent studied painting with the American Impressionist William Merritt Chase and with Ashcan School painter Robert Henri. He is perhaps best known for his illustrations of books such as *Candide* and *Moby Dick*.

MAL

Suggested Reading:

West, Richard V. **An Enkindled Eye: The Paintings of Rockwell Kent**. Santa Barbara, CA: Santa Barbara Museum of Art, 1985.

Charles Shaw
(1892-1974) American
PAINTING, *around 1940s-1950s*
Oil on board
20 x 24 inches
Gift of Mr. Paul Ganz, 1961.27

Heir to a considerable fortune based partially on the Woolworth empire, Charles Shaw was one of the so-called "Park Avenue Cubists" in New York during the 1930s. He attended Yale University and went on to study with Thomas Hart Benton and George Luks. He began his career as a writer for *Vanity Fair* and *The New Yorker* and traveled abroad extensively to research articles for those magazines. Shaw was particularly impressed by the work of Paul Cezanne and Pablo Picasso and *Painting* reflects his interest in those artists. Cezanne and Picasso were largely responsible for introducing Shaw and other American artists to the possibilities of Geometric Abstraction.

Painting was very likely created during the 1940s or 1950s. The spare, flat geometry of the piece is in contrast to his Cubist works of the early 1930s, in which the volume of his shapes was more pronounced. The planes of color, which overlap with one another but combine to form an overall shape within the square canvas, reassert the two-dimensionality of the picture plane. At the same time, the painterly brush strokes reflect the loosening and broadening in Shaw's style that occurred in the late 1940s. The work is also a study in color harmony and contrast: the subtle mauves are offset by varying shades of green and punctuated by areas of black and deep red.

Shaw was a founding member of the American Abstract Artists group in 1937. This group attempted, through exhibitions and publications, to bring public attention and understanding to Abstract art during an era of economic depression and cultural conservatism. Shaw, like many other members of this group, believed painting should appeal to aesthetic emotions rather than sentimentality or anecdote. As such, Shaw stood in the vanguard of American painting during the era in which American Abstraction developed and gained acceptance.

MAL

Suggested Reading:

Lane, John R. and Susan C. Larsen. **Abstract Painting and Sculpture in America, 1927-1944**. *Pittsburgh: Carnegie Museum of Art, 1983.*

Marsden Hartley
(1877-1943) American
FLOWER AND STAR ON WINDOW, *1941*
Oil on canvas
40 x 30 1/4 inches
Bequest of Virginia Rike Haswell, 1977.46

When Marsden Hartley settled in Maine permanently in 1937, the accompanying dedication to the creation of a "truly" Maine style in his art arose from, among others, a desire to establish himself as <u>the</u> artist from Maine. Long regarded as an American artist who relished in European Modernism, Hartley, like others in the mid-1930s, was experiencing a decline in his sales due to a backlash against the perceived decadence of European aesthetics. With the popularity of the Regionalist-type paintings of Thomas Hart Benton and Grant Wood, the art and general publics had become leery of works that were not rooted in American subjects, scenery, and style. Writing on the heels of his 1936 exhibition at Alfred Stieglitz's American Place Gallery, which featured his representations of both New England and Alpine scenery, and acknowledging the poor reception of the latter, the artist noted, "I propose a 100% Yankee show next year—to cram the idea down their throats until it chokes them even."

As Dorinda Cassidy suggests, the economic problems resulting from slumping sales, critical disfavor, patronage strife (Stieglitz wanted less European-derived and more American-inspired works), and the public demand for Americanism were all channeled by Hartley into his "rebirth" as a nativist painter. Citing Winslow Homer and Albert Pinkham Ryder as his predecessors in Maine, Hartley set about to construct an art which was based in the experiences he felt particular to his home state. It is in such images as *Flower and Star on Window*, which partake in an action of the refashioning of the artist's image.

The clamoring for Regionalism extended beyond the art world. In an age when the city and modernity had come to signify a way of life quite removed from the roots of American culture, the corrective, for many of the regionalist apologists, included a glorification of the folk traditions and a renewed interest in American mythology. For Hartley, this became a driving force behind his fascination with the sea, the fishing families, and the simple, rustic pleasures.

TDS

Suggested Readings:

Ames, Polly Scribner. **Marsden Hartley in Maine**. *Orono: University of Maine Press, 1972.*

Haskell, Barbara. **Marsden Hartley**. *Exhibition catalogue. New York: Whitney Museum of American Art, 1980.*

Scott, Gail R. **Marsden Hartley**. *New York: Abbeville Publishers, 1988.*

Niles Spencer
(1893-1952) American
CONNECTICUT SHORE, 1941
Oil on canvas
20 x 36 inches
Bequest of Virginia Rike Haswell, 1977.68

Connecticut Shore exemplifies Niles Spencer's understated style and his intellectual approach to art. For his many depictions of the modern industrial landscape, Spencer preferred a muted palette; in this painting, all the colors have an underlying gray tonality. Also characteristic of Spencer's work is the lack of a specific light source, an absence that imbues the landscape with a quality of stillness. Spencer simplified the architectural forms, omitting details in order to reduce the scene to its basic geometric relationships. The artist's typically balanced composition is comprised of a series of diagonals, most notably those created from the implied line that moves between the smokestacks and the wooden pole (at the left foreground), and the line caused by the road. The simplified geometric forms, subdued colors, and controlled, unified composition of *Connecticut Shore* create a strong sense of order and timelessness. Despite its title, this landscape has an anonymous quality—its buildings could be located anywhere in the United States.

Spencer, a native of Pawtucket, Rhode Island, studied at the Rhode Island School of Design and with Robert Henri and George Bellows at the Art Students League in New York. In the early 1920s, Spencer traveled to Europe, where he saw firsthand many Cubist works. Upon his return, he became one of a group of artists who, beginning in the 1920s, created works glorifying industry, vernacular architecture, and the streamlined shapes of modern design. Sensing the fundamental element of abstraction in their chosen subject matter, these American artists combined realism with a Cubist-influenced emphasis on the underlying geometric shapes of objects. Known as the Precisionists, their paintings are ordered and still, and, as is true of *Connecticut Shore*, paint surfaces are smooth and unvaried. Highly respected by his fellow artists and critics, Spencer was not so well-known by the public, perhaps because of his understated style and slow working method (he averaged two paintings a year) that led to a small body of work.

MAR

SUGGESTED READINGS:

Freeman, Richard B. **Niles Spencer**. Exhibition catalogue. Lexington: The University of Kentucky, 1965.

Friedman, Martin B. **The Precisionist View in American Art**. Exhibition catalogue. Minneapolis: The Walker Art Center, 1960.

Niles Spencer. Karol Ann Marling and Wendy Jeffers essays. Exhibition catalogue. New York: The Whitney Museum of American Art at Equitable Center, 1990.

Tsujimoto, Karen. **Images of America: Precisionist Painting and Modern Photography**. Exhibition catalogue, San Francisco Museum of Modern Art. Seattle and London: University of Washington Press.

Charles Ephraim Burchfield
(1893-1967) American

BUDDING POPLAR BRANCHES, 1942

Watercolor on paper
32 7/8 x 29 inches
Museum purchase, 1947. 93

In this watercolor, a realistic style is united with an emotional response to the beginnings of spring. The tree's angular branches express growth and energy, while the blue-gray, cloudy sky hints at the kind of blustery weather that is associated with the season. The painting exemplifies Charles Burchfield's late style, one that resolved his early, highly expressive, romantic tendencies with the realism of his middle years. About this work, Burchfield wrote in a letter to the Art Institute:

> This picture was painted outdoors in my own backyard, and was the result of a determination on my part to do a painting outdoors that would have some of the quality of a carefully wrought still-life, with the added interest of actual life, of a growing plant, stirred to "life" by the quickening action of a spring sun, and the watering from melting snow.

A painter of American farmlands, from an early age Burchfield was interested in the everyday world around him, both natural and manmade. Because his watercolors depict places in which he lived and visited, especially Salem, Ohio (his hometown), and Buffalo, New York, he is sometimes considered part of the "American Scene" movement. In the 1920s and 1930s, this group of painters sought specifically "American" subject matter, often portraying scenes of the Midwest. Burchfield disavowed the label for himself, however, stating that he did not select subject matter to celebrate our national character. Rather, he painted what appealed to him or provoked an emotional response, as *Budding Poplar Branches* reflects.

MAR

SUGGESTED READINGS:

Baigell, Matthew. **Charles Burchfield**. New York: Watson-Guptill Publications, 1976.

Baur, John I.H. **Life and Work of Charles Burchfield**, 1893-1967: The Inlander. New York and London: Cornwall Books, 1984.

Charles Burchfield's Journals: The Poetry of Place. J. Benjamin Townsend, ed. Albany: State University of New York Press, 1993.

Yasuo Kuniyoshi
(1889-1953) Japanese

I LIKE IT HERE, *1945*

Oil on canvas

16 1/4 x 12 inches

Bequest of Virginia Rike Haswell, 1977.73

Repeatedly drawn to women as subject matter for his paintings, during the late 1930s and 1940s Yasuo Kuniyoshi portrays them as increasingly melancholic in nature. Shown in repose, the solitary woman in *I Like It Here* is absorbed in her own thoughts and emotionally distanced from the viewer. The optimistic title forms a striking contrast to the painting's melancholy tone, perhaps reflecting Kuniyoshi's own conflicted feelings during the war years. Born in Japan, he was unable to become an American citizen because of longstanding U.S. immigration laws that did not permit Japanese to apply for citizenship. Nonetheless, he was a firm believer in democracy and supporter of the American government, and watched the rise of militarism in Japan with great alarm. The melancholy mood that pervades many of his works in the 1940s, including *I Like It Here*, is undoubtedly an indication of the inner turmoil he felt.

Kuniyoshi's interest in art developed after he came to America in 1906, and his training was entirely American. He studied at the Los Angeles School of Art and Design and at several art schools in New York, including the Society of American Artists and the Art Students League. In his paintings, drawings, and prints, his preferred subjects were still-lifes, landscapes, and women. In his early paintings, Kuniyoshi's interest in American folk art was evident in an emphasis on line, extremely flattened space, and bright colors. In later works such as *I Like It Here*, Kuniyoshi's style was one of subtle coloration and a greater sense of depth, but in which the expressive qualities of line remained a central focus. Kuniyoshi's linear style and preference for flattened space and understated colors may also be the result of his intuitive understanding of traditional Japanese aesthetics.

MAR

Suggested Readings:

Goodrich, Lloyd, Susan Lubowsky and Tom Wolf. **Yasuo Kuniyoshi, Retrospective Exhibition**. *Exhibition catalogue. New York: The Whitney Museum of American Art at Philip Morris, 1986.*

Uchiyama, Takeo, Susan Lubowsky, Alexandra Munroe and Tom Wolf. **Yasuo Kuniyoshi**. *Exhibition catalogue. Kyoto: The National Museum of Modern Art, 1989.*

Wolf, Tom. **Yasuo Kuniyoshi's Women**. *San Francisco: Pomegranate Artbooks, 1993.*

Yasuo Kuniyoshi. *Shigemi Asano. ed. Okayama: Fukutake Publishing Company, Ltd., 1991.*

Rockwell Kent

(1882-1971) American

ENDLESS ENERGY FOR LIMITLESS LIVING, *around 1945*

Oil on canvas

44 x 48 inches

Gift of Dane and Kerry Dicke, 1994.60

Brandishing a large lump of coal, a male figure emerges from a burst of clouds. The coal produces an explosion of light that beams down on a coal generator and from which the holder must protect his face. Such a unique composition and subject matter actually is part of a series that Rockwell Kent executed in 1945. These nine paintings were commissioned by the Bituminous Coal Institute and the Benton and Bowles Advertising Agency in New York City as illustrations for an advertising campaign that ran in magazines such as *Saturday Evening Post*, *Newsweek*, and *Liberty*. The purpose of these spots was to boost the reputation of the coal industry and argue for the centrality of this energy source for the modern, postwar society. Other works in the series included *Power for the Wheels of Progress*, *Heat for the Steel That Shapes Our Lives*, *To Make Dream Homes Come True*, and *Light for Tomorrow's Lincolns*. Their titles suggest society's perceived total reliance on coal. Likewise, other utilities and heavy-manufacturing industries, such as steel, copper, and natural gas, competed in the public arena of advertising for public loyalty and recognition.

What is the most intriguing aspect of this series of works is Kent's own political history with relation to coal and the plight of union workers. Known throughout the 1930s as a political leftist, Kent was actually a major spokesperson for the Communist Party in America. Answering his own rhetorical question of "What is an American?" in *The New Masses* in 1936, Kent states that "to be a true American a man must have the will to right our social wrongs. For me, the way is Communism." Also in 1936, Kent, in making the claim for the unionization of artists, draws upon the example of the United Mine Workers with the following caveat: "Coal is to be sure a first necessity. Yet it is hardly realized what a necessity art is . . . Not only are the workers in coal organized, but the workers in diamonds. Are diamonds a greater necessity to man than art?" Finally in 1935 and 1936, Kent aided the striking marble workers in Rutland, Vermont. Against such a backdrop, one might wonder of the place of this 1945 work that seemingly celebrates the power of industry over the common people, the workers. The question remains: was Kent caught up in the optimism of the postwar victory and promise of a bright future?

TDS

SUGGESTED READING:

West, Richard U. **An Enkindled Eye: The Paintings of Rockwell Kent**. *Exhibition catalogue. Santa Barbara Museum of Art, 1985.*

Reginald Marsh
(1898-1954) American

CONEY ISLAND BEACH, *1948*

Wash drawing on paper
27 1/16 x 40 1/4 inches
Museum purchase with funds provided by Mr. and Mrs. Anthony Haswell, 1961.2

Beginning in the 1920s and continuing until near the end of his life, Reginald Marsh was fascinated with capturing the energy, excitement, and sensuality of the bathers at Coney Island. This interest in a single subject, a subject that the artist claimed represented more than one-sixth of his artistic output, found several parallels in Marsh's career. Whether it was lower-class female shoppers on Fourteenth Street, or the performers and spectators at burlesque shows, Marsh's subjects always were engaged in an urban existence at odds with Marsh's own background. Born in Paris with two artist parents, Marsh was raised within a privileged circle. Educated at Yale, patronized by a millionaire advertising executive, and the son-in-law of the curator of paintings at The Metropolitan Museum of Art, Marsh's life intersected those of his subjects only on the canvas. His treatment of women, in particular, represents a thorough knowledge of the emerging place of women within a consumer culture—as both object and subject.

Coney Island, the five-mile stretch of beach on the shore of Long Island, had begun to lose some of its glamour by the late 1920's. The ratio between the upper- and lower-class visitors to the beach had undergone a major readjustment during the 1920s with the extension of the New York City subway system to Coney Island, affording a massive influx of lower-class bathers. The addition of the boardwalk ensured crowds, but with these crowds came beggars, vagabonds, and the homeless who often lived under the boardwalk.

In Marsh's 1948 *Coney Island Beach*, one can witness the last stages of the artist's fascination with the subject. His style had, at this point, become highly free and expressive. The figures are exaggerated and the treatment of the line and form sketchy. For some, such a scene and style indicates Marsh's nostalgic viewing of a quickly vanishing moment. Toward the end of his life—the period of this work—Marsh began questioning his own standing within contemporary art. While attending a conference and after listening to the other speaker's address on the accomplishments of Abstract Expressionism and abstraction in general, Marsh rose to the podium and reportedly stated: "I am not a man of this century." With such an announcement, Marsh made clear that his style and his interest in the figure and the social environment had come to occupy an unprivileged place within contemporary art.

TDS

Suggested Reading:

Goodrich, Lloyd. **Reginald Marsh**. *New York: Whitney Museum of American Art, 1955.*

Edward Hopper
(1882-1967) American

HIGH NOON, 1949
Oil on canvas
27 1/2 x 39 1/2 inches
Gift of Mr. and Mrs. Anthony Haswell, 1971.7

Edward Hopper is best known for his poignant yet curiously detached paintings of modern life, such as *High Noon*. The painting is characteristic of Hopper's mature style of simplified planes, broad blocks of color, isolated figures, and detached viewpoint. The strongly geometrical quality of his paintings is augmented here by the interplay of lines made by junctions of sunlight and shadow and the interest in architectural features. While a seemingly realistic depiction of the scene, in reality the composition is highly ordered, and many details, such as vegetation and a pathway to the door, have been left out. That nothing about the painting has been left to chance is also seen in Hopper's use of at least four preparatory studies. Although *High Noon* was painted in Cape Cod, Hopper later said that the locale was really "Hopper-Land," a term that probably refers to the personalized landscapes he created through his distinctive treatment of light, color, composition, and subject matter.

Hopper depicted American subjects, believing that artists should respond to their own surroundings and heritage. Having studied with Robert Henri, he was familiar with the work of The Eight, the exhibiting circle with whom Henri was associated. Like The Eight's core group of urban realists, who focused on paintings of ordinary city life, Hopper found inspiration in prosaic subjects such as gas stations, hotel rooms, train compartments, and offices: images familiar and yet overlooked in everyday existence. Hopper's works differ from the earlier works, however, in their more ordered compositions, lighter tonality, and omission of detail. His scenes are peopled by anonymous human beings, usually physically or psychologically isolated from their environment. All activity is suspended; indeed, the absence of movement is the event.

Hopper's fascination with solitude and specific times of day is apparent in *High Noon*. The woman stands alone at her doorway, seemingly removed from civilization. Although his isolated, generic figures sometimes reflect the alienation present in modern society, Hopper enjoyed being alone. In *High Noon*, solitude is a positive state, for the woman's air of expectancy and hope seems to be generated by the sunlight and adds a quality of sexual tension to the painting.

MAR

SUGGESTED READINGS:

Goodrich, Lloyd. **Edward Hopper**. New York: Harry N. Abrams, Inc., 1987.

Levin, Gail. **Edward Hopper: The Art and the Artist**. Exhibition catalogue, The Whitney Museum of American Art. New York and London: W.W. Norton & Company, 1980.

O'Doherty, Brian. **American Masters: The Voice and the Myth in Modern Art**. New York: Dutton, 1982.

Norman Lewis
(1909-1979) American

PREHISTORY, 1952

Oil on canvas
25 3/4 x 49 3/4 inches
Gift of the James F. Dicke Family, 1996.13

The floating, amorphous areas of color punctuated by what appear to be ancient sea creatures are an abstract evocation of what Norman Lewis saw as "prehistory." This interest in exploring a time and creating a world that predates civilization, or perhaps even the emergence of man, was common among Abstract Expressionist artists such as Lewis. Abstract Expressionism was the first major American post–World War II art movement and its artists were immersed in the ideas of Sigmund Freud, Carl Jung, Existentialism, and European Surrealism. Despite the abstract nature of many of the works by the Abstract Expressionists, content was of vital importance to them. As Mark Rothko and Adolph Gottlieb stated in a letter to *The New York Times* in 1943: "There is no such thing as a good painting about nothing. We assert that the subject is crucial." Like his Abstract Expressionist colleagues, Lewis often took his subject matter from primitive life and cultures, the fascination of which was expressed by Gottlieb:

> All primitive expression reveals the constant awareness of powerful forces, the immediate presence of terror and fear, a recognition of the brutality of the natural world as well as the eternal insecurities of life . . . to us an art that glosses over or evades these feelings is superficial and meaningless. That is why we insist on subject matter, a subject matter that embraces these feelings and permits them to be expressed.

Lewis was also influenced heavily by the work of the early 20th century Russian master, Wassily Kandinsky. The Museum of Non-Objective Painting, now the Solomon R. Guggenheim Museum in New York, exhibited Kandinsky's work regularly and mounted a major memorial exhibition of Kandinsky in 1945, one year after his death. The museum also published his two influential treatises, *Concerning the Spiritual in Art* and *Point and Line to Plane* in the late 1940s. Lewis visited the memorial exhibition and was very attracted to Kandinsky's work and ideas. The free-flowing lines and amorphous areas of color are Lewis's debt to Kandinsky's ideas.

Lewis was the only African-American member of the Abstract Expressionist movement. In the 1930s, he worked in a Realist style with social-realist subject matter. He taught at a variety of art schools and, like other Abstract Expressionists, was a member of the Works Progress Administration (WPA) art program.

MAL

SUGGESTED READINGS:

Norman Lewis: From the Harlem Renaissance to Abstraction. New York: Kenkeleba Gallery, 1989.

Sandler, Irving. *The Triumph of American Painting*, New York: Harper and Row, 1970.

Charles Sheeler
(1883-1965) American

STACKS IN CELEBRATION, 1954

Oil on canvas
22 x 28 inches
Signed and dated lower: Sheeler 1954
Museum purchase with funds provided by the Eloise Spaeth Fund, the
Virginia Rike Haswell Fund through exchange, and other sources, 1998.52

Charles Sheeler is one of the most important painters of the so-called Precisionist movement, which originated in the United States in the years following the 1913 Armory Show in New York City. It was at this seminal exhibition (later seen in Chicago and Boston) where many American artists and critics had their first exposure to such European trends as Post-Impressionism, Fauvism, and Cubism. It was the latter, intellectual Cubism, with its interest in fractured matter and multiple viewpoints, that became translated on this side of the Atlantic by artists like Sheeler, Charles Demuth and Georgia O'Keeffe. These painters gave the style a distinctly American character, stressing clarity, sharply defined shapes, and cool and balanced color schemes, all tempered with an eye for industrial precision. In many ways, Precisionism was a perfect style to extol the growing American urban landscape surrounded by booming factories and power plants.

Although Sheeler was equally drawn to rural America as well as intimate and personal studies of his home and studio interiors, he seemed best-suited to depicting the great achievements of American industry. As a photographer, he produced prints that he often translated into painted works. *Stacks In Celebration* was made from photographs he took at a power plant in New Bedford, Massachusetts around 1938-1939. The combination of elegantly tall stacks and horizontal buildings accented by a peaked-roof cylindrical squat tower excited Sheeler. He walked around the site for several hours and called it "breath-taking." In fact, his experience at this plant was the genesis for a number of works, including *Fugue*, 1940 (Museum of Fine Arts, Boston), *Fugue*, 1945 (Regis Collection, Minneapolis), and the Art Institute's *Stacks in Celebration* of 1954.

The differences between Sheeler's *Fugue*, 1940 and *Stacks in Celebration* are worth noting. In *Fugue*, Sheeler seems to be recreating his initial experience in a fairly direct and realistic—albeit purified—manner. Although he has reduced much extraneous detail for the benefit of the greater whole, the work remains a nearly photographic depiction of an industrial site. However, 14 years later, Sheeler returned to the same subject in *Stacks*, creating a much more dynamic and cerebral work. The horizontal buildings are flattened into rectangular shapes, which are punctuated by the multitude of vertical stacks with an almost musical rhythm. Even the sky behind is fractured into great diagonal planes and shards relieving the regularity of horizontal and vertical elements, helping to create an ensemble of great visual and intellectual power.

DHV

SUGGESTED READINGS:

Friedman, Martin. **Charles Sheeler: Paintings, Drawings, Photographs**. New York: Watson-Guptill Publications, 1975.

Troyen, Carol and Erica S. Hirshler. **Charles Sheeler: Paintings and Drawings**. Exhibition catalogue. Boston: Museum of Fine Arts, Boston, 1987.

Milton Avery
(1885-1965) American

QUARRY, 1955

Oil on canvas
30 x 48 inches
Gift of the Milton Avery Trust, 1995.9

*Q*uarry is an example of Milton Avery's mature style that favored large areas of rich, luminous color and sophisticated interlocking shapes. This style was developed around 1944 shortly after Avery joined the gallery of art dealer Paul Rosenberg, who had supported the work of such Modernists as Pablo Picasso, Georges Braque, and Fernand Léger in Paris. Rosenberg was impressed by the structure of Avery's paintings and encouraged him to abandon the graphic detailing and brushy quality of works, such as the Art Institute's *The Tree, Vermont* (see page 90), in favor of dense, even areas of flattened color. Avery's post-1944 works are more abstract than his previous paintings, but he never abandoned his ties to nature. While these late works often appear to be abstractions, a landscape, a tree, a bird, or figure is always present.

In *Quarry*, the white cliffs of the far side of a quarry are set against a green-black foreground and a background of trees. The division of these color fields flatly rendered on the canvas reminds us of the pure abstractions of Mark Rothko, with whom Avery was very close friends. During the late 1920s and 1930s, Avery exerted a strong influence on Rothko and contributed greatly to the development of what is now known as Color-Field painting in the United States.

Avery was an independent artist, often working at odds with prevailing artistic trends. Thus, in the 1930s when the Social Realism and Regionalism of artists such Ben Shahn or Thomas Hart Benton was in vogue, Avery was uninterested in such themes and concentrated on pure landscapes, still lifes, and portraiture. In the 1940s and 1950s, as Abstract Expressionism came to the artistic forefront, Avery refused to give up the subject and paint pure abstractions. The artist was extremely well-versed in the entire history of modern art, however, and in his work the influence of Picasso and Henri Matisse can be noted. Avery's commitment to an art based on rich color, the interplay between recognizable forms and abstract shapes, and his belief that a painting should be flat and lie on one plane makes his work unique in American art of the 20th century.

MAL

SUGGESTED READING:

*Haskell, Barbara. **Milton Avery**. New York: Whitney Museum of American Art, 1982.*

Alfred Jensen
(1903-1981) American
MADONNA AND CHILD, *1958*

Oil on canvas

75 x 40 inches

Museum purchase, 1960.23

Alfred Jensen's checkerboard images are the result of a life-long exploration of a wide variety of optical, theoretical, and mystical teachings. The theories of Leonardo da Vinci and Johann Wolfgang von Goethe, ancient Chinese and Mayan numerical systems, the optics of the prism and the discoveries of 19th century scientists like Michael Faraday, James Clerk Maxwell, and Konrad Lorenz all played a role in Jensen's development as a painter. *Madonna and Child* was painted at a pivotal point in Jensen's career. In 1957, Jensen's previously dark, swirling abstractions gave way to canvases that synthesized his interest in Goethe's color theories and his own experiments using the prism. By looking through a prism, Jensen found the light and dark ends of the color spectrum. The transitional areas from black to white appeared to Jensen like the image of a checkerboard. From this, Jensen went on to develop families of color that ultimately found a place in his canvases: the "children" of black are blue, green, and violet; of white—red, orange, and yellow. Jensen's prismatic checkerboard combined with his use of arcane numerical systems determines the overall shape and pattern of works such as *Madonna and Child*. The title was likely derived from the seated silhouette image, resembling a seated Madonna, created by the checkerboard system in this piece.

Jensen was born in Guatemala City and arrived in the United States in 1925. In the course of his studies and career, he came into contact with some of the most important painters of the 20th century. He studied at the San Diego Fine Arts School for a year before he moved to Germany and studied with Hans Hofmann in 1926. Throughout the 1930s and 1940s, Jensen traveled extensively and studied painting with French figurative painters Othon Friesz and Charles Dufresne. In 1952, Jensen befriended Mark Rothko and was exposed to the work of other members of the Abstract Expressionist School. These contacts did not alter the direction of Jensen's thinking or painting, however, and his work retains a unique place in the history of modern American art.

MAL

SUGGESTED READING:

Cathcart, Linda L., and Marcia Tucker. **Alfred Jensen: Paintings and Diagrams from the Years 1957-1977**. *Buffalo: Buffalo Fine Arts Academy, 1978.*

Joan Mitchell
(1926-1992) American
UNTITLED, *around 1961-1963*
Oil on canvas
76 1/2 x 51 inches
Gift of Mr. Max Pincus in honor of Mr. and Mrs. Elton F. MacDonald, 1964.25

Untitled is typical of Joan Mitchell's work in the early 1960s and reflects many qualities of what is sometimes called the "second generation" Abstract Expressionist or New York School. These artists' work was more extroverted, nature-based, and objective than that of the earlier generation whose orientation was mythical, introspective, and symbolic. But the younger artists responded to the gestural brushstrokes, open surfaces, and vivid colors of "first generation" artists such as Franz Kline, Hans Hofmann (with whom Mitchell briefly studied), Willem de Kooning, and Clifford Still. Thus the emphatic, energetic brushstrokes of *Untitled* are reminiscent of Kline or de Kooning, but the overall effect is an objective, not a subjective one.

Mitchell used nature and landscape as a vehicle through which she expressed, or objectified, her feelings and emotions. In this sense, her work is related to such early Expressionists as Vincent van Gogh or Chaim Soutine.

Mitchell was born in Chicago and trained at The Art Institute of Chicago. Impressed at a very early age by the view from her parents' apartment on Lake Michigan, her affinity for using landscape as a means to express her emotions and feelings did not waver throughout her career. Mitchell arrived in New York in the late 1940s and became friends with other artists who shared an Abstract Expressionist aesthetic legacy, as well as an interest in landscape. Mitchell became an integral part of a group of artists that included Grace Hartigan, Norman Bluhm, Alfred Leslie, Helen Frankenthaler, Michael Goldberg, and the poet and curator Frank O'Hara. In 1954, she began to spend a great deal of time in Paris, where she met Sam Francis and Paul Jenkins. She moved permanently to France in 1959.

MAL

SUGGESTED READINGS:

Bernstock, Judith E. **Joan Mitchell**. New York: Hudson Hills Press, 1988.

Schimmel, Paul. **Action, Precision: The New Direction in New York, 1955-60**. Exhibition catalogue. Newport Beach, CA: Newport Harbor Art Museum, 1985.

Hans Hofmann
(1880-1966) American
ENCHANTED FIRE II, 1962
Oil on paperboard
21 3/4 x 23 3/4 inches
Museum purchase, 1963.29

German émigré Hans Hofmann came to the United States in 1930 and quickly became one of this country's most influential teachers and artists. While an art student in Paris from 1904 to 1918, Hofmann was exposed to the work of the French avant-garde. Personally acquainted with Henri Matisse and Pablo Picasso, he assimilated the former artist's bold, rich colors and the latter's discoveries of the potential for Cubist composition. He also knew and learned from the work of Piet Mondrian, Wassily Kandinsky, and Robert Delaunay. Hofmann is perhaps best known as an important member of the Abstract Expressionist group that flourished in New York in the 1940s and 1950s. His theory of "push-pull," based on the fact that warm colors tend to advance and cool colors tend to recede on the picture plane, allowed Abstract Expressionist artists to create spatial tension and interest without denying the two-dimensional quality of the picture plane.

Enchanted Fire II is an example of Hofmann's late style, which is characterized by lyrical or geometric compositions on small canvases. While these works tend to be smaller than Hofmann's heroically sized paintings of the 1940s and 1950s, their energy and vitality create a dimension that appears to go beyond the limits of the canvas. The dark, swirling forms in the center of the canvas draw the eye in while the cooler blues and whites recede. The thick and expressive brushstrokes (a process often referred to as gestural painting) reveal Hofmann's continued involvement with the Abstract Expressionist desire for spontaneity, personal disclosure, and vibrant energy as fundamental elements of modern painting.

MAL

SUGGESTED READING:

Goodman, Cynthia. **Hans Hofmann**. New York: Whitney Museum of American Art in association with Prestel Verlag (Munich), 1990.

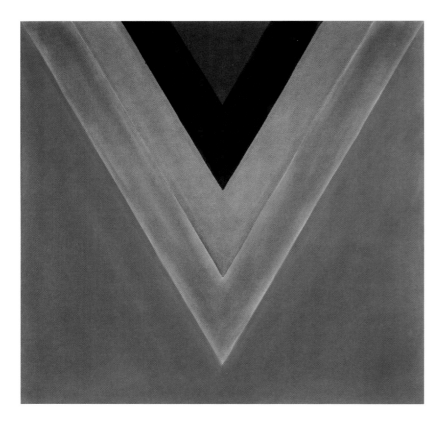

Kenneth Noland
(b. 1924) American
NIGHTWOOD, 1964
Acrylic on canvas
45 x 45 inches
Museum purchase, 1967.95

Kenneth Noland studied art at Black Mountain College with two of the leading Geometric Abstractionists working in America in the late 1940s: Joseph Albers, a former Bauhaus teacher; and Ilya Bolotowsky, an American whose work was informed by Mondrian's abstractions. Noland's later work, such as *Nightwood*, in its purity, optical effects, and color relationships owes much to this background, as well as to his exposure to the work of Paul Klee and Henri Matisse. Color was a primary concern for Noland and the chevron motif, which the artist introduced in his work in 1962, was—like the circle motif that preceded—a neutral vehicle for his exploration of color.

Noland evolved his own personal style through his exposure to the gestural painting of Jackson Pollock, the ideas of the critic Clement Greenberg, and his exposure to the stained canvases of Helen Frankenthaler. Frankenthaler, whose work Noland viewed in 1953 with his friend and fellow painter Morris Louis, was influential in Noland's ideas about how to work with large areas of color poured directly onto raw canvas. Rejecting the rigid geometry of Albers' squares and the highly personal gestures and all-over painting of Pollock, Noland began to work with vibrant hues of color circles focused in the center of the canvas. With the emergence of the chevron series, the organizational focus of the painting is shifted from the center to the midpoint or bottom edge of the canvas. The chevrons, which may have been influenced by Louis' diagonal color areas in his "Unfurl" series, are thoroughly integrated with the shape of the canvas and thus have no meaning as a motif. Color, shape, and canvas become united as a singular expressive medium.

MAL

Suggested Readings:

Moffett, Kenworth. **Kenneth Noland**. New York: Harry N. Abrams, Inc., 1977.

Waldman, Diane. **Kenneth Noland: A Retrospective**. New York: The Solomon R. Guggenheim Museum, 1977.

Michael Goldberg
(b. 1924) American

FRUITS AND FLOWERS, *1965*

Canvas (mixed media)

60 x 57 3/4 inches

Gift of Mr. Bernard Linn in memory of Claire Linn, 1968.78

Fruits and Flowers depicts a traditional still-life theme: a bowl of fruit and some flowers on a table. Here, however, the still-life is not still. Vivid abstract color splashes, and frenetic brush strokes, done with a large brush, animate the canvas. The overall effect seems more abstract than figurative and is reminiscent of the work of Abstract Expressionist painters Hans Hofmann and Willem de Kooning. In fact, Goldberg had studied painting with Hans Hofmann and knew the work of de Kooning well. Goldberg's indebtedness to the so-called "action painting" associated with those artists can be seen in the broad swaths of active color that sweep across the surface—both animating and structuring it in the process. One can also detect a structural interest in the experiments of Cubism.

Goldberg, like his contemporaries Robert Rauschenberg, Helen Frankenthaler, and Larry Rivers, matured as an artist during a time in which the lessons of Abstract Expressionism were either being aggressively challenged or actively expanded and enhanced. Many artists reintroduced figures into their work (Rauschenberg, Rivers, and Goldberg), but continued to use the highly personalized, expressive brush strokes favored by older artists such as Franz Kline and de Kooning (who actually had never given up the figure completely in his painting). Adopting everyday subject matter and themes and even drawing on mass media for their imagery, these artists combined aspects of Pop Art with an Abstract Expressionist sensibility. Thus Goldberg paints a subject that few of the original Abstract Expressionists found to be of any interest—the still-life. Goldberg uses the still-life as a starting point in his ongoing struggle between himself and the canvas: "it's only when a painting is able effectively to fight back, when it begins to have an existence that can counter what I want to impose on it, that it becomes a life and death proposition."

Goldberg was born and raised in New York City. He had his first solo exhibition at Poindexter Gallery in 1956 and counted poets such as Frank O'Hara among his friends and artistic collaborators. He continues to work and live in New York and Tuscany, Italy.

MAL

Suggested Readings:

Michael Goldberg. *Exhibition catalogue. Los Angeles: Manny Silverman Gallery, 1994.*

Schimmel, Paul, et al. **Action/Precision: The New Direction in New York 1955-60.**
Newport Beach, CA: Newport Harbor Art Museum, 1985.

Jules Olitski
(b. 1922) American

INTIMACY, *1965*
Acrylic on canvas
93 1/2 x 71 inches
Museum purchase with funds provided in part by the Associate Board's 1970 Art Ball,
1969.45

I ntimacy was created during a pivotal period in Jules Olitski's career as a Color-Field painter. Beginning in 1961, Olitski created large-scale paintings with circular images "stained" or soaked into the canvas. His goal, like that of other Color-Field painters such as Kenneth Noland or Helen Frankenthaler, was to achieve a unity between the support (i.e. the canvas) and the image being painted on it. In 1965, as a result of his stated goal to have his paintings appear to be pure color sprayed and suspended in the air, Olitski began to spray paint onto canvas in large areas of rich, expansive colors. The effect is an ethereal, evanescent one that invites meditation of the canvas' subtle hue changes and evaporating space. The beads of paint spray create a grainy texture and give a sculptural quality to the work.

Like other Color-Field painters, Olitski was indebted to predecessors such as Jackson Pollock, whose all-over poured paintings unite the background and foreground, and no visual center or focal point exists. At the same time, Olitski differed from the earlier Abstract Expressionists in his seemingly impersonal, nongestural technique. The mechanical, impersonal means of spray painting itself is completely at odds with the autobiographical, existential gesture of Willem de Kooning, Jackson Pollock, or Franz Kline. This self-removal characterized the work of the "second generation" Abstract Expressionists, Color-Field painters, and Pop artists.

Olitski was born in Snovsk, Russia, and his father, a commissar, was executed by the Russian government in 1921. In 1923, Olitski and his mother immigrated to the United States. Olitski, like many other Color-Field painters, studied painting in France after World War II. The influential art critic Clement Greenberg noted in 1966 that Olitski's paintings of the period were modern masterpieces in painting with color.

MAL

Suggested Reading:

*Greenberg, Clement. **Post Painterly Abstraction**. Exhibition catalogue. Los Angeles: Los Angeles County Museum of Art, 1964.*

Friedel Dzubas
(1915-1994) American

BEYOND, *1966*
Acrylic on canvas
27 1/2 x 165 inches
Gift of Andre Emmerich, 1969.82

Friedel Dzubas was born in Germany, came to the United States in 1939, and ultimately settled in New York. In the mid-1940s, he became familiar with Abstract Expressionism and admired the work of Jackson Pollock, Mark Rothko, and other members of that group. In 1948, Dzubas made the acquaintance of the critic Clement Greenberg and through him met Pollock and Helen Frankenthaler, with whom he later shared a studio. Dzubas, like Kenneth Noland, discovered the potential of the stained painting technique from Frankenthaler. *Beyond* demonstrates Dzubas's use of large areas of rich color applied to unprimed canvas in a manner similar to Frankenthaler's.

One of the striking features of *Beyond* is the unusual canvas size and shape that Dzubas (as well as other artists such as Noland and Jules Olitski) used frequently during this period. The elements of the painting move flowingly across the horizontal expanse of the picture plane but seem to be squeezed back in again by the outer edges of the frame. This containment within a very expansive format lends a density and immediacy to the image. Landscape painting comes to mind with *Beyond*. A cove of azure blue water set against a green background and intersected by a mauve peninsula-like shape reminds us of a bucolic lake or ocean front unmarred by human habitation.

Dzubas is one of the major protagonists of the "second generation" Abstract painters. His work, with its open, spatial qualities differs from the more centrifugal, gestural aspects of the "first generation." The fact that his color shapes appear to be emerging, merging, expanding, and contracting at the same time attests to the artist's concerns with process as opposed to the final product of the painting.

MAL

SUGGESTED READINGS:

Carmean, E.A. Jr., **Friedel Dzubas: A Retrospective Exhibition**. Houston: The Museum of Fine Arts, 1974

Wilkin, Karen. **Friedel Dzubas: Four Decades, 1950-1990**. Exhibition catalogue. New York: Andre Emmerich Gallery, Inc., 1991.

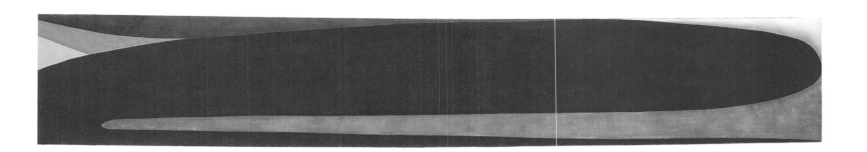

Frank Stella
(b. 1936) American
WOLFEBORO II, *1966*
Fluorescent alkyd and epoxy on canvas
160 x 100 inches
Museum purchase with funds provided by the Associate Board's 1979 Art Ball, 1979.1

*W*olfeboro II belongs to the "Irregular Polygon" series that Stella painted in 1966 and 1967. Consisting of 11 different-shaped canvases, each named for a different town in New England, this series marked an important departure in Stella's artistic development. In his earlier paintings, he employed colored stripes that followed the shape of the canvas; in this series he uses large areas of unbroken color that may or may not relate to the shape chosen for the canvas. Although artists had experimented with shaped canvases since the 1920s, Stella and Kenneth Noland were the first to fully explore and develop a nonrectangular, non-windowlike painting field. The primacy of the support over the shapes in the work itself and the dialogue between those two elements was a major concern for artists in the 1960s.

The colors used in *Wolfeboro II*, like others in the series, have a factory-produced, industrial quality that reinforces the artist's depersonalized approach to the work of art. Between the color fields, Stella allowed for thin unpainted strips by placing one-quarter-inch masking tape between them. But to avoid a "hard-edge" painting effect, Stella permitted the paint thinner to eat through the inexpensive tape, giving the color an irregular edge and allowing the paintings to "breathe." The thickness of the stretcher (the work extends four inches out from the wall) and the shaping of the canvas give *Wolfeboro II* a sculptural quality, thus challenging the boundaries between painting and sculpture.

Stella, who matured in the period following the peak of Abstract Expressionism, belongs to a generation of painters who sought to simplify painting and to treat a work of art as an object like any other. While Stella rejected Abstract Expressionism's heroic mannerism and painterly impastos, his artistic roots are to be found in the directness and "wholeness" of the work done by Jackson Pollock and Mark Rothko. The monumental scale of Stella's work also reflects his debt to Abstract Expressionism. But Stella, like his contemporaries Noland and Ellsworth Kelly, took painting one step further by eliminating incidental passages in a painting's composition in order to create large patterns that "stamp" themselves immediately on the viewers eye. *Wolfeboro II* makes a bold, yet neutral, statement characteristic of the art of the 1960s and early 1970s.

MAL

Suggested Reading:

Fried, Michael. "Shape As Form: Frank Stella's New Paintings" in **Frank Stella: An Exhibition of Recent Paintings**. Seattle: Seattle Art Museum Pavilion, 1967.

Mark Rothko
(1903-1970) American
UNTITLED, *1967*
Oil on paper, mounted on canvas
23 1/2 x 18 inches
Museum purchase, 1968.80

Mark Rothko was one of the leading figures of the Abstract Expressionist movement that developed primarily in New York following World War II. Rothko is known for large canvases with luminous rectangles floating on fields of rich color. Scale was important to the artist because he believed that a large painting was more capable of drawing the viewer into a powerful, but intimate, dialogue. The modest size and the paper media of *Untitled* were unusual for Rothko, however. He had worked on paper since the late 1920s, and during the last years of his life, frequently applied his evocative color fields to works on a small scale. While many of the small works-on-paper done after 1950 were sketches for larger canvases, most were created as works of art in themselves.

In his large canvases, Rothko often used several thin washes of paint to cover the surface. These washes blended and overlapped to create a soft, misty effect. This blending and overlapping was not possible with his works-on-paper, as paper absorbs the pigment. Thus, in *Untitled* and other works like it, Rothko applied only two layers: the background and the floating, rectangular forms on top. This simplification of process, combined with the increase in artistic control that comes with working on a smaller surface, lend a directness and clarity to his works-on-paper.

MAL

Suggested Reading:

Clearwater, Bonnie. ***Mark Rothko Works on Paper***. *New York: Hudson Hills Press, 1984.*

Joseph Albers
(1888-1976) American
HOMAGE TO THE SQUARE: SENTINEL, 1968
Oil on canvas mounted on masonite
48 x 48 inches
Gift of Society Bank, 1986.15

In the last 25 years of his life, Joseph Albers made more than 1,000 paintings and prints entitled *Homage to the Square*. Albers' interest was not in the square, however, but in the mysterious, luminous qualities of colors and their interactions with one another: "I'm not paying 'homage to the square.' It's only the dish I serve my craziness about color in." Exploring, to the fullest extent, the way solid colors are altered by their position in the square and the effect of surrounding colors, Albers ultimately produced an iconic body of work that evokes both mystery and spirituality. The subtitle of the Art Institute's painting, *Sentinel*, suggests caution and the corresponding red color underlines the association with this sentiment.

Albers was born in Bottrop, Germany, and began studying at the Bauhaus in 1920. He later became a teacher at both the Dessau and Berlin locations. When the school was closed by the Nazis in 1933, the American architect Philip Johnson brought Albers and his wife to teach at Black Mountain College in North Carolina. There, and later at Yale University, Albers became a highly influential teacher; among his student artists were Kenneth Noland and Robert Rauschenberg. In his own work and teaching, Albers stressed a high level of craftsmanship—the value of which he learned from his craftsman father. For example, he began all his *Homages* in the center so that he could catch the drips and avoid getting his shirt cuffs dirty—a lesson from his father who was, among other things, a housepainter.

Homage to the Square: Sentinel, like the other *Homages*, is done with an economy of means and emotional detachment that set Albers' work apart from other artists of the period. After applying six coats of white ground to make the colors brilliant and luminous, Albers would then apply pure, unmixed color to the panel with a painter's knife. Albers would examine each piece under warm and cool fluorescent light to ensure the consistency of the color effects in different light conditions. The result is an art of unprecedented consistency and simplicity.

MAL

Suggested Reading:

Weber, Nicholas Fox, et al. **Joseph Albers: A Retrospective**. *New York: The Solomon R. Guggenheim Museum, 1988.*

Carl Andre
(b. 1935) American

SLOPE 2003, *1968*

Hot rolled steel plate

5 pieces: 36 x 36 x 3/8 inches (each)

1 piece: 36 x 27 x 3/8 inches

Gift of Carl Andre, 1969.102

C arl Andre's sculpture is striking in its minimal means, common materials, and strict horizontality. Andre, who attended and was expelled from Kenyon College, was introduced to the New York art world in 1957 where he made the acquaintance of Frank Stella. Working in Stella's studio, Andre explored the work of Constantin Brancusi as well as the Russian Constructivists. The anthropomorphic, vertical orientation of Brancusi's work ultimately dissatisfied Andre, however, and he began seeking ways to create a sculpture devoid of those qualities. In 1960, Andre went to work for the Pennsylvania Railroad as a brakeman and conductor. His exposure to the horizontal rails and ties brought Andre to the conclusion that he wished to create sculpture that looked "more like roads than like buildings." Andre's ideas about a nonvolumetric, democratic aesthetic can be seen in his statement that, "Most sculpture is priapic with the male organ in the air. In my work, Priapus is down on the floor. The engaged position is to run along the earth." Implied, however, is the volume of space above the work with the metal plates serving as bases.

Slope 2003 exemplifies Andre's conception of sculpture as "place." Its placement not only creates the specific environment in which it is experienced but also determines the viewer's reception of it as a work of art. The series of metal plates, depending on their position in the room, arranges and actually creates a specific place; and seen outside the context of a gallery or museum, this work would seem a mere assortment of scrap metal rather than a work of art. The use of repeated, identically sized metal plates illustrates Andre's principle of "anaxial symmetry," in which each part, identical in shape, size, and material, can replace any other part of the sculpture.

MAL

Suggested Reading:

Bourdon, David. **Carl Andre: Sculpture 1959-1977**. *New York: Jaap Rietman, Inc., 1978.*

Sam Gilliam
(b. 1933) American

3 POINT, *1970*

Acrylic on canvas
24 feet, 8 inches x 9 feet, 10 inches
Museum purchase, 1987.57

With its abstract, decorative splashes of soaked-in color, *3 Point* can be firmly rooted within the context of post–World War II Abstract Expressionist and Color-Field painting. After studying art at the University of Louisville, Gilliam moved in 1962 to Washington, D.C., where he came into contact with what is known as "Washington color art." Identified with artists such as Morris Louis, Kenneth Noland, Anne Truitt, and others, this style favored large, clean-edged expanses of pure color. Gilliam developed from this style his own exuberant, gestural works that began to emerge in the late 1960s. By this time, he had also incorporated Helen Frankenthaler's lessons in applying soaked-in paint to canvas.

In 1970, Gilliam began to make wall-bound, "draped" paintings. These works launched Gilliam's career and made him an internationally recognized artist. The introduction of an unsupported canvas stands as a unique innovation that has influenced other artists greatly. The work becomes part painting, part sculpture and allows Gilliam to partake in a lyric quality inherent in the large, draped fabric. *3 Point* demonstrates Gilliam's success in combining vibrant color, an active, gestural painting style, and draped canvas.

Born in Tupelo, Mississippi, Gilliam is one of this country's leading African-American artists. He continues to live and work in Washington, D.C.

MAL

SUGGESTED READING:

Gilliam/Edwards/Williams: Extensions. *Exhibition catalogue. Hartford: CT: Wadsworth Atheneum, 1974.*

Alexander Liberman
(b. 1912) American

FIRMAMENT, 1970
Painted steel sculpture
H: 88 inches
Museum purchase with funds provided by the National Endowment for the Arts and
matching funds from various sources, 1976.1

Firmament exemplifies Alexander Liberman's lifelong interest in simple geometric forms—the circle and the triangle—and the structural logic of ancient architecture. Six cylinders, five of which are sliced diagonally so that they read as triangles, are welded to four square steel platforms arranged so that the spaces between them create thin, triangular shapes on the ground. The bold cadmium red color gives the sculpture a weightless quality and underscores its abstract geometry. This visual language of simple forms, monumentality, and primary color that can quickly and easily be apprehended by the eye are typical of much of Liberman's painting and sculpture, placing him squarely within the development of Abstract art in America and Europe in the second half of the 20th century.

Liberman, who was born in Moscow, studied art in Paris, and emigrated to the United States in 1941, began to paint a series of circle paintings in the early 1950s. Liberman, like other Eastern European artists such as Wassily Kandinsky, Kasimir Malevich, and Frank Kupka, sought to express spiritual and universal ideas through non-objective, geometric art. For Liberman, the triangle and the circle implied the "elevation of the spirit into realms beyond the material." His emphasis on the circle was related to its ability to be "visible in its totality instantly." This emphasis on simple signs, or signals, that communicated directly and simultaneously with the eye and mind prefigured the Minimalist work of artists such as Donald Judd and Frank Stella, but it was also key to Liberman's later development of monumental sculpture. Liberman's interest in an art of emotional content and personal metaphor also developed through his contact with Robert Motherwell, Mark Rothko, Barnett Newman, and other members of the Abstract Expressionist group.

Firmament demonstrates Liberman's integration of architectural, geometric, and philosophical concerns in a large, public sculpture that is simultaneously massive and transparent, classical and industrial.

MAL

SUGGESTED READING:

Rose, Barbara. **Alexander Liberman**. New York: Abbeville Press, 1981.

Edward Kienholz
(1927-1994) American

SAWDY, *1971*

Car door, mirrored window, automotive lacquer, polyester resin, screenprint,
fluorescent light, galvanized sheet metal
39 1/2 x 36 1/2 inches
Museum purchase, 1987.73

Edward Kienholz grew up on his family's farm, where he learned to work with a variety of materials from everyday life. This predilection for combining humble everyday materials into assemblages compounded with his early experience as a hospital orderly, car salesman, bootleg club manager, and vacuum cleaner salesman—among other things—is central to the social/human content of his tableaux. The presence of the mundane, sometimes tawdry, elements of everyday life place him in line with Pop Art, but the strong emotional or social content of many of his tableaux makes him an heir of the American Social Realist tradition prevalent in the 1930s.

Sawdy is a multiple developed from one of Kienholz's installations called *Five Card Stud*, which the artist considered "symbolic of minority strivings in the world today." *Sawdy* presents us with a disembodied Datsun car door. The viewer is on the "inside" of the Datsun looking out. Out the half-open car window is a scene of racial violence in which a black man is beaten by whites for drinking alone with a white woman. Should we attempt to roll up the window we are confronted, and thereby implicated, with our own mirrored reflection. The work indicates not only the violence associated with the automobile but reveals the distancing from reality that the automobile makes possible. The number "20" on the window in *Sawdy* refers to the number of this piece in the edition of 50 that were produced.

Sawdy was produced as a multiple at Gemini GEL in Los Angeles where Kienholz lived in the late 1960s and early 1970s. Gemini was a major force in producing high-quality art lithography for outstanding artists during this period. Robert Rauschenberg, Joseph Albers, Frank Stella, Donald Judd, and Claes Oldenburg all produced multiples (lithographs or objects) with Gemini.

MAL

SUGGESTED READING:

Desmarais, Charles. **Proof: Los Angeles Art and the Photograph, 1960-1980**. *Laguna, CA: Laguna Art Museum, 1992.*

Pat Steir
(b. 1940) American
BORDER LORD, 1972
Oil on canvas
69 1/2 x 92 inches
Museum purchase, 1987.139

Border Lord presents a series of disjointed, unrelated images together with splotches of paint in a variety of colors, pencil scribblings, and phrases ("Can never be beautiful," "Morning Glory, Glory, Save me, save me, love me, love me," "I miss you"). The artist neither chose, nor arranged, the various elements of the picture in such a way that they can be interpreted symbolically or narratively. Instead, the viewer must bring his or her own experience, feelings, and insights to the work and discover its personal meaning. For Pat Steir, artistic intention does not create meaning. This philosophy reveals the influence of composer John Cage, whose ideas about random sound composition inspired Steir to try to do the same with visual art. Steir chose to make only the most basic artistic choices in advance and then allowed the unconscious flow of images to emerge at random.

The work has various sources for its imagery and composition. The bird is likely a reference to Steir's "lucky bird" pet that was a gift from a friend and appears in a number of the artist's works of the period. The use of words, random lines, and scribbling were, for Steir, equivalents to her images of things. Writing was a form of a picture just as a picture was a form of writing: "I was seeing all lines as figures, whether they formed letters or pictures," Steir said. The color charts are what art historian Marcia Tucker described as: "a way of indicating the difference between the actual and the illusory . . . [they] are another way of letting the painting speak its own language, of refuting imitation."

The composition of Border Lord is organized by a series of grids, within which the random elements are contained. These grids were done under the influence of Steir's friend, the Minimalist artist Agnes Martin, whom Steir visited in her New Mexico studio in 1971. The mountain and cloud images in Border Lord are to be found in numerous works by Steir from 1971 to 1972. The emblematic presence of the mountain may be related to an incident in which Steir became lost while looking for Martin's house in the New Mexico desert, with her only landmark being the mountain at the base of which Martin lived. While Border Lord cannot be definitively analyzed, its elements speak in a way that invites the viewer to wander through a world of Steir's personal experiences and random musings and find ones's own meaning there.

MAL

Suggested Readings:

Ratcliff, Carter. **Pat Steir Paintings**, New York: Harry N. Abrams, Inc., 1986.

Tucker, Marcia. "Pat Steir: 'The thing itself, made by me,'" **Art in America** (Vol. 61, January-February 1973: 70-74.

William T. Wiley
(b. 1937) American
YOU ARE AS CLOSE AS YOU WILL BE, 1972
Mixed media (wood, lead, hide, ceramic, acrylic paint)
87 x 50 inches
Museum purchase, 1987.160

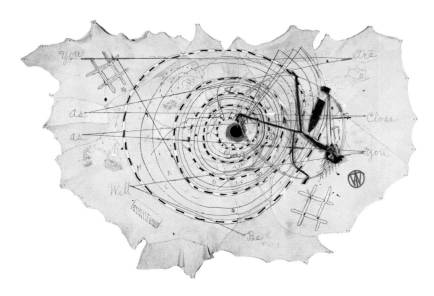

William Wiley's work calls upon a complex and enigmatic set of personal symbols, art historical reference, and metaphor. In the course of his career, Wiley has explored several themes that remain distinct, but interrelated: the West, traveling over land and sea, magic, and Wiley's own art. *You Are As Close As You Will Be* incorporates a number of Wiley's recurrent themes and symbols, but, like most of his work, resists any clear-cut interpretation or fixed analysis.

Predominant in this work is Wiley's interest in using travel as a metaphor for the life cycle. Hides sewn together in a shape that approximates the outline of the United States serve as a backdrop for Wiley's arcane mapmaking, puns, and personal symbolism. The tic-tac-toe marks in the upper right and lower left, for example, were initially a reference to W.C. Westermann's work. Later, they took on a variety of other meanings for Wiley: the four elements (his wife, his two sons, and himself), space (as in typesetting), innocence (as referred to in the *I Ching*), and a scuffle mark. The black and white spiral form, a variant on a picket or range pole that was part of Wiley's father's surveying equipment, "relates to the highway markings in the landscape." As in many of Wiley's works, nautical references abound. A small sailboat on the left side alludes to being out at sea and looking back at the landscape.

Wiley, who was born in Bedford, Indiana, and lived in Washington State before settling down in San Francisco, often alludes to the West in his work. This interest in themes of the Old West can be seen in the hides, scabbard, and self-invented Indian artifacts in *You Are As Close As You Will Be*. But like Wiley's maps, the pioneering flavor is one of the spirit rather than the actual past. The journey Wiley invites us to share is more likely to lead us towards a Zen (which Wiley has said has "been a great source of inspiration in resolving things") experience as it is to a destination in time or place.

MAL

Suggested Readings:

Beal, Graham W.J., and John Perreault. **Wiley Territory**. *Minneapolis: Walker Art Center, 1979.*

Tooker, Dan. "How to Chart a Course: An Interview with William T. Wiley." **Artscanada** *(Spring 1974): 82-85.*

Roger Brown
(1941-1997) American

TOURIST TRAP, *1974*

Oil on canvas

70 x 72 inches

Museum purchase with funds provided by the 1987 and 1988 Associate Boards, 1987.27

Although he was born in Alabama and raised in the South, Roger Brown was known as one of the leading members of a loosely associated group of Midwest artists known as the "Chicago Imagists." Like other members of the group, Brown rejected the idea that New York is the center of the contemporary American art world. In addition, Brown's work represents a conscious turning away from classical Modernism with its emphasis on abstract images and art-for-art's-sake position. Instead, Brown exploited techniques and attitudes derived from folk art, commercial art, comic strips, and American Scene painting of the 1930s and 1940s in order to provide wry commentary on contemporary American life.

In *Tourist Trap*, Brown places his figures in a uniform, yet disjointed, landscape in which the logic of scale, Renaissance perspective, and natural color relationships is discarded. The puppet-like figures gesture toward, and regard with awe, a towering mountain landscape with an arid uniformity that makes it a worthy, but also a difficult, object of attention or praise. Unusually small in relation to the mountains and fields that surround them and from which there is no apparent escape, the figures become enigmatic visitors to a familiar, yet mysterious, land. *Tourist Trap* was executed after separate trips Brown made to the South Dakota Badlands and the Southwest. The brown, denuded mountains, scrubby vegetation, and brilliant blue sky reflect the impact of those trips and can be found in a number of Brown's landscapes.

It is the combination of sophistication and naivete that gives *Tourist Trap* its formal and narrative power. Brown often uses isometric perspective (a technique in which the lines of perspective recede into depth but remain parallel, as opposed to converging in the center as in Renaissance perspective) in his paintings. This archaic perspective system, the simple patterning, and limited color scheme combined with Brown's wry social commentary make this and other Brown works innovative expressions of contemporary figurative painting.

MAL

Suggested Readings:

Bowman, Russell. "An Interview with Roger Brown." **Art in America** *(January-February 1978): 106-111.*

Lawrence, Sidney. **Roger Brown**. *New York: George Braziller, Inc., in association with the Hirshhorn Museum and Sculpture Garden, Smithsonian Institution, 1987.*

Robert Morris
(b. 1931) American

UNTITLED, *1974*
Felt, metal
98 1/2 x 76 x 36 3/4 inches
Museum purchase, 1987.96

Robert Morris, noted for his Minimal sculptures constructed of spare geometric forms in aluminum, steel, and fiberglass, added felt as a medium in 1967. In this untitled work, Morris has maintained the autonomy and integrity of his materials while minimizing his own artistic role in the object's creation. Felt, a soft, malleable fabric that forms itself, allows Morris to create a work that does not appear preconceived or artistically manipulated. The dull, almost nondescript color testifies to Morris' belief that neutral hues "do not call attention to themselves [and] allow for the maximum focus on those essential physical decisions that inform sculptural works." All this contributes to Morris' vision of an art that contains no mystery (other than that inherent in the materials themselves), a sense of impersonality, and an emphasis on the process as opposed to the product of creation.

The elimination of content or subject matter, the lack of overt artistic manipulation, and the humbleness of materials all contribute to a work of art that is physically assertive and demands in return a physical response from the viewer. Only after coming to terms with its presence and placement do we begin to interact with it as an art object. The clarity, unity, and ultimate harmony of the piece exemplify the Minimalist view of what art should be.

MAL

SUGGESTED READINGS:

Battock, Gragory. **Minimal Art: A Critical Anthology**. New York: E.P. Dutton, 1968.

Tucker, Marcia. **Robert Morris**. New York: Whitney Museum of American Art, 1970.

Sol Lewitt
(b. 1928) American

331/313, 1975

Baked enamel on steel

Eight cubes: 54 x 18 x 18 inches (each)

Gift of Mr. Sol Lewitt 1976.13

In *331/313*, the seemingly mundane, straightforward quality of the materials and composition actually disguise a subtle and highly sophisticated artistic vision by Sol Lewitt. Lewitt is considered to be a conceptual artist, for whom the idea behind a work of art is greater than its visual manifestation. As Lewitt stated: "Ideas can be works of art; they are in a chain of development that may eventually find some form. All ideas need not be made physical." Lewitt's work can also be allied, in its spare forms and seeming lack of any personal touch by the artist, to Minimal Art, as exemplified in the work of Donald Judd and Carl Andre. For Lewitt, the important thing is not to dazzle the eye, but to express an idea: "Anything that calls attention to and interests the viewer in [the object's] physicality is a deterrent to our understanding of the idea . . ." Lewitt's choice of neutral, nonexpressive white enamel for his structures underlines the clinical, cerebral approach.

331/313 is a set of eight modules. Each module containing three stacked cubes demonstrates variations on a solid cube, a cube with opposite sides removed, and a cube with one side removed. In 1967, the artist conceptualized 47 variations and had them produced in aluminum. Nine more variations were added and incorporated in 1974, when the original aluminum version was destroyed and remade in steel. The Art Institute has eight of these later 56 variations. The modules are independent of one another and are displayed in autonomous rows. Lewitt's mathematical, geometric concepts are expressed through structures that mirror not only Minimal sculpture but International Style architecture, familiar to Lewitt from his work in I.M. Pei's office from 1955 to 1956.

MAL

Suggested Reading:

Sol Lewitt. *Exhibition catalogue. New York: The Museum of Modern Art, 1978.*

Andy Warhol
(1930-1987) American
AMERICAN INDIAN SERIES (RUSSELL MEANS), 1976
Acrylic and silkscreen on canvas
84 x 70 inches
Museum purchase with funds provided by the C.F. Kettering Fund, 1987.153

Andy Warhol has been credited with reviving the tradition of grand portraiture from the moribund state it had fallen into during the 20th century. Warhol's interest in portraiture began in the early 1960s when he began to make drawings and paintings from publicity photographs of celebrities such as Troy Donahue, Marilyn Monroe, and Elvis Presley. These images, which he collected from books and magazines, appealed to Warhol due to their simple, straightforward presentation of the subject. By using a photograph from a magazine or his own Polaroid of the subject, Warhol distances the portrait from its subject, thus allowing him to explore the relationship between the genuine and the fake, the real and the simulated. Like many of Warhol's portraits, *Russell Means* was done as a multiple. Warhol would often display these multiple images in decorative rows or grids—a device that further distanced the unique reality of the person from the image. The process of making his portraits was also journalistic and impersonal: Warhol would send the snapshot or Polaroid to a laboratory where it was enlarged in black and white and then transferred to a silkscreen. From the silkscreen, the image was printed on canvas and embellished with touches of artist-applied paint.

Russell Means, an Oglala Sioux, gained wide visibility in 1973 when he led a group of Native Americans in a symbolic takeover of Wounded Knee. The siege lasted 71 days. Warhol's image presents Means as a giant celebrity whose noble features have been softened and glamorized. In Warhol's portrait, Means' status as celebrity hero takes precedence over his actuality as a person and his political importance.

MAL

Suggested Readings:

McShine, Kynaston. ed. **Andy Warhol: A Retrospective**. *New York: Museum of Modern Art, 1989.*

Whitney, David, ed. **Andy Warhol: Portraits of the 70s**. *New York: Museum of Modern Art, 1989.*

Louise Nevelson
(1900-1988) American
RAIN GARDEN #7, 1978
Wood, painted black
44 1/2 x 31 1/2 x 7 inches
Museum purchase with funds provided by the Kettering Fund, 1987.101

Louise Nevelson was a master of wood. A forager and collector of discarded remnants of furniture, building materials, and architectural fragments, Nevelson created relief sculptures that explore shape, scale, texture, light, and shadow. Nevelson worked intuitively, arranging and juxtaposing her materials, inventing and reinventing them through the process: "I'd be defeated right away if I had to remember that this is a leg from a chair . . . I'd be defeated immediately with that association." Nevelson uses wood scraps in the same way a painter uses color, line, shape, and paint texture.

Rain Garden #7 is the result of an artistic evolution that began in the 1940s when Nevelson visited Central America and was struck by the totemic columns and indecipherable inscriptions of the Mayan ruins. The power of these relief images to transmit the mysterious forces of life and the universe was inspirational. The 1950s saw the development of her interest in wood and by 1958, she had created her first large-scale, wood environmental work.

Rain Garden #7 exemplifies Nevelson's inventive use of wood scraps of various shapes (circles, triangles, rectangles-inscribed with the manufacturers' inscriptions), sizes, and textures to create a landscape for the spirit, mind, and eye. The intuitive, immediate quality of the work is the result of Nevelson's working style: "I go to the sculpture and my eye tells me what is right for me. When I compose, I don't have anything but the material, myself, and an assistant. I compose right there while the assistant hammers. Sometimes it's the material that takes over; sometimes it's me that takes over. I permit them to play, like a seesaw . . . It was always a relationship—my speaking to the wood and the wood speaking back to me."

While Nevelson also created wood sculptures using white or gold paint, she often used black, as she felt it gave order to her work: "One of the reasons I originally started with black was to see the forms more clearly. Black seemed the strongest and the clearest." But black was more than just a compositional tool—it also connoted for Nevelson "the shadow of the universe." Nevelson took ordinary objects and through artistic manipulation elevated and imbued them so that they transcend the ordinary and speak to our minds and senses.

MAL

Suggested Reading:

Nevelson, Louise. **Dawns & Dusks**, *taped conversation with Diana Mackown. New York: Charles Scribners' Sons, 1976.*

John Torreano
(b. 1941) American
EXPLODING GALAXY, 1981
Acrylic paint, glass jewels on canvas
84 x 84 inches
Museum purchase with funds provided by the 1987 and 1988 Associate Boards, 1987.147

Using the most obvious symbols—fake jewels—of our increasingly remote relationship to the precious and the genuine, John Torreano draws the viewer into a (not mutually exclusive) contemplation of materialism, kitsch, and transcendental mysticism. The key to an appreciation of Torreano's art comes through an examination of the interrelationship of the material, low art, and the mystical in works such as *Exploding Galaxy*.

Torreano was born in Flint, Michigan, and was brought up in a Catholic home. He received a master's degree in Fine Art from The Ohio State University in 1964. Torreano's ongoing dialogue with his Catholic upbringing can be seen in a number of glass-jewel encrusted objects with a cruciform shape. These objects are not meant to mock or denigrate religious artifacts of the past; instead they inform us anew of their original spirit, namely religious glorification through the use of scarce (but real) gems. Torreano's fake gems confront us with our society's material abundance and spiritual impoverishment.

In *Exploding Galaxy*, Torreano works on the heavens in a similar way. Using dots of paint and clear and colored jewels against the tan canvas, Torreano creates a cosmic cataclysm. The awe generated by an explosion in the heavens, the movement and force in our universe, are rendered through simple daubs of paint and glitzy plastic. Torreano calls upon our association of stars and jewels to make the connection between his "heavenly vision" and vulgar ornament more poignant.

Exploding Galaxy is also of interest from a purely formal standpoint. Torreano has used a number of techniques—principles of color and application of paint in small dots to create an overall pattern—developed by 19th century Pointillist painters such as Georges Seurat. The center of the "explosion," for example, appears to be a brighter white than other parts of the canvas. Torreano has achieved this effect through the use of white, rather than dark, daubs of paint in this central area. The underlying canvas, however, is the same color as in the darker-appearing areas. And, like the Pointillist paintings of Seurat, what appears to be a meaningless assemblage of dots and colors when viewed at close proximity becomes a coherent image when viewed from a distance.

MAL

Suggested Reading:

Torreano: Gems, Stars & Perceptual Trackings. *Grand Rapids, MI: Grand Rapids Art Museum, 1989.*

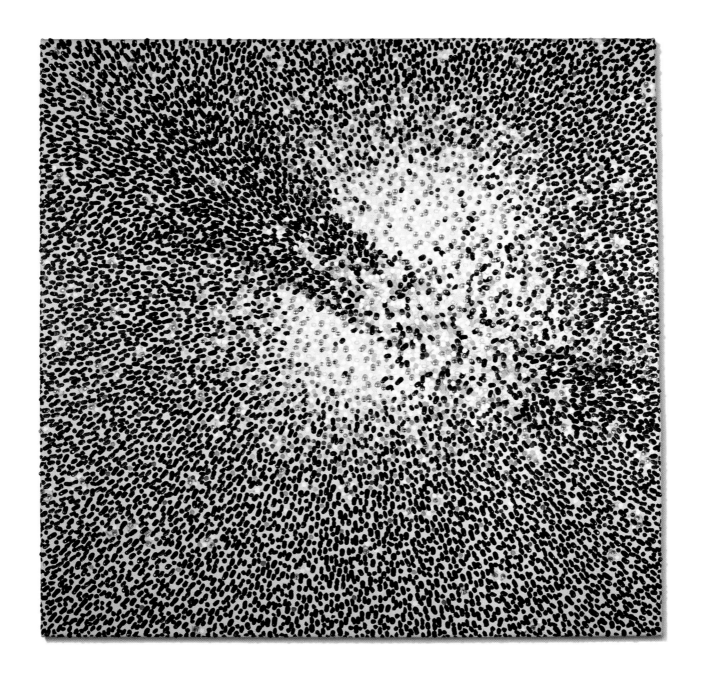

Helen Frankenthaler
(b. 1928) American

SEA CHANGE, 1982

Acrylic on canvas

38 x 116 1/2 inches

Museum purchase with funds provided by the 1987 and 1988 Associate Boards, 1987.53

Helen Frankenthaler is widely recognized as the first painter to use and fully realize the importance of the soak-stain technique. This process, in which thinned-down, watery paint is spilled on and allowed to soak into raw canvas, had a profound effect not only on Frankenthaler's work, but on that of her contemporaries Kenneth Noland and Morris Louis. Through the soak-stain technique, Frankenthaler was able to actually merge her images with the canvas and allow color to float in and out of the surface, creating as well as denying space in the process.

Sea Change, executed 30 years after Frankenthaler's first stained canvas, demonstrates well Frankenthaler's artistic concerns during the early 1980s. Against rich, layered fields of green and blue, the artist has applied clumps of pigment that move across the canvas and animate its surface. Like other works of the period to which it is related (such as *Parrot Jungle* [1981] and *Grey Fireworks* [1982]), *Sea Change* reflects Frankenthaler's interest in painterly, almost lyrical, effects. It looks forward to 1983 paintings such as *Madame Matisse* and back toward Frankenthaler's own works of the 1950s and her interest in Jackson Pollock.

Born in New York, Frankenthaler grew up in an affluent family that encouraged her artistic interests. After graduating from Bennington College, she studied with Hans Hofmann in Provincetown, Massachusetts. In 1950, she began a five-year liaison with the influential art critic Clement Greenberg, who introduced her to Pollock and other Abstract Expressionists. Frankenthaler's early and continued success has made her an influential figure in American art during the last four decades.

MAL

Suggested Reading:

Elderfield, John. **Frankenthaler**. New York: Harry N. Abrams, Inc., 1989.

Donald Judd
(1928-1994) American

UNTITLED, *1982*

Brass and anodized aluminum
40 1/2 x 84 x 6 3/4 inches
Museum purchase with funds provided by the NCR Corporation, 1987.72

Donald Judd's reductive artistic style epitomizes the formal concerns of the Minimalist artists who emerged in America in the 1960s. Working from the view that he could only express artistically what he knew empirically, Judd limited his sculpture to rigorous visual truth devoid of any subjective, personal content. *Untitled* demonstrates Judd's rejection of traditional ideals of sculpture in the elimination of a pedestal—which isolates the work of art in an ideal, separate realm—and in its constructed, industrial execution that denies former sculptural techniques such as carving, molding, and modeling.

Untitled occupies the ambiguous territory, like the shaped canvases of Frank Stella, of being neither sculpture nor painting. Judd's experimentation with progressive wall reliefs took place in 1963 when he produced a horizontal bar punctuated with holes on either end that projected out from the wall. This wall relief was followed by works such as *Untitled* with its series of square vertical projections joined across the top by a hollow tube open at the sides to reveal the thickness of the aluminum. The regular intervals between the vertical bars eliminate questions of artistic subjectivity or personal choice in their arrangement. The use of industrial anodized aluminum, with its shimmery and rich, yet inexpressive, color effects and surface, contribute to what the critic Hilton Kramer called, "minimal forms at the service of glamorous, hedonistic effects of light." But such effects are not at odds with Judd's empirical focus: each material has its own unique texture, weight, and color and these intrinsic qualities and their effects do not deny the logic of art. With all hierarchical relationships and associative values avoided, Judd's sculpture severs the connection between what one feels about an object and the object's actuality.

MAL

Suggested Reading:

Haskell, Barbara. **Donald Judd**. *New York: Whitney Museum of American Art, 1988.*

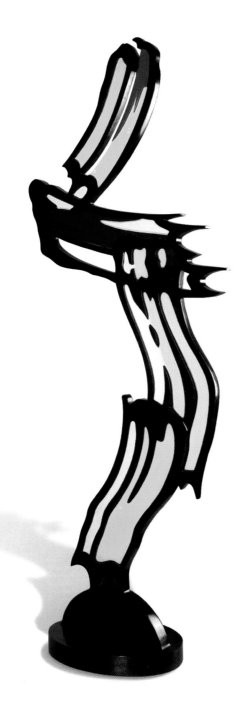

Roy Lichtenstein
(1923-1997) American
HOMAGE TO PAINTING, 1983
Bronze sculpture, painted, second in an edition of six
H: 55 1/4 inches
Gift of Ponderosa, Inc., 1987.6

This sculpture is actually a three-dimensional recapitulation of the "Big Painting" series Roy Lichtenstein did in the mid-1960s. The "Big Painting" series, rendered in the harsh, "commercial" fashion of Pop Art, parodied the thick, gestural brushstrokes of the Abstract Expressionists. Lichtenstein's brushstrokes are a parody of and an homage to an earlier art movement that saw the application of paint on canvas as a highly personal and emotionally charged gesture. Like other Pop artists such as Andy Warhol, Lichtenstein rejected personal statements in favor of a cooler, more objective viewpoint: "I want my painting to look as if it had been programmed. I want to hide the record of my hand." *Homage to Painting* pays tribute to and mocks our ideas of what art is and what it means.

MAL

SUGGESTED READINGS:

Coplans, John, ed. **Roy Lichtenstein**. New York: Praeger, 1972.

Lippard, Lucy. **Pop Art**. New York: Praeger, 1966.

Selected
Works from
ANTIQUITIES
The Dayton Art

Institute Permanent

Collection

Cycladic Islands (Spedos)
STANDING FEMALE IDOL, *3rd millennium B.C.*
Carved yellow marble
H: 23 3/4 inches
Museum purchase with funds provided by the Associate Board's 1969 Art Ball, 1969.36

Although this simple, female figure is today considered as a kind of Mother Goddess, the function of this sculpture and others like it is not known. Found in tombs usually in horizontal positions, Cycladic idols, as they are called, are incapable of standing upright alone. Conceived in a starkly schematized way, these svelte marble goddesses are carved virtually in one plane. Human anatomy is reduced to a formula of repeated features: a broad, shovel-shaped head tilted backward; an arched nose projecting from the facial plane; long, cylindrical neck; breasts in low relief; folded, flattened arms; slim hips, legs bent slightly at the knee, swelling calves, and often pigeon-toed feet. So abstracted and chaste are these figures that even the genitalia may be omitted. Some examples of Cycladic idols and figures show vestiges of painted details, although this one does not.

The Cyclades, from which this figure came, is composed of 24 islands in the central Aegean sea, and is one of three groups of islands that surround mainland Greece. As early as the Neolithic period or "New Stone Age" (around 4th millennium-2700 B.C.), these islands were sources of various important stones: obsidian (especially from Melos), emery of corundum (from the mines on Naxos), and the fine-grained marble of Paros. The availability of these natural resources in the Cyclades made them an ideal birthplace for sculpture in prehistoric Greece.

By the middle Bronze Age (around 2100-1600 B.C.), Cycladic art was entirely eclipsed by the Minoan culture on the island of Crete, which became the dominant culture of the Aegean world. Although these creations of the 3rd millenium B.C. had, by then, become obsolete, their strikingly abstracted form has made them especially appealing to modern eyes. Twentieth century artists, such as Pablo Picasso, Jean Arp, and Constantin Brancusi, found Cycladic sculpture mysterious and beautifully abstract, and their works often demonstrate its compelling influence.

DHV

SUGGESTED READINGS:

Getz-Preziosi, Pat. **Early Cycladic Art in North American Collections**. *Exhibition catalogue. Richmond: Virginia Museum of Fine Arts, 1987.*

Renfrew, Colin. **The Cycladic Spirit**. *New York: Harry N. Abrams, Inc., 1991.*

Egyptian
New Kingdom XVIII-XIX dynasty (1570-1197 B.C.)

A NOBLE COUPLE, around 1210-1162 B.C.
Carved limestone relief, painted
16 x 13 1/4 inches
Museum purchase with funds provided by the Jefferson Patterson Endowment Fund,
1972.48

The vertical inscription at the left of the carved figures of a nobleman and his wife reads, "The bakers of the goddess Mut, Iny"; however, the inscription may not refer specifically to the figures shown here, who appear to be persons of rank. To the right of the noblewoman are the legs, feet, and hand of another seated, unknown family member. This incised, painted relief sculpture may have come from the necropolis of Thebes where similar painted reliefs are found. The people depicted here may have been gathered to partake in a funerary banquet— a subject befitting a burial chamber. The nobleman, possibly the owner of the tomb from which this relief was taken, is seated on a chair with lion feet, a style that was especially popular from the time of the Old Kingdom (2680-2258 B.C.) onward. The elegant, graceful gestures and overlapping design characterizes the taste of the XVIII dynasty.

Egyptian wall reliefs and paintings are characterized by a style not reliant upon one-point, Renaissance linear perspective. Egyptian artists depicted reality by its most characteristic, individual components, balancing what one knows with what one sees against the limitations of the medium. For example, we know that the nobleman and his wife would have been seated side-by-side at a banquet or official gathering; however, the artisan who carved this relief knew that if he were to attempt to render this, the profile of the wife would obscure that of her husband. Therefore, he shifts the wife to her husband's right, while implying to the viewer that the figures, nevertheless, are seated next to each other.

DHV

SUGGESTED READINGS:

Aldred, Cyril. *Egyptian Art*. London: Oxford University Press, 1980.

Smith, W. Stevenson and revised by William Kelly Simpson. *The Art and Architecture of Ancient Egypt*. New York: The Pelican History of Art, Penguin Books, 1981.

Greek

Attic ("The Dayton Painter")

BLACK-FIGURE NECK AMPHORA, *around 520 B.C.*

Earthenware, painted and fired

H: 13 inches

Museum purchase, 1963.84

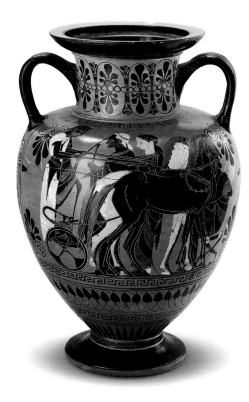

Pottery was an essential component of everyday life in Greece; terra-cotta (fired clay) containers of various shapes were used to hold or serve wine and store grain, honey, oil, and other commodities. This *amphora* (which may originally have had a cover) for example, would have been used to store food. Usually a pottery vessel was produced by one craftsman and painted by another. Although some vessels were signed by the artisan, most were not; in modern times, as a way of helping to identify them, vessels are often named for the collection in which the piece is located. In 1964, Greek pottery specialist Dietrich von Bothmer baptized the unnamed craftsman who painted this particular *amphora* as "The Dayton Painter." Consequently, Dayton's piece is known as the "name vase" which helps to identify other works by the same hand. A companion vase by "The Dayton Painter" of similar shape and decoration is in the collection of the Museum of Fine Arts, Boston.

The early Greeks were fond of decorating these vessels with stories taken from their religious myths or scenes of daily life; often they extolled the beauty or heroic deeds of a particular person. One side of this *amphora* shows a crowded chariot scene, while the other is decorated with a figure of Apollo, Greek god of music, poetry, and dance, playing a *kithara* (lyre), accompanied by two gesturing female figures. The neck and lower part of the vessel are decorated with bands of geometric and highly stylized plant forms.

This *amphora* was decorated with its male figures painted in black and detailed with elegantly incised lines; women, however, are depicted in a cream-colored glaze. The background has been left the natural red color of the fired-clay body. Consequently, this style of vase painting is called "Black-Figure"—in contrast to "Red-Figure" decorations in which the background is painted out and the figures are left the natural color of the terra-cotta. These decoration styles were employed during 6th and 5th century B.C. respectively, in Attica, one of the most important production sites of ancient Greece pottery.

DHV

Suggested Readings:

Boardman, John. **Athenian Black Vases**. *New York: Oxford University Press, 1974.*

Moon, Warren G. and Louise Berge. **Greek Vase-Painting in Midwestern Collections**. *Exhibition catalogue. Chicago: The Art Institute of Chicago, 1980.*

Etruscan (Praeneste)
ENGRAVED MIRROR, *late 4th century B.C.*

Bronze

L: 13 inches

Museum purchase with funds provided by the Zimmerman Foundation, 1970.34

This bronze hand mirror with its incised, decorated back came from an Etruscan tomb probably in Praeneste (the ancient name of Palestrina) not far from Rome. Unlike mirrors today that are made of silvered glass, this one would have had a highly polished reflecting surface. Like most Etruscan hand-mirrors, its decoration depicts a mythological subject and while the three figures are not identified by name, they most certainly represent Minerva (or Athena), Bacchus (or Dionysus), and a *maenad*, a female devotee of Bacchus.

The seated Bacchus is about to be crowned with a laurel wreath by the attendant maenad. Between them stands a *thyrsos*, a pinecone-topped staff, which was a symbol of the followers of Bacchus. Watching the scene at the left is Minerva, goddess of wisdom, armed with a spear and shield upon which an owl—Minerva's symbolic animal—seems about to perch. At Minerva's feet, a dog raises his paw begging attention. Any particular symbolism that may have been implied by the grouping of these three figures is now lost.

The people of ancient Etruria, a region in Italy corresponding to what is now Tuscany and part of Umbria, are known as the Etruscans. Little is known of their culture except through their funerary art. Although heavily borrowed from Greek art, Etruscan art is individualized by an interest in lively action and introduction of a new naturalism, illustrated here by the addition of the dog asking Minerva's attention. The simple and confident drawing style of the incised figures is reliant upon Greek antecedents and technical requirements imposed upon the craftsman who engraved the decoration.

DHV

Suggested Readings:

Del Chiaro, Mario. **Re-exhumed Etruscan Bronzes**. *Exhibition catalogue. Santa Barbara: University Art Museum, Santa Barbara, 1981.*

Wellard, James. **The Search for the Etruscans**. *New York: Saturday Review Press, 1973.*

Greek

STELE OF THEAGENES, 2nd century B.C.

Carved marble

26 3/4 x 15 1/2 inches

Gift of the Honorable Jefferson Patterson, 1930.110

The practice of honoring the dead with a monument or grave marker of some sort is perhaps as long as human history itself. The ancient Greeks used standing stone markers or *stelae* to commemorate battles, to worship their gods, and to honor the dead. This particular *stele* is a grave monument that takes its pedimented form from the architecture of the time. The simplicity and clarity of its carving make it as moving today as it was when it was first erected. The marker is clearly inscribed in ancient Greek with the name of the person it commemorates: Theagenes, Son of Theagenes. We will probably never know who this person was, yet by his dress we can assume that he was a warrior or military leader.

Theagenes is shown as a relatively young man, wearing a long tunic tied with a belt. Over the tunic he wears a *chlamys*, an oblong mantle worn by the men of ancient Greece, fastened by a pin at the shoulder. Theagenes extends his right arm to touch his sword that is suspended from a cord in the upper left corner of the *stele*. Below the sword, a young servant dressed in a short tunic brings Theagenes his lance. Theagenes would appear, therefore, to be arming himself for battle, and perhaps it was in this way that he met his death.

Alexander the Great's conquests (336-323 B.C.) in the Near East greatly expanded the Greek empire. During the 2nd and 3rd centuries B.C., Greek culture spread throughout Persia, Egypt, and Syria, mingling with local cultures and producing a rich amalgam. As a result, Greek art from the Hellenistic period (after Alexander's death in 323 B.C.) was produced in cities far from Athens, the birthplace of Greek art. The Art Institute's *stele* was, in fact, found in Byzantium, or present-day Istanbul, Turkey.

DHV

Suggested Readings:

Bieber, Margarete. **The Sculpture of the Hellenistic Age**. *New York: Columbia University Press, 1951.*

Vermule, Cornelius C. **Greek and Roman Sculpture in America: Masterpieces in Public Collections in the United States and Canada**. *Exhibition catalogue, The J. Paul Getty Museum. Malibu and Berkley: University of California Press, 1981.*

Greco-Roman

APHRODITE PUDICA WITH EROS ASTRIDE A DOLPHIN, *A.D. 1st century*

Carved white marble

H: 35 inches

Museum purchase with funds provided by Mr. and Mrs. Ralf Kircher, 1968.112

Though fractured and fragmented, this remains a lovely image of Aphrodite, the Greek goddess of love, and her son, Eros (or Cupid). Probably sculpted by a Greek artisan for the Roman market, this goddess must have graced a niche in a garden or nymphaeum somewhere in Italy, the seat of the Roman Empire. Although the base is unfinished in the rear where it would have touched the back of the niche, the work is completely finished—inviting the viewer to enjoy the work from all angles. Carved from a solid block of marble, Aphrodite and Eros now are separated. The smaller figure of Eros is seated on a dolphin that served not only as physical support for the weight of the figure but also as a visual reference to the mythological story of Aphrodite's birth from sea foam.

This particular type of Aphrodite shows her covering her breasts and groin; therefore, she is termed "pudica" or the modest Aphrodite. Sandro Botticelli used the pose of the Aphrodite Pudica to depict the goddess in his *Birth of Venus* (Galeria degli Uffizi, Florence). As in many classical sculptures, the arms of this Aphrodite are broken and missing, although the thumb of her right hand remains coyly attached to her left breast where it would have provided the support and attachment for the hand and arm.

DHV

SUGGESTED READINGS:

Richter, Gisela M.A. *A Handbook of Greek Art*. New York: Phaidon Press, 1960.

Toynbee, J.M.C. *Roman Art*. Baltimore: Penguin Books, 1976.

Vermule, Cornelius C. *Greek and Roman Sculpture in America: Masterpieces in Public Collections in the United States and Canada*. Exhibition catalogue, The J. Paul Getty Museum. Malibu and Berkley: University of California Press, 1981.

*Selected
Works from*

ASIAN ART

*The Dayton Art

Institute Permanent

Collection*

India, Mathura

Kusāna period (A.D. 320-550)

PILLAR WITH DESIGN OF YOUNG WOMAN, 2nd century

Red sandstone

H: 36 1/2 inches

Museum purchase with funds provided by the Virginia V. Blakeney Endowment, 1968.79

This tree goddess is portrayed in an unusual pose with her back to the viewer. Standing on a crouching gnome, she turns to look over her shoulder with her arm resting on her hip. The goddess is clothed with a skirt and decorated with pieces of jewelry. Her hair is arranged in an elaborate coiffure and gathered in a ponytail in the back, a popular hairstyle during the Kusāna period in Mathura.

The reverse of the pillar is faceted following the octagonal design and decorated with lotus medallions. The angular cuts at the top and bottom of the pillar and the diagonal alignment of the crossbar slots on both side faces indicate that it once formed part of a staircase leading to the terraced level of a Buddhist burial mound where the circular walkway was located. The red sandstone is characteristic of the Mathura region in Central India.

Many similar representations of female deities exist within the Kusāna artistic vocabulary of the Mathura region. These images are symbols of fertility, their presence causing the tree to bear fruit and, in turn, offering symbolically the same to the faithful. The sensuously exposed back and dramatic hips seen in this goddess represent a sophisticated ideal of feminine beauty evident throughout Indian sculpture.

CWK

SUGGESTED READINGS:

Czuma, Stanislaw J., with the assistance of Rekha Morris. **Kushan Sculpture: Images from Early India**. Cleveland: The Cleveland Museum of Art, 1985.

Rosenfield, John M. **The Dynastic Arts of the Kushans**. Berkeley and Los Angeles: University of California Press, 1967.

van Lohuizen-de Leeuw, J.E. Leiden: "Gandhara and Mathura: Their Cultural Relationship" in **Aspects of Indian Art**. Pratapaditya Pal, ed. E.J. Brill, 1972: 27-43.

Vogel, Jean P. "The Woman and Tree or Salabhanjika in Indian Literature and Art." **Acta Orientalia Ediderunt Societates Orientales Batava Danica Norvegica** (Vol. 7, 1929): 201-231.

India, Gandhāra
Kusāna period (A.D. 320-550)
HEAD OF A BODHISATTVA, *5th century*
Stucco with traces of paint
H: 15 inches
Gift of the Honorable Jefferson Patterson, 1944.46

In ancient times, the region known as Gandhāra, which today incorporates parts of northern India, Pakistan, and Afghanistan, was a major center of creativity in the Kusāna empire. The area also possessed economic and political links to the Mediterranean world, and contact with the Greco-Roman world is reflected in Gandhāran art of the Kusāna period. Legacies of this influence are expressions of idealized physical beauty based upon Western forms and idioms.

This unusually large stucco head, with its wavy locks and benign expression, is representative of the commingling of foreign and native Indian idioms. Although predicated upon standards in schist examples from the region, such as the sharpness of the nose, full lips, and repetitive display of locks in the hairstyle, Indian elements found in classic Gupta sculpture are also evident. These latter ingredients include the ovoid silhouette of the face, arc of the eyebrow, full and fleshy cheeks, and heavy-lidded, almond-shaped eyes. The effect is contemplative and serene.

The face has been made from a mold, thus accounting for its similarity with other stucco faces from the period and Taxila area. Its body, now lost, would have reached an imposing height and required a core support. The cores were generally comprised of sand, clay, and gravel mixed with lime and straw (or animal hair), over which the stucco was applied. As was standard, the head was made separately and attached to the torso with straw or pegs.

The hair was fashioned by hand; the plastic fluidity of the stucco permitted the artist to individualize the work. The facial features were painted and traces of red paint are still visible on the lips, along the hairline, and lining the eyes. The pupils and the hair were painted a deep bluish-black color. A fragment of a clasp or buckle is still visible over the right profile, indicating that the figure originally wore a diadem.

CWK

Suggested Readings:

Czuma, Stanislaw J., with the assistance of Rekha Morris. **Kushan Sculpture: Images from Early India.** *Cleveland: The Cleveland Museum of Art, 1985.*

Lyons, Islay, and Harald Ingholt. **Gandhāran Art in Pakistan.** *New York: Pantheon Books, 1957.*

Rosenfield, John M. **The Dynastic Arts of the Kushans.** *Berkeley and Los Angeles: University of California Press, 1967.*

India, Gujarat

SHIVA AND PARVATI, *late 8th - early 9th century*

Red sandstone

23 1/2 x 16 1/2 inches

Museum purchase with funds provided by the Honorable Jefferson Patterson, the 1966
Art Ball and other sources, 1966.26

Seated images of Shiva embracing his consort Parvati constitute one of the more popular themes in Indian sculpture. Shiva is a divine being of the Hindu trinity, a god of destruction and creation. His spouse Parvati is the daughter of Himalaya, also called "goddess of the mountain." Seated on Shiva's sacred bull, Shiva embraces Parvati with his primary left hand. In a gesture of intimate trust, Parvati places her hand upon Shiva's leg. Both deities are sumptuously adorned with jewelry.

This carving captures the intimacy of the divine lovers in the disposition of the faces, fixed gazes, and tender embrace. On an ontological level, this exalted embrace represents the union of spirit and matter, essence and substance. While the stylized facial features and elegant coiffures are slightly reminiscent of the classic Gupta style, the well-modeled plasticity of forms and somewhat expansive quality of physical volumes indicate a post-Gupta date of the late 8th to early 9th centuries.

CWK

SUGGESTED READINGS:

Deva, Krishna. "Extensions of Gupta Art and Architecture in the Pratihara Age." in **Seminar on Indian** Art History. Moti Chandra ed. New Delhi: Lalit Kala Akademi, 1962: 85-106.

Gods, Guardians, and Lovers: Temple Sculptures from North India, A.D. 700-1200. Vishakha N. Desai and Darielle Mason,s eds. New York: The Asia Society Galleries, 1993.

Kramrisch, Stella. **Manifestations of Shiva**. Philadelphia: Philadelphia Museum of Art, 1981.

Kramrisch, Stella. **The Presence of Shiva**. Princeton: University Press, 1981.

India, Rajasthan

GANGĀ AND ATTENDANT, *8th - 9th century*

Red sandstone

29 1/2 x 19 inches

Museum purchase with funds provided by the Associate Board's 1966 Art Ball, 1966.25

The Ganges is considered the holiest river in India, flowing from its celestial source to wash away the sins of mankind. It is personified in Indian art by Gangā, goddess of purity and purification. In this piece, Gangā stands on a lotus flower carrying a divine water pot. Gangā's sacred character is indicated by her elaborately ornamented headdress and extreme, thrice-bent pose with her weight borne on her right leg. Standing beside is an attendant holding a parasol to shield Gangā. The clarity of carving, richness of decorations, compactness of composition, exaggerated stances, and benign expressions of the figures are characteristic of 8th and 9th century carvings of the Gurjara-Pratihāra period. The mottled, red sandstone is typical of the stones from northern Indian quarries.

Images of Gangā are often depicted on the door jambs of entrances to temples and shrines. Usually, Gangā is paired with an image of Yamuna, goddess of devotion and personification of the Yanuma River. Upon entering the temple and thus crossing the threshold framed by the two river goddesses, the devotee is symbolically purified. The symbolism of devotion to Gangā is more poignant in cremation services when the ashes of the deceased are spread upon the waters of the Ganges River. In this final act of purification, all sins are washed away, borne by the goddess so that one may enter the eternal sanctum of salvation.

CWK

SUGGESTED READINGS:

Deva, Krishna. "Extensions of Gupta Art and Architecture in the Pratihāra Age" in **Seminar on Indian History**. Moti Chandra ed. New Delhi: Lalit Kal ~ Akademi, 1962: 85-106.

Vishakha N. Desai, and Darielle Mason, eds. **Gods, Guardians, and Lovers: Temple Sculptures from North India**, A.D. 700-1200. New York: The Asia Society Galleries, 1993.

Huntington, Susan L., with contributions by John C. Huntington. **The Art of Ancient India**. New York and Tokyo: Weatherhill, 1985.

Lanius, Mary C "Rajasthani Sculptures of the Ninth and Tenth Centuries" in **Aspects of Indian Art**. Pratapaditya Pal, ed. Leiden: E.J. Brill, 1972: 79-84.

India, Tamil Nadu
Cōla period (around 850-1150)
VAISNAVI, 11th-12th century
Granite
42 1/4 x 17 1/4 x 11 1/4 inches
Museum purchase with funds provided by the Junior League of Dayton, Ohio, Inc.,
Tour of Three Great Historic Houses and the Sale of Contents and Contributed Gifts at
the Frank M. Tait House, 1964.12

This imposing image is the personification of the wife, or female version, of the Hindu deity Visnu, Preserver of the Universe. Vaisnavi's principal left hand rests upon her leg while her corresponding right hand, although now lost, was likely raised. The goddess' secondary left arm holds a conch shell, the battle horn that spread terror among the deity's enemies. Her secondary right arm raises the disc, Visnu's weapon in slaying his enemies. The goddess is richly ornamented with an elaborate headdress, armbands, wrist bracelets, anklets, a multistrand necklace, and diaphanous skirt. Vaisnavi stands with her weight supported on her left leg in a characteristic thrice-flexed pose.

The modeling of Vaisnavi is especially sensuous in the curves of her triple-bent posture, the gentle, full curves of her breasts, and the rich ornamentation. Her relaxed, serenely proud pose and harmonious proportions are typical of Cōla sculpture of the 11th century. Intended to be seen from the front, this grand relief image may have originally been paired with an image of Visnu, or may have been one of a larger sculptural set, depicting a standardized group of female deities known as the Seven Mother-Goddesses.

CWK

SUGGESTED READINGS:

Dehejia, Vidya. **Art of the Imperial Cholas**. New York: Columbia University Press, 1990.

de Lippe, Aschwin. "Divine Images in Stone and Bronze: South Image, Chola Dynasty (c. 850-1280)." **Metropolitan Museum Journal** (Vol. 4, 1971): 29-79.

de Lippe, Aschwin. **Indian Medieval Sculpture**. Amsterdam, New York, Oxford: North Holland Publishing Company, 1978.

Pal, Pratapaditya. "South Indian Sculptures: A Reappraisal." **Bulletin, Museum of Fine Arts, Boston** (Vol. 67, No. 350, 1969): 151-173.

India, Tamil Nadu

Cōla period (around 850-1150)

THE GODDESS PARVATI, *12th century*

Bronze

H: 30 3/4 inches

Museum purchase with funds provided by Mrs. Theodore C. Dye in memory of her husband Theodore Cole Dye, 1966.46

It is difficult to identify this freestanding female figure with certainty. Although images of Parvati, the quintessential Hindu goddess, are abundant in Cōla period bronzes, this example, isolated from her sculptural context, could be a portrait of any one of five goddesses. In her graceful stance and dignified elegance, however, she is the epitome of the female deity found in South Indian bronzes of the Cōla period. On holy festival days, poles were slid through the lugs on the base and the statute was paraded as part of a procession.

The goddess stands on a double lotus base with upturned petals on a double pedestal in the traditional triple-bent (*tribhaga*) stance reserved for Indian deities. Her conical headdress is studded with jewels and pendant earrings touch her shoulders—emblems of her divinity. She also wears an elegant necklace and bracelets typical of Hindu deities. An elaborate belt secures her diaphanous skirt which is visible at the hemline above her ankles. The sacred thread of divinity mirrors the triple flection of her stance as it crosses her shoulder and falls downward.

Typical of late 12th century Cōla bronzes is the exaggerated bending of the figure's stance. The tubular, distended character of the left arm and the stylized formulations of simplified body parts such as the spherical breasts, short, cylindrical neck, the oval face, and conical headdress are also indications of a 12th century date. By this time, Cōla bronzes, while still vital, had lost the sinuous quality of earlier centuries for an assembled coordination of masses and a style defined by the simplification of established idioms as seen here.

CV/K

Suggested Readings:

Khandalavala, Karl J. "The Chronology of South Indian Bronzes." **Lalit Kal** ~ (Vol. 14, 1969): 26-37.

Kramrisch, Stella. **Manifestations of Shiva**. Philadelphia: Philadelphia Museum of Art, 1981.

Nagaswamy, R. **Masterpieces of Early South Indian Bronzes**. New Delhi: National Museum, 1983.

Waghorne, Joanne Punzo. "Dressing the Body of God: South Indian Bronze Sculpture in Its Temple Setting." **Asian Art** (Summer 1992, Vol. V, No. 3): 8-33.

China

Majiayao culture, Neolithic period

PAINTED JAR, *around 2500 B.C.*

Banshan-type ware: earthenware with painted decoration

H: 14 inches; Dia: 16 inches

Gift of the Estate of Mrs. Harrie G. Carnell, 1959.45

As one of many large clay vessels recovered in northwestern China from the Neolithic burial site at Banshan in Gansu Province, this jar has a globular body with two loop handles attached to the sides.

Built up by a series of clay coils, this lightweight vessel has a characteristically robust, handsome shape. Made of a coarse, reddish buff clay, the upper half is decorated in a bold, running spiral pattern that is centered around four evenly spaced circles. This sense of movement is made even more dramatic by the alternating use of color and the finesse of broad, sweeping bands contrasted with narrower, calligraphic lines with cilia-like motifs. The lower portion of the vessel is undecorated.

Archaeological evidence of the earliest Majiayao culture was first recovered in 1924 at Majiayao, Gansu Province and the site lends its name to this ancient Neolithic culture. Painted vessels of this culture have since been found in widely dispersed areas in Gansu and Qinghai provinces. The Banshan-type ware, one of the distinguished type of pottery produced by this culture, is characterized by the use of black paint mixed with red and patterns of spirals and saw-teeth as seen in this jar. Archaeological finds suggest that a vessel of this type was used as a storage jar for grain and water.

CWK and LJ

SUGGESTED READINGS:

Chang, K.C. **The Archaeology of Ancient China**, 4th ed. New Haven: Yale University Press, 1986.

Feng, Xianming. **Chinese Ceramics**. Shanghai: Shanghai Ancient Books Press, 1994.

Huber, Louisa G. Fitzgerald. "The Traditions of Chinese Neolithic Pottery." **Bulletin of the Museum of Far Eastern Antiquities** (No. 53, 1981): 1-256.

Shangraw, Clarence F. **Origins of Chinese Ceramics**. New York: China Institute in America, 1978.

Shih, Hsio-Yeh. "Stylistic and Regional Development of Neolithic Painted Pottery." **Orientations** Vol. 22, No. 10 (October 1991): 40-46.

China

Western Han dynasty (206 B.C.- A.D. 9)

HU (STORAGE VESSEL), *2nd half of the 2nd century B.C.*

Henan ware: gray earthenware with painted and molded decoration

H: 19 1/4 inches; Dia: 14 inches

Purchased with funds provided by various sources, 1959.44

During the Han period (206 B.C.-A.D. 220), ceramic works often imitated ancient Chinese bronze vessels in both form and ornamentation. This particular form is known as the *hu*, characterized by a tall base usually with a footring, spreading foot, and expanding body that narrows along the neck. Around its bulging waist is a series of fantastic beasts, including dragons and tigers, prancing amid swirling polychrome and arabesque bands. To either side, a pair of molded *taotie* escutcheons serve as modest handles as well as decorative accents. Regrettably, the lid of the vessel is now missing.

This substantial grain vessel was intended to accompany the deceased into the afterlife. As such, it belongs to a group of mortuary objects placed in the tomb as a substitute for the more valuable bronze and lacquer vessels of Han China. There was a belief in Han China that the soul temporarily wandered after death throughout the celestial realm, as illustrated here by the swirling cloud patterns. The heavens are additionally identified by the presence of the White Tiger, cosmological symbol of the western quadrant of the universe, and, similarly, the Green Dragon of the East. On a metaphysical level, the spiral-patterned clouds represent a state of existence free of corporeal and temporal limitations. This spiritual existence was the Great Beginning—the state of immortality also know as the Dao or "The Way."

CWK

SUGGESTED READINGS:

Loewe, Michael. **Ways to Paradise: The Chinese Quest for Immortality**. London: George Allen & Unwin, 1979.

Sturman, Peter C. "Celestial Journeys—Meditations on (and in) Han Dynasty Painted Pots at the Metropolitan Museum of Art." **Orientations** (May 1988): 54-67.

Watson, William. **Pre-Tang Ceramics of China: Chinese Pottery from 4000 B.C. to 600 A.D.** London: Faber and Faber Limited, 1991.

Yaw, Lu, Chi-yun Chen, Abu Ridho, Eng-lee Seak Chee, Rosemary E. Scott, Candace J. Lewis and Chen Huasha. **Spirit of Han: Ceramics for the After-Life**. Singapore: Southeast Asian Ceramic Society, 1991.

China

Western Han dynasty (206 B.C.- A.D. 9)

KNEELING WOMAN, *2nd century B.C.*

Earthenware

H: 13 inches

Gift of Mrs. Virginia W. Kettering, 1996.225

Modeled hollow in gray clay, this pottery figure depicts a kneeling woman with her arms raised, sitting upright on her folded legs. The woman wears layers of garments with wide sleeves, a stylistic costume for women during the Western Han dynasty. The deeply recessed sleeves are sculptured in contrast to the plain, smooth modeled surface of the body. The woman is depicted with her hair parted neatly in the center and coiled, bound on the back, a characteristic hairstyle for women since the Qin dynasty (221-206 B.C.). Her face is modeled softly to reveal a serene, gentle expression, often seen on the female figures dating to the Western Han Dynasty. Although both hands of the figure are missing, her arm posture suggests that she is perhaps an attendant, likely holding some type of tribute.

In terms of pose, size, and treatment, this female figure is rendered in a manner similar to the kneeling figures excavated in 1966 at Rejiapo, Xi'an, near the tomb of Empress Dou (died 135 B.C.) Her facial features are identical to a standing female figure excavated from Langjiagou near Xi'an. These similarities suggest this figure may have come from the Xi'an area. Indicated by the white pigment around the ears, this figure seems to have been originally colorfully painted like the figures from Renjiapo. Based on texture, coloration, and stylistic differences, the entire left arm and sleeve appear to have been restored in an attempt to match the original on the right.

LJ

Suggested Readings:

ETERNAL CHINA: Splendors from the First Dynasties. *Exhibition catalogue. Dayton, OH: The Dayton Art Institute, 1998.*

Wang, Xueli, and Wu Zhenfeng. "Excavation of the accompanying pits for a Han mausoleum at Rejiapo, Xi'an." **Kaogu** *(No. 2, 1976).*

Zhou, Baoxi. **History of Ancient Chinese Costume.** *Beijing: China Drama Publishing House, 1984.*

China, Henan province
Eastern Han dynasty (A.D. 25-220)
MORTUARY TOWER, *2nd century*
Henan ware: earthenware with green glaze
44 1/2 x 13 1/2 x 16 inches
Museum purchase in recognition of all The Dayton Art Institute volunteers and in special memory of Kit Johnston, 1992.18

This impressive, multi-storied watchtower rises from an enclosed courtyard. Compelling details, such as the figures peering out from openings in the facade, make this a particularly fine example. Other realistic details include a front gate decorated with auspicious masks and two guard-dog openings on each flank. The first story has a post and lintel doorway and triangular window openings. The right doorway is closed with a figure peering from behind it. Standing on the second story are two long-robed officials; another figure peers through the large open window. The tiled roof is of a traditional Chinese style with large, overhanging eaves and half-circular tiles. Latticed windows at each of the four sides ventilate each story.

The Han Chinese believed in an afterlife. To prepare for the spirit's journey into the hereafter, the Chinese furnished the tomb with as many of life's comforts as possible. Like many other cultures, humans and animals were interred with the deceased in ancient periods; but by the time of the Han dynasty (206 B.C.-A.D. 220) ceramic substitutes were used. In northern regions of China, this type of tower would have been a familiar part of the landscape, providing a high vantage point to spot invading enemies. This ceramic watchtower suggests that even in death the Chinese believed that they would have to protect themselves against their raiders.

The impressive height of this tower, well-articulated details, and modeling make it one of finest examples of this type. Its quality production indicates that it was likely made for a wealthy family. This tower is similar to several Han towers recovered near Zhangwan and Shanxian in Henan Province. They are all characterized by the same method of construction, clay body, glaze, architectural details, and types of figures. These similarities suggest that the tower may have the same provenance of production and date.

CWK

SUGGESTED READINGS:

Berger, Patricia. **Ancestral Dwellings: Furnishing the Han Tomb**. *Asian Art Museum of San Francisco, 1987.*

Loewe, Michael. **Ways to Paradise: The Chinese Quest for Immortality**. *London, Boston & Sydney: George Allen & Unwin, 1979.*

Pirazzoli-t'Serstevens, Michéle. Janet Seligman trans. **The Han Dynasty**. *New York: Rizzoli International Publications, Inc., 1982.*

Yaw, Lu, Chi-yun Chen, Abu Ridho, Eng-lee Seak Chee, Rosemary Scott, Candace Lewis and Chen Huasha. **Spirit of Han: Ceramics for the After-Life**. *Singapore: Southeast Asian Ceramic Society, 1991.*

China
Late Sui (581-618)/early Tang dynasties (618-907)

GUARDIAN WARRIOR, 7th century

Henan ware: earthenware with painted decoration

H: 14 inches

Gift of Mr. Brainerd B. Thresher, 1942.131

Tomb guardian figures such as this standing warrior were placed at the entrance to burial chambers. They served a similarly symbolic function in the burial rites—to assist the deceased as they had during the lifetime of the tomb occupant. Dressed in typical regalia, this figure wears long trousers and a knee-length cassock. A midriff guard is tied tightly around his waist. His chest is protected by opposing pectoral plaques with circular designs while the earlier armorial style of shoulder guards has been diminished to long sleeves. The head is protected by a collar and helmet with shoulder-length earflaps. A banner, or lance, was originally held in the left hand, as indicated by the closed fist, which is not tightly clenched and forms an opening for such a purpose.

The strength, cosmopolitan nature, and vast wealth of the Tang empire attracted many foreigners. Mortuary models reflecting this international gathering are abundantly illustrated by recovered artifacts. The delicately modeled facial features as seen on our warrior have been identified as Central Asian, an ethnic extraction of Tocharian and Altaic mix. A similar warrior excavated from an early Tang period tomb at Dasikongcun, near Anyang in Henan Province, was accompanied by a coin datable to the year of 621, and provides an approximate time period for our figure.

CWK

SUGGESTED READINGS:

Dien, Albert E. "A Study of Early Chinese Armor." **Artibus Asiae** (Vol. XLIII, Nos. 1/2, 1981-82): 5-66.

Fong, Mary. "Antecedents of Sui-Tang Burial Practices in Shaanxi." **Artibus Asiae** (Vol. LI, Nos., 3/4, 1991): 147-198.

Fong, Mary. "Tomb-Guardian Figurines: Their Evolution and Iconography," in **Mortuary Traditions of China: Papers on Chinese Ceramic Funerary Sculptures**. George Kuwayama, ed. Los Angeles: Far Eastern Art Council, Los Angeles County Museum of Art, 1991: 84-105.

Mahler, Jane Gaston. **The Westerners Among the Figurines of the T'ang Dynasty in China**. Rome: Instituto Italiano per il Medio ed Estremo Oriente, 1959.

The Quest for Eternity: Chinese Ceramic Sculptures from the People's Republic of China. Exhibition catalogue, Los Angeles County Museum of Art. Los Angeles and San Francisco: Museum Associates, Los Angeles County Museum of Art and Chronicle Books, 1987.

Schloss, Ezekiel. **Ancient Chinese Ceramic Sculpture: From Han through T'ang**, 2 Vols. Stamford: Castle Publishing Co., 1977.

China

Tang dynasty (618-907)

HORSE, *7th century*

Earthenware with traces of painted decoration and gold

21 1/2 x 24 inches

Gift of Mrs. Howard C. Davidson in honor of her mother, Mrs. Harrie G. Carnell, 1943.39

S uch was the importance of the horse to the Chinese empire that the *Tang Shu* (History of the Tang) states, "Horses are the military preparedness of the state; if Heaven takes this preparedness away, the state will totter to a fall."* Especially prized for their military advantage, chargers were imported from Samarkand and Farghana in Central Asia. Horses were also sent to the Tang empire as diplomatic gifts by foreign powers eager to align themselves under the auspices of Tang protection. The abundance of such gifts allowed the emperor to refuse them when diplomatically expedient.

Early in the Tang period, the stylistic development of mortuary horses advanced rapidly from the thin-legged, yet exaggerated, body types of the Six Dynasties (220-589) into robust and energetic steeds. As with other funerary animals and human representations, there is a sense of life, natural movement, anatomical correctness, and elegant proportions in this ceramic horse. The fully delineated features of this horse, especially at the knee and hoof joints, the musculature of the face, the swept-back forehairs, and braided tail all point to the early Tang period. The restrained, plastic qualities of the 7th century exhibited here would soon become highly exaggerated as these mortuary figures became overly dynamic.

CWK

SUGGESTED READINGS:

Juliano, Annette L. *Art of the Six Dynasties: Centuries of Change and Innovation*. New York: China Institute in America, 1976.

The Quest for Eternity: Chinese Ceramic Sculptures from the People's Republic of China. Los Angeles and San Francisco: Museum Associates, Los Angeles County Museum of Art and Chronicle Books, 1987.

Schloss, Ezekiel. *Ancient Chinese Ceramic Sculpture: From Han through T'ang*. 2 Vols. Stamford: Castle Publishing Co., 1977.

Watson, William. *Tang and Liao Ceramics*. New York: Rizzoli International Publications, Inc., 1984.

*Cited in Edward H. Schafer, *The Golden Peaches of Samarkand: A Study of T'ang Exotic*. Berkeley, Los Angeles, London: University of California Press, 1963, p. 58.

China

Tang dynasty (618-907)

BOTTLE, *early 8th century*

Silver with parcel-gilt

H: 7 1/2 inches

Gift of Mrs. Harrie G. Carnell, 1935.23

Only four examples of this type of silver bottle from the Tang dynasty are known in Western collections. Made of several sheets of hammered silver soldered together, the bottle is decorated with playful felines and birds scattered amid rinceaux grapevines. The animals have been gilded, highlighting them against the finely punched, ringmatted background typical of early Tang dynasty silverware. Additional decorative details have been chased. The rollicking creatures and arabesque floral tendrils, idioms of foreign expressions, hint at the cosmopolitan nature of the period when Tang China was at the apex of its international reputation—wealthy, powerful, and lavish.

This vessel shape was widely popular in Tang China and abundant representations are available in bronze and ceramic wares. Silver, however, was a rare and expensive commodity in China, and silver objects were the embellishments of the wealthy life of the nobility. Internal unrest over the decadent lifestyles of the imperial court resulted in the An Lushan rebellion of 755 that forced the emperor to flee the capital. Recovered caches of hastily buried silverware dating to the time of the rebellion illustrate the panic within imperial circles. Following the restoration of government control, several edicts proscribing the manufacture of precious metal objects were issued.

Bottle-shaped vases such as this are known as *baoping* or "ambrosia bottles" and have their origin in India amongst Buddhist circles. It was believed the ambrosia of immortality could restore the faithful to life. As such, ambrosia bottles are frequently depicted in the hands of the Buddhist deity Guanyin, the Bodhisattva of Mercy. The spiritual promise of salvation offered by Buddhism soon gained many new faithful followers, as well as generous monetary donations. In an effort to lessen and to control the influence of the Buddhist church within the empire, the Tang government enacted several pogroms aimed at the wealthy Buddhism centers. As a result, the ambrosia bottle soon disappeared from the repertoire of Tang manufacture.

CWK

SUGGESTED READINGS:

Gyllensvard, Bo. "T'ang Gold and Silver." **Bulletin of the Museum of Far Eastern Antiquities**. (No. 29, 1957): 1-230.

Kelley, Clarence W. **Chinese Gold and Silver from the Tang Dynasty in American Collections**. The Dayton Art Institute, 1984.

Rawson, Jessica. **The Ornament on Chinese Silver of the Tang Dynasty (AD 618-906)**. British Museum Occasional Paper (No. 40). London: Trustees of the British Museum, 1982.

China

Tang dynasty (618-907)

JAR, *early 8th century*

*Henan or Shaanxi ware: (**sancai**) "three-color" lead glazed stoneware*

H: 12 1/4 inches; Dia: 9 7/8 inches

Museum purchase, 1964.36

The rounded jar known as the *wan nian guan* (myriad year jar) was favored among Tang funerary vessels. The name of this type of jar refered to the desired and offered benevolence for the deceased in the afterlife. *Wan nian guan* wares. especially prevalent from the northern kilns of Henan and Shaanxi provinces, continued to be made in North China during the succeeding Liao dynasty (907-1125).

Our example is a slightly elongated version of the *wan nian guan*, but has a characteristically short neck and the pronounced, rolled lip. The body tapers to a slightly flared foot, which is cut back under at the edge of the flare. The bottom is flat. The buff-colored earthenware is covered in a white slip and transparent glaze that imparts a faint yellow tint. Imposed on this are green, blue, and mustard-yellow lead glazes, applied with a wax-resist technique. During the firing, wax melts and allows the colored glazes to blend and form various drip patterns so each piece has a unique color and decoration scheme. Although this technique is known as *sancai* or "three-color" glazing, the number of glazes actually used varied between three and five. The control of wax-resist techniques and the mastery in glaze application seen in the diamondlike, polychrome drip pattern is a hallmark of Tang skill and finesse of the early 8th century. The jar likely had a lid that is now lost.

CWK

SUGGESTED READINGS:

Feng, Xianming. **Chinese Ceramics**. *Shanghai: Shanghai Ancient Books Press, 1994.*

Medley, Margaret. **The Chinese Potter: A Practical History of Chinese Ceramics**. *Oxford: Phaidon Press Limited, 1976.*

Watson, William. **Tang and Liao Ceramics**. *New York: Rizzoli International Publications, Inc., 1984.*

China

Late Northern Song (960-1127)/Jin (1125-1234) dynasties

BOWL, *12th century*

Ding ware: porcelaneous white stoneware with transparent ivory glaze, molded decoration, copper lip band

Dia: 6 15/16 inches

Gift of the Honorable Jefferson Patterson, 1952.132

In China and the West, the production of a fine white ceramic ware has long been a preoccupation. Records dating from the Tang (618-907) and Song (960-1279) dynasties indicate that a hard, ivory-colored stoneware of fine quality was produced at several kilns located in northern China. These ceramics are known as Ding ware since they were produced at Dingzhou, present-day Juyangxian, Hebei Province. Although these northern wares were undistinguished during the late Tang dynasty, wares from Dingzhou kilns came into their own by the Song period.

The pursuit of a whiter vessel with a more delicately thin side posed new technical problems, especially for a vessel with a sharply flaring profile and diminutive foot, as seen in this example. The thinness of the side not only made it delicate, but also fragile and susceptible to buckling during the firing process. To overcome this, Ding bowls were placed upside-down on their rims to provide a larger diameter of support for firing. In order to increase the number of wares fired at the same time, vessels were placed on saggers (firing blocks) and then stacked on top of each other. To further increase the economic advantage of Ding production, wares were mold pressed, as seen in this example, which features lotus flowers in the center surrounded by a pair of phoenixes among blooming peonies, and a band of running fret design. Overall, these production innovations ensured regularity of design, streamlined production, moderated labor costs, and minimalized clay waste.

Characteristic of Ding glazes, the glaze on this bowl is virtually bubbleless. Applied by dipping, the glaze has pooled in areas near the lip as a result being inverted during the firing process. To prevent the ware from sticking to the sagger, the glaze was wiped from the lip before firing. This may also account for the uneven areas of glaze on the exterior of this bowl near the lip. After removal from the kiln, the rim of the bowl was lined with copper or silver to conceal the unglazed portion. Firing the bowl rimside down eliminated the need for a base ring, as seen in this bowl, the footring was reduced to tiny proportion.

CWK

SUGGESTED READINGS:

Liu, Liang-yu, "Ting Ware: The White Queen Among Porcelains." **Arts of Asia** (Vol. 17, No. 4, July-August 1987): 107-113.

Medley, Margaret. **Illustrated Catalogue of Ting and Allied Wares in the Percival David Foundation of Chinese Art**, Section 4. London: Percival David Foundation, 1980.

Tregear, Mary. "The Classic Northern White Wares of the Northern Song and Jin Dynasties." **Bulletin of the Oriental Ceramic Society of Hong Kong** (Vol. 6, 1982-84): 22-25.

Tregear, Mary. **Song Ceramics**. New York: Rizzoli International Publications, 1982.

Wirgin, Jan. **Sung Ceramic Designs**. London: Han Shan Tang Ltd., 1979.

China
Northern Song (960-1127)/Jin (1125-1234) dynasties

BOWL, *12th century*
Jun ware: porcelaneous stoneware with blue glaze and double crimson-purple splash
Dia: 7 1/8 inches
Museum purchase with funds provided by the Honorable and Mrs. Jefferson Patterson, 1963.32

China
Northern Song (960-1127)/Jin (1125-1234) dynasties

BOWL, *12th century*
Jun ware: porcelaneous stoneware with blue glaze and purple splash
Dia: 7 1/4 inches
Gift of Mrs. Virginia W. Kettering, 1969.12

Elegant yet simple bowls, such as these with their striking glazes, were made during the 12th century. The finely levitated clay has a thick, robin's egg-blue glaze, approaching a pale lavender color with splashes of crimson and purple— distinctive marks of Jun glazing. The deliberate addition of copper produced the crimson and purple splashes. Applied in successive layers, numerous minute bubbles are suspended in the glaze that lends an opacity characteristic of Jun ware.

Jun vessels were produced at a great number of kilns scattered throughout Henan Province, especially those centered primarily at Linru and Yuxian. Under Jin dynasty rule, Yuxian was renamed Junzhou, thus lending the Jun name to these wares.

Jun ware was one of the major ceramic wares introduced and perfected in the Song dynasty; and the manufacture continued beyond the demise of the dynasty. The popularity of Jun ware is attested to by its wide distribution dating from the 11th through 13th centuries and by the existence of Jun wares recovered from distant kiln sites. These latter sites include the kilns at Yixing in Anhui Province dating to the Ming dynasty (1368-1644), and the kilns of the Qing dynasty (1644-1911) far to the south at Guangzhou in Guangdong Province.

CWK

SUGGESTED READINGS:

Gray, Basil. **Sung Porcelain and Stoneware**. Boston: Faber and Faber, 1984.

Medley, Margaret. **The Chinese Potter: A Practical History of Chinese Ceramics**. Oxford: Phaidon Press Limited, 1976.

Tregear, Mary. **Song Ceramics**. New York: Rizzoli International Publications, Inc., 1982.

China

Jin (1125-1234)/Yuan (1279-1368) dynasties

TRUNCATED VASE, *13th to 14th century*

Cizhou ware: stoneware with cut-glaze designs

H: 13 inches; Dia: 12 1/2 inches

Gift of Mary and Jack A. Diamond in memory of the late H.S. Mori, 1960.73

This vase has a globular shape with decorations of condensed floral scrolls on the shoulder. Three panels, serving as open windows, contain peonies, lotus, and plum blossoms on the upper part of the vase. The gray stoneware was covered with a dark brown glaze. Before the glaze dried, the design was incised and cut away to the level of the body, which was covered by a creamy white slip. The effect after firing is a boldly contrasting design of both luster and texture between the glazed and unglazed areas.

Although this piece shares some similarities in design to pieces produced in the Northern Song dynasty, it differs in its depressed shape and condensed design with a more naturalistic representation of motifs. The naturalism of the floral designs with its finely incised detail is in striking contrast to the conventionalized design of overlapping floral scrolls on the shoulder, seen commonly in the vessels of the Northern Song dynasty (960-1127). The floral design of the later period, as seen in this vase, tends to be more condensed than that of the earlier. Accompanying the format of the panel, a novel addition to the latter representation, the design points to newer artistic concerns of the Jin and Yuan dynasties in the 13th and 14th centuries.

CWK

SUGGESTED READINGS:

Kwan, Simon. "The Meiping in Song Ceramics." *Bulleting of the Oriental Ceramic Society of Hong Kong (Vol. 8, 1986-88, Vol. 8): 27-35.*

Lee, Sherman E., and Wai-kam Ho. *Chinese Art Under the Mongols: The Yuan Dynasty (1279-1368).* Cleveland: The Cleveland Museum of Art, 1968.

Mino, Yutaka, and Katherine R. Tsiang. *Freedom of Clay and Brush through Seven Centuries in Northern China: Tz'u-chou Type Wares, 960-1600 A.D.* Indianapolis: Indianapolis Museum of Art, 1980.

Tregear, Mary. *Song Ceramics.* New York: Rizzoli International Publications, Inc., 1982.

Chinese

Yuan dynasty (1279-1368)

JAR, late 13th - early 14th century

Cizhou ware: stoneware with white slip and painted designs

H: 11 1/2 inches; Dia: 7 1/4 inches

Gift of the C.F. Kettering Fund, 1928.3

The decorative scheme of this wine or oil jar with its four, double-looped handles consists of double concentric bands that define four registers. The top register at the shoulder is plain except for splashes of dark slip on the loop handles. The two center registers are painted with rudimentary grass and leaf motifs, highlighting the skillful mastery of brush. The bottom register is unadorned. The short foot is slightly flared.

A widespread design technique among Cizhou family wares was slip painting. Slip is a clay solution applied onto the body of a vessel for a smooth, desired surface. A white underlayer slip has been applied to the body, providing the ground or "canvas" for the dark brown or black overlayer slip painting. Although frequently described as utilitarian, the quality of Cizhou ware was such that it became virtually the only "folk art" to attract the scholarly elite—possibly because the potter's hand, like that of a calligrapher and painter, is so evident in the vigorous and calligraphic motifs that decorate the surface.

CWK

SUGGESTED READINGS:

Lee, Sherman E., and Wai-kam Ho. **Chinese Art Under the Mongols: The Yuan Dynasty (1279-1368)**. Cleveland: The Cleveland Museum of Art, 1968.

Mino, Yutaka, and Katherine R. Tsiang. **Freedom of Clay and Brush through Seven Centuries in Northern China: Tz'u-chou Type Wares, 960-1600 A.D.** Indianapolis: Indianapolis Museum of Art, 1980.

China

Yuan dynasty (1279-1368)

STEM CUP, *early 14th century*

Jingdezhen ware: porcelain with molded decoration and underglaze blue designs

H: 3 11/16 inches; Dia: 4 5/8 inches

Gift of Mrs. Virginia W. Kettering, 1969.42a

The stem of this elegant porcelain cup is gently flared and decorated with three convex moldings, each finely incised with a double ring in imitation of a bamboo stalk. Like many similar examples of this type, the bowl has steeply rounded sides with a slightly everted rim. Painted in a vivid underglaze blue over molded designs is a freely drawn, sketchy scroll motif on the inside lip and a flaming pearl in the center of the well—all symbols of merit, prosperity, and the universe. The cavetto has molded designs of chrysanthemums alternating with marguerites. On the exterior of the bowl is a three-clawed dragon chasing a flaming pearl amidst clouds. The interior of the stem is unglazed and fired to an orange-red.

The type and decoration as seen here are known to date from the 14th century. Although the manufacture of these cups spanned the entire century, they are generally attributed to the Yuan dynasty. This cup is unique for its successful application of molding and blue underglaze decorative techniques. This cup is most likely a court vessel produced at Jindezhen, Jiangxi Province under the supervision of the Fuliang Ceramic Bureau, which was established in 1278 by the Yuan authority. A few similar cups excavated at the archaeological sites near Jingdezhen are inscribed with the character for "wine," which suggests the function of this type of vessel.

CWK and LJ

SUGGESTED READINGS:

Carswell, John, with contributions by Edward A. Maser and Jean McClure Mudge. **Blue and White: Chinese Porcelain and Its Impact on the Western World**. Chicago: The David and Alfred Smart Gallery, The University of Chicago, 1985.

Feng, Xianming. **History of Chinese Ceramics**. Beijing: Wenwu Press, 1987.

Jingdezhen Wares: The Yuan Evolution. Hong Kong: The Oriental Ceramic Society of Hong Kong, 1984.

Lee, Sherman E., and Wai-kam Ho. **Chinese Art Under the Mongols: The Y,an Dynasty (1279-1368)**. Cleveland: The Cleveland Museum of Art, 1968.

Valenstein, Suzanne G. **A Handbook of Chinese Ceramics**. New York: The Metropolitan Museum of Art, 1989.

China

Song dynasty (960-1279)

HEAD OF GUANYIN, *early 11th century*

Earthenware with traces of polychrome

H: 25 inches

Museum purchase with funds provided by Mrs. Harrie G. Carnell, 1959.41

Among the deities of the Buddhist faith is one known as Guanyin, an enlightened being who assists the faithful as they strive for salvation. Guanyin was originally depicted in India where the deity was called Avalokitesvara. It spread to China in the 3rd century and has been used in worship since. Most early Guanyin were depicted with simple male characteristics. Since the Song dynasty (960-1279), Guanyin has been treated realistically as a secular woman with a fashionable hair style, flowing ribbons, robe, and sometimes even richly adorned with jewelry.

The *Head of Guanyin* in the Art Institute's collection fits into the stylistic aspects of the Song dynasty as described above. This exquisite Guanyin wears an elaborate coiffure, diadem of ornate jewels, shawl, and ribbons falling at the shoulders. Traces of a rich, indigo blue are visible throughout the hair; the eyes are darkened with color, and the lips are shaded with red touching. The ethereal grace and inward, contemplative expression, conveyed by the downcast eyes, and the full, yet slender, form of the bust with its lyrical cascades of hair and ribbons, richly exemplifies the salvation and calm of Buddhist teachings. The youthfulness of the image, the lifelike realism, and the sensitive modeling of its features are typical of the best Song dynasty Buddhist sculpture during the 11th century. Although the image has lost the lower torso and most of the painted decoration, this piece still remains a rare example of Chinese Buddhist sculpture of the Song dynasty.

CWK

Suggested Readings:

Siren, Osvald. **Chinese Sculpture from the Fifth to the Fourteenth Century**, 2 Vols. New York: Hacker Art Books, 1970.

Siren, Osvald. "Chinese Sculpture from the Sung, Liao and Chin Dynasties." **Bulletin of the Museum of Far Eastern Antiquities** (Vol. 14, 1942): 45-67.

China

Ming dynasty (1368-1644)

SIDDHARTHA (BABY BUDDHA), *15th century*

Gilt bronze

H: 6 1/2 inches

Gift of Mrs. Virginia W. Kettering, 1978.121

This sculpture depicts Prince Siddhartha, who would become the Buddha, at a moment shortly after birth. According to legend, Siddhartha sprang fully formed from the side of his mother. Here, the infant Buddha stands triumphant with his left hand raised and his index finger, now broken and lost, pointing skyward; his right index finger points toward the earth. The depiction is of that momentous occasion immediately following his birth when he strode forth. As indicated by his gesture, he proclaimed that he was Siddhartha, the honored one who would redeem the suffering of those in this world as well as those who had passed into another existence.

The child is marked by several distinctive signs of his Buddhahood: the long arms, fingers, and toes, golden skin, and rounded head with a mark between his eyebrows. His earlobes are already elongated—presaging the time when he would relinquish his royal garbs and heavy earrings that distended his lobes. Of solid cast, Siddhartha is clad only with a stomach warmer, tied at the back and secured around his neck. The naturally rendered, chubby body, and the elaborately engraved lotus blossom and leaves on his warmer are part of the Ming artistic repertoire. The original base of the piece is most likely a lotus pedestal.

CWK

Suggested Readings:

Karetzky, Patricia Eichenbaum. ***The Life of the Buddha: Ancient Scriptural and Pictorial Traditions***. *Lanham, NY and London: University Press of America, 1992.*

Lee, Sherman E. "The Golden Image of the New-Born Buddha." ***Artibus Asiae*** *(1955, Vol. 18, No. 3/4): 224-237.*

Pal, Pratapaditya with essays by Robert L. Brown, Robert E. Fisher, George Kuwayama and Amy G. Porter. ***The Light of Asia: Buddha Sakyamuni in Asian Art***. *Museum Associates, Los Angeles County Museum of Art, 1984.*

von Schroeder, Ulrich. ***Indo-Tibetan Bronzes***. *Hong Kong: Visual Dharma Publications Ltd., 1981.*

China

Ming dynasty (1368-1644), Shanxi province

PAIR OF DRAGON GATES, *late 15th - early 16th century*

Stone with relief carving decoration

54 x 90 inches (each)

Gift of Mrs. Harrie G. Carnell, 1928.48.1-2

These stone carvings and a set of door, window, and ceiling panels in the Art Institute's collection were originally part of a private mausoleum in Shanxi Province. Similar stone carvings are seen as part of exterior walls or architectural gateways. These stone panels may have once stood beneath the windows to the inner sanctum, thus the unsullied sharpness of the carving seems to support the suggestion of an interior setting. The powerful, expressive style of the carvings, the varying heights of relief, and the compositional diagonals indicate a Ming dynasty date of the 15th to 16th centuries.

On each panel, a pair of five-clawed dragons rise above the churning waters of the universe, guarding a pearl of immortality. Although carved in coiled postures, each pair of dragons is compositionally aligned along parallel diagonals, completely filling the space. Two diagonals are defined by their spines while a third bisects the stone extending along their heads and through the central pearl. In a masterful display of skill, the panels are carved with a changing series of relief heights that adds to the tension and dynamism of the works.

The dragon is one of the most popular motifs found in Chinese art and representations of this mythical creature reach far back in Chinese culture. It is associated with auspiciousness as the bringer of rain and the herald of spring, and thus the provider of life and plentitude. Traditionally, it is the representative of the emperor and the supreme symbol of prosperity, virtue, wisdom, strength, and power. The pearl in Chinese art is ultimately derived from Buddhist sources where it is known as the wish granting jewel. In its Buddhist context, it represents transcendent wisdom and, by extension, the tenets of Buddhist enlightenment. The combination of the dragon and pearl, as shown on these carvings, creates an association between supernatural power and knowledge, and, on an imperial level, is the embodiment of the emperor.

CWK

Suggested Readings:

Paludan, Ann. **The Chinese Spirit Road: The Classical Tradition of Stone Tomb Statuary**. *New Haven and London: Yale University Press, 1991.*

Steinhardt, Nancy Shatzman, Fu Xinian, Else Glahn, Robert L. Thorp and Annette L. Juliano. **Chinese Traditional Architecture**. *New York: Chinese Institute in America, 1984.*
Zhao, Qiguang. "Dragon: The Symbol of China." *Oriental Art (N.S., Vol. XXXVIII, No. 2, Summer 1991): 72-80.*

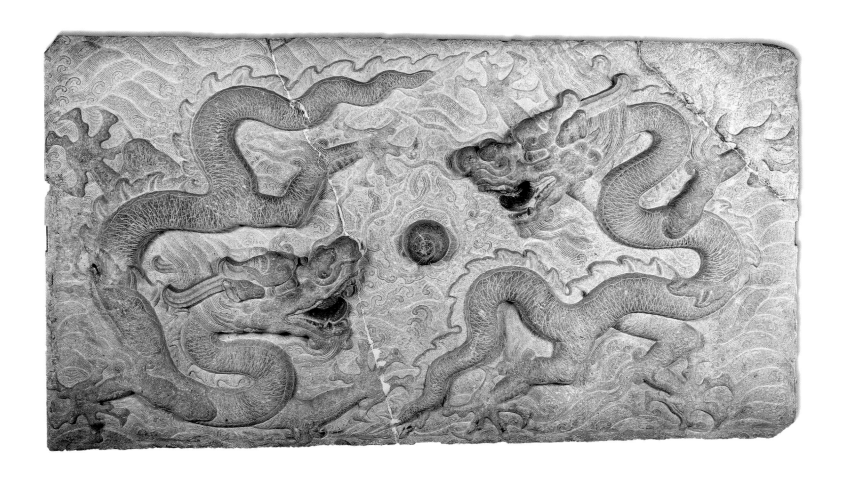

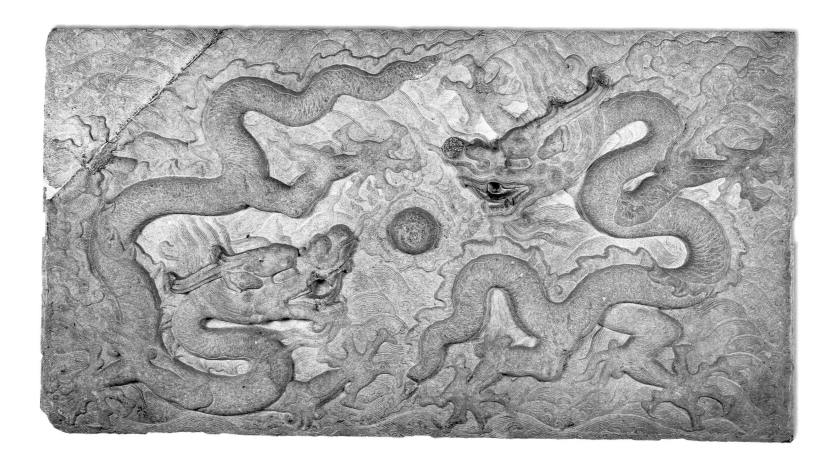

Kuncan

Chinese (1612-1674 or later)

MOUNTAIN LANDSCAPE, *around 1663-1664*

Hanging scroll: ink and colors on paper

41 5/8 x 11 1/8 inches

Gift of Mrs. Virginia W. Kettering, 1976.277

Inscription:

Heaven creates mountains and rivers,
Settled down in the South.
Being able to sustain a square house,
The married couple shares the candles.
The auspicious influences [of the sovereign] are luxuriant,
As if the Emperor shepherds the people.
The divine waterfalls are full with waves,
Which can be used for cleansing and bathing.
Trees, torrents and shoals,
Are the bones of snow-fed creeks.
The roads are hidden in the rushes,
Built a thatched hut and set up a whisk.
Never destroyed for a thousand years,
The Divine Glory again in charge.
Here is a wise man,
Who obtains a divine cave.
Carrying a fan to get rid of influences,
Bless my native land.
After countless years,
The true models [principles] always fragrant.
Done in the winter of the *guimao* year, the twelfth
month [December 29, 1663-January 27, 1664] at the
monastery in Changgan Temple [Nanjing].*

Signature: Shiqi; Can Daoren*
Artist's seals: Jieqiu; Shiqi*

Kuncan, also named Shiqi, was a monk painter of the late Ming dynasty. A native of Wuling, Hunan Province, Kuncan was a devout practitioner of Chan (Zen) Buddhism. In 1654, he moved to Nanjing where he was associated with the artistic and literary circles of Ming loyalists. He traveled extensively in the Jiangsu and Zhejiang provinces and also visited the Huangshan Mountains, Jiangxi Province in early 1660. After his return, he lived alone in a hut near a Buddhist temple in Nanjing, and produced more than 300 works during 1660-1663. Seemingly, this painting is one of his works painted during that period of time.

Unlike the orthodox painters of the late Ming and early Qing dynasty who tended to emulate the great masters of the past (cf. Wang Jian, 78.14), others such as Kuncan chose to view nature as an inspiration and model. His landscapes, often executed in seclusion, are characterized by a sense of controlled compositional complexity—a reflection of the complexity of nature itself. His landscape elements, such as rocks, trees, and mist, are depicted in dynamic animation as if possessed of life forces. The vibrancy of his brushstroke and his lively use of color heighten this sensation. Only a monk painter, alone in his mountainous retreat, seems to be able to create works like this, inspired by nature and charged with his profound insights.

CWK and LJ

SUGGESTED READINGS:

Cahill, James. **The Restless Landscape: Chinese Painting of the Late Ming Period**. Berkeley: University of California Press, 1971.

Ho, Wai-kam, Sherman E. Lee, Laurence Sickman, and Marc F. Wilson essays. **Eight Dynasties of Chinese Painting: The Collections of the Nelson-Atkins Museum , Kansas City and The Cleveland Museum of Art**. Cleveland: The Cleveland Museum of Art, 1980.

Roger, Howard and Sherman Lee. **Masterworks of Ming and Qing Painting from the Forbidden City**. Lansdale, PA: International Arts Council, 1988.

Xie, Zhiliu. **The Four Monk Painters: Paintings of Hongren, Kuncan, Bada Shanren and Shitao from the Shanghai Museum Collection**. Shanghai and Hong Kong: Shanghai People's Fine Art Publishing House and Tai Yip Company, 1990.

*Translation provided by Nora Ling-yun Shih of New York with additional assistance from Dr. Tsing Yuan of Wright State University (Dayton, Ohio) and Mr. Joseph Chang of Kansas City, Missouri.

173

Wang Jian
Chinese (1598-1677)

LANDSCAPE, 1674

Fan painting: ink on gold paper
10 3/8 x 22 1/2 inches
Museum purchase with funds provided by the Associate Board's 1978 Art Ball, 1978.14
Inscription: "Second month of Spring in the year of Jiayin [1674], after Huanghe
Shanqiao (Wang Meng [1308-1385]). Wang Jian."
Artist's seal: "Wang Jian Jiayin"

In this fan painting, Wang Jian has constructed a densely forested landscape and babbling brook below mountain peaks rising above clouds. A small hermit's cottage stands beneath pines. The work is a masterful achievement in rhythm, movement, and brush handling. The viewer's eye is led into the painting at the right through the cascading stream across the landscape and into the distance through a subtle play of varying brush strokes, gray washes, and dark accents. The panorama unfolds visually just as the fan would have unfolded to reveal the painting within.

Wang Jian belonged to a prominent family of Taicang, Jiangsu Province. After attaining his *jinshi* degree, the highest level of the civil service examinations, Wang Jian served as a prefect in Guangdong Province. Following the collapse of the Ming dynasty, he entered a life of self-imposed retirement and devoted himself to his art. He emulated a lineage of the revered *literati* masters of the past. One of the most distinguished masters was the Yuan dynasty (1279-1368) artist Wang Meng, on whose style this painting is based, as acknowledged in the inscription.

CWK

Suggested Readings:

Contag, Victoria. **Chinese Masters of the Seventeenth Century**. Rutland and Tokyo: Charles E. Tuttle, 1969.

Ecke, Tseng Yu-ho. **Poetry on the Wind: The Art of Chinese Folding Fans from the Ming and Ch'ing Dynasties**. Honolulu: Honolulu Academy of Arts, 1982.

Hay, John. "Chinese Fan Painting." **Colloquies on Art and Archaeology in Asia**. Margaret Medley, ed. London: University of London, Percival David Foundation of Chinese Art, School of Oriental and African Studies, 1975: 95-117.

Ho, Wai-kam, Sherman E. Lee, Laurence Sickman, and Marc F. Wilson (essays). **Eight Dynasties of Chinese Painting: The Collections of the Nelson-Atkins Museum, Kansas City and The Cleveland Museum of Art**. Cleveland: The Cleveland Museum of Art, 1980.

China

Qing dynasty (1644-1911), Kangxi period (1662-1722)

IMPERIAL DRAGON TEXTILE, *late 17th century*

Silk tapestry weave: **kesi** *("cut silk") with metallic thread*

60 x 48 inches

Gift of the Honorable Jefferson Patterson, 1952.97

This magnificently woven silk textile is the front panel of what was intended to be a formal robe for official ceremonies. The central portion of this panel, with powerful dragons, flaming pearls and churning waters, is the focal point of this piece. Had the textile been cut and assembled, nine five-clawed dragons would have decorated the robe.

The design is a diagram of the Chinese concept of the universe and is replete with cosmological symbols. The dragons, which live among the clouds, symbolize the element air. During the Qing dynasty, the five-clawed dragon would become reserved for the imperial family and its authority. The number nine was a symbol of supreme power and potency. Each dragon grasps a flaming pearl, symbol of eternal light, omnipotent wisdom, and unerring truth. The pearl is also the emblem of the Universal Sovereign, which to the Chinese is the emperor. Along the bottom are triple-peaked mountains rising above swirling waves that represent the primordial seas and the earth.

The robustness of the dragons in their twisting posture are characteristic of Kangxi period dragons. The fungus-shaped wave bursts and cloud motifs likewise indicate an early Qing date. During the Qianlong reign (1736-1795), strict regulations on design and decoration were established and more motifs were introduced for such robes. The absence of later Qing dynasty motifs, such as the eight auspicious emblems, also pushes the date of this robe fragment back.

Kesi weaving is the most elaborate type of Chinese tapestry weaving. The term *kesi* means "cut silk," which refers to the technique in color weaving. In *kesi* weaving, the design is achieved by covering the warp or longitudinal threads with polychrome weft or horizontal threads. The weft threads, however, are only woven across the warp strands in their specific pattern area rather than across the entire warp structure. Thus, one row of weft may contain as many as four or more different-colored threads, a tiny slit or cut in the silk appearing where one colored weft thread ends and another begins. The technique was likely introduced from Central Asia along the silk route during the 10th century.

CWK

Suggested Readings:

Cammann, Schulyer. **China's Dragon Robes**. *New York: The Ronald Press Company, 1952.*

De Verboden Stad: Hofcultuur van de Chinese keizers (1644-1911)/The Forbidden City: Court Culture of the Chinese Emperors (1644-1911). *Rotterdam: Boymans-van Beuningen Museum, 1990.*

Vollmer, John. **In the Presence of the Dragon Throne: Ch'ing Dynasty Costume (1644-1911) in the Royal Ontario Museum**. *Toronto: Royal Ontario Museum, 1977.*

Wilson, Verity. **Chinese Dress**. *London: Victoria and Albert Museum, 1986.*

Sino-Tibet
MYRIAD AMITAYUS, *18th century*
Thanka: colors and gold on sized cotton
45 1/2 x 30 1/2 inches
Gift of Mrs. Harrie G. Carnell, 1944.101

Tibet has been an important source of inspiration for Chinese art since the Yuan dynasty (1279-1368). In the following centuries with the cultural and religious exchange between the two regions, objects including sculpture, metalwork, and painting were made in the Tibetan style, known as "Sino-Tibetan." During the reign of the Emperor Qianlong (1736-1795), Sino-Tibetan works reached heights in quality and quantity when they were produced in the palace workshop in Beijing with the supervision of and advice from Tibetan scholars and high Lamas.

The *thanka* (Tibetan term for painting on cloth) in the Art Institute's collection is one of the products from that period. In the center of this thanka is a magnificent, gold image of Amitayus, Buddha of Eternal Life. According to traditional iconography, his hair is colored blue and gathered in a chignon with jewels and flowers. Resplendently attired, Amitayus is seated in the yogi position, meditating. Surrounding Amitayus are 54 images of the Buddha of Infinite Life, similarly depicted against a red background. Scattered throughout the lower portion of the painting are landscape elements, animals, and other auspicious Buddhist emblems; the upper section is filled with clouds, the sun disc, and the crescent moon.

Amitayus is the Dispenser of Infinite Life and an extremely popular figure in Tibetan Buddhism. He is the Buddha of the western direction; and his paradise is known as the Western Pure Land. The Buddha manifests himself in a myriad of means. Traditionally, there are 108 Buddha images of virtue and salvation, a number expressive of the omnipresent nature of the Buddha and his law. This *thanka* contains half this number and thus is likely one of a pair. An image of Amitabha, Buddha of Eternal Light, with 54 subsidiary images, may have originally accompanied this painting because Amitabha is closely linked to Amitayus in Buddhist concept.

The use of color is symbolic. Red is the common color for rituals and passion, particularly compassion. The red lotus is likewise associated with the wisdom of Amitabha, the fountain source of Amitayus, and is probably intended here to illustrate the beneficence of their wisdom and compassion conjoined.

CWK

Suggested Readings:

Bartholomew, Teresa Tse. "Sino-Tibetan Art of the Qianlong Period from the Asian Art Museum of San Francisco." **Orientations** (1991,Vol. 22, No. 6): no pp.

Pal, Pratapaditya. **Art of the Himalayas: Treasures from Nepal and Tibet**. New York: American Federation of Arts and Hudson Hill, 1992.

Pal, Pratapaditya. **Tibetan Paintings: A Study of Tibetan Thankas Eleventh to Nineteenth Century**. Basel: Ravi Kumar, 1984.

Rhie, Marylin M., and Robert A.F. Thurman. **Wisdom and Compassion: The Sacred Art of Tibet**. San Francisco and New York: Asian Art Museum of San Francisco and Tibet House in association with Harry N. Abrams, Inc., 1991.

Korea
Old Silla dynasty (57 B.C.-A.D. 668)
FUNERARY VESSEL WITH COVER, *5th - 6th century*
Ash-glazed gray stoneware with beaten decoration
H: 12 1/4 inches
Gift of Mr. Harold W. Shaw, 1984.93

This unassuming mortuary urn has five lugs on the shoulder and a cover in the shape of an inverted, footed bowl with perforations. The vessel is decorated with paddle markings, the result of being patted with a wooden mallet with carved striations on the head. With no attempt to form a regular pattern and the rather casual nature of the design, this vessel is typical of the Korean pottery of the Three Kingdoms period. There are traces of a natural-ash glaze covering the body, a result of the drifting gases in the kiln. The shape, decoration, and glaze are similar to the vessels excavated at the burial sites in Silla, in the southeast Korean peninsula, dated to the 5th and 6th centuries.

This type of vessel was produced with the introduction and the influence of Buddhism. Although not given official sanction until 527, Buddhism was likely introduced into the Kaya kingdom by the 5th century. One of its impacts was the substitution, with increasing frequency, of cremation rites around the middle of the 6th century, replacing the former preference for imposing mound burials. This urn is an example of such a cinerary tomb furnishing.

CWK

Suggested Readings:

Griffing, Robert P. **The Art of the Korean Potter: Silla, Koryo, Yi**. *New York: The Asia Society, 1968.*

Henderson, Gregory. **Korean Ceramics: An Art's Variety**. *Columbus, OH: The Ohio State University, 1969.*

Lefebvre d'Argence, Rene-Yvon, ed. **5,000 Years of Korean Art**. *San Francisco: Asian Art Museum of San Francisco, 1979.*

Moes, Robert J. **Korean Art from the Brooklyn Museum Collection**. *Brooklyn: The Brooklyn Museum, 1987.*

Korea
Unified Silla dynasty (668-918)
COVERED STORAGE BOX, *8th century*
Gray stoneware with stamped decoration
H: 6 inches; Dia: 6 3/4 inches
Gift of Mrs. Virginia W. Kettering, 1969.55

This circular box is decorated with elaborate, stamped patterns. The top of the lid consists of a central medallion with patterns of radiating circles and floral motifs. The sides of the cover have triangular pendants formed by circles, beneath which is a double row of additional circles. The decor on the sides of the box consists of a band of evenly spaced, floral motifs similar to those found on the lid, a wide band of closely spaced circles, and two lower registers of floral designs.

The Korean pottery produced during the Unified Silla dynasty is characterized by simple forms and impressed ornaments. The impressed designs are applied to accessories of these vessels, such as lugs, or even the entire surface. The popular decorative motifs are stamped circles, dotted lines and geometric floral motifs as seen in this covered box. As the Unified Silla dynasty progressed, stamped designs became the standard form of decoration, replacing the earlier, incised designs of the Three Kingdoms period (57 B.C.-A.D. 668). The result, however, is that the designs appear to be more mechanical in nature, replacing the more casual designs found on works of the early period.

CWK

SUGGESTED READINGS:

Griffing, Robert P. **The Art of the Korean Potter: Silla, Koryo, Yi.** New York: The Asia Society, 1968.

Lefebvre d'Argence, Rene-Yvon, ed. **5,000 Years of Korean Art**. San Francisco: Asian Art Museum of San Francisco, 1979.

Moes, Robert J. **Korean Art from The Brooklyn Museum Collection**. Brooklyn: The Brooklyn Museum, 1987.

Korea
Koryo dynasty (918-1392)
VASE, early 12th century
Iron-black ware: porcelaneous stoneware with iron-oxidized slip and celadon glaze
H: 11 inches; Dia: 6 1/2 inches
Gift of Mrs. Virginia W. Kettering, 1969.101

Koryo experiments in iron black ware began late in the 11th century and achieved the best results at the end of the 12th and early 13th centuries. Covered completely with an iron slip and then a celadon-type glaze, this vase was fired to a lustrous bluish-black with a bluish-green hue and fine crackles. The surface has an overall worn appearance, a distinguishing characteristic of early iron black wares. The glaze did not take in places and air bubbles surfaced, adding another decorative dimension to the surface adornment.

The shape of this elegant vase is a splendid example of the so-called *maebyng* form, derived from the Chinese appellation *meiping* which means "plum vase." A vase of this type was commonly thought to have been used for a single branch of blossoms. However, the small mouth of this piece suggests they were actually used as wine containers. The silhouette of this vase closely follows the classical Chinese form with its more cylindrical outline, a reflection of its early 12th century date. Later Korean examples possess a more constricted lower portion and emphasize a more globular, swelling shape.

CWK

SUGGESTED READINGS:

Gompetz, G.S.G.M. "Black Koryo Ware," **Oriental Art** *(1950, Vol. III, No. 2): 61-67.*

Griffing, Robert P. **The Art of the Korean Potter: Silla, Koryo, Yi**. *New York: The Asia Society, 1968.*

Itoh, Ikutaro, and Yutaka, Mino, with contributions from Jonathan W. Best and Pamela B. Vandiver. **The Radiance of Jade and the Clarity of Water: Korean Ceramics from the Ataka Collection**. *Chicago: The Art Institute of Chicago, 1991.*

Kwan, Simon. "The Meiping in Song Ceramics." **Bulletin of the Oriental Ceramic Society of Hong Kong** *(1986-88, Vol. 8): 27-35.*

Korea
Koryo dynasty (918-1392)
WINE BOTTLE, *12th century*
Porcelaneous stoneware with inlaid white and black slip decoration under a
celadon glaze
H: 15 1/4 inches; Dia: 6 1/4 inches
Gift of Mrs. Virginia W. Kettering, 1976.172

One of the most striking and aesthetically pleasing achievements of the Koryo potters was inlaid decoration known as *sanggam*. This decorative technique became widely popular during the Koryo dynasty from the 12th through 14th centuries. Fine examples are also seen in other media, such as bronzes inlaid with silver and lacquer wares inlaid with mother-of-pearl, tortoiseshell, and metals. Although the origin of this technique in Korea is still debated, it is likely to have been a product introduced from the Chinese Tang dynasty (618-907), metal inlay on lacquer, with contemporaneous Chinese lacquer inlay from Hangzhou. For inlaid decoration, design elements were incised into the clay and filled with a slip that oxides either white or black in firing.

The simple, yet robust, form of the vessel, as well as the balance of design, is indicative of its 12th century date. The relative sparseness of design is typical of early inlaid wares. The base of the neck region has a single, thin, inlaid band beneath which is a collar of fungi motifs. On the body of the bottle are three flowering branches in white and black slip inlay. A fine celadon glaze with crackles covers the entire surface. The mouth area has been restored, as has the loop through which a cord once passed to secure the now-missing lid.

CWK

SUGGESTED READINGS:

Gompetz, G.S.G.M. **Korean Celadon and Other Wares of the Koryo Period**. New York: Thomas Yoseloff, 1964.

Griffing, Robert P. **The Art of the Korean Potter: Silla, Koryo, Yi**. New York: The Asia Society, 1968.

Itoh. Ikutaro and Yutaka Mino, with contributions from Jonathan W. Best and Pamela B. Vandiver. **The Radiance of Jade and the Clarity of Water: Korean Ceramics from the Ataka Collection**. Chicago: The Art Institute of Chicago, 1991.

Mowry, Robert D. "Koryo Celadons." **Orientations** (May 1986, Vol. 17, No. 5): 24-39.

Korea

Koryo dynasty (918-1392)

BRIDAL BOWL, *late 12th - early 13th century*

Porcelaneous stoneware with inlaid and reverse inlay slip decoration under a
celadon glaze

H: 2 3/4 inches; Dia: 7 7/8 inches

Gift of Mrs. Virginia W. Kettering, 1976.161

This bowl with gently sloping sides and a straight footring is decorated on the interior well with a pair of fish, a symbol of prosperity and good luck, and a band of fungi heads, a symbol of immortality. In the four medallions are blossoming peony sprays, representative of an enduring matrimonial bliss. Other decorative motifs are swans, foliage, and willow trees. All these paired elements are subtle symbols of happiness, prosperity, and progeny, suggesting that the bowl was likely a wedding or commemorative gift. Originally, this may have been one of a pair of such bowls. The tendency to cover the entire surface with decor indicates its late 12th or early 13th century date.

The slip inlay decoration is one of the perfected characteristics of Koryo celadon ware. Design elements were incised or stamped into the damp clay. White or black slip (clay suspended in a watery solution) was applied. Once dried, the object was lightly polished to remove all excess slip from the surface, leaving a smooth surface and only the incised areas filled. The glaze was then applied by a dipping method, and the vessels were rotated to ensure an even application.

Part of the design elements on the exterior of the bowl have been worked in a technique called "reverse inlay," seen in the leafy tendrils between the large chrysanthemum sprays in the double roundels. In this system of decoration, the background elements—rather than the leafy tendrils—have been cut away from the clay and filled with a white slip so that after firing, the tendrils are celadon colored against a white slip background. The presence of both techniques also suggests a late 12th to early 13th century date.

CWK

Suggested Readings:

Gompetz, G.S.G.M. **Korean Celadon and Other Wares of the Koryo Period**. *New York: Thomas Yoseloff, 1964.*

Griffing, Robert P. **The Art of the Korean Potter: Silla, Koryo, Yi**. *New York: The Asia Society, 1968.*

Itoh, Ikutaro and Yutaka Mino, with contributions from Jonathan W. Best and Pamela B. Vandiver. **The Radiance of Jade and the Clarity of Water: Korean Ceramics from the Ataka Collection**. *Chicago: The Art Institute of Chicago, 1991.*

Korea

Koryo dynasty (918-1392)

WATER DROPPER IN THE FORM OF A TURTLE

late 12th - early 13th century

Porcelaneous stoneware, molded with carved, incised, and applied decoration under a
celadon glaze

H: 2 1/4 inches

Gift of Mrs. Virginia W. Kettering, 1976.159

This water dropper in the shape of a turtle is one of the most charming Koryo celadon vessels in the Art Institute's Collection. The pale, evergreen-blue glaze is crazed throughout the entire body and thinned along the edges of the molded and applied elements. The turtle's carapace is incised with an hexagonal design, believed to contain the hidden trigrams of magical divination. Water is admitted through the opening on the turtle's back into the center of the lotus plant, the curled edges acting as a natural funnel. The head, with a small hole at the mouth, acts as the spout. The water dropper was used with an inkstone for calligraphy and painting.

The turtle is a favored animal in Korean art. Often depicted with the head of a different species, serpent-like in this water dropper, the tortoise is one of the ten symbols of long life. This is an appropriate association as giant turtles are known to live for centuries. The ancient Chinese tradition of divination by interpreting the cracks found on tortoise shells after application of a hot poker established the animal's shamanistic context, and associations of mythological benevolence are similarly found in Korean beliefs. The turtle is also one of the four animals of good luck and one of the four animals of the cardinal directions. It is moreover the messenger of the Dragon King, otherwise known as the Water Spirit, whose dwelling is the Dragon Palace at the bottom of the sea.

CWK

SUGGESTED READINGS:

Gompetz, G.S.G.M. **Korean Celadon and Other Wares of the Koryo Period.** *New York: Thomas Yoseloff, 1964.*

Griffing, Robert P. **The Art of the Korean Potter: Silla, Koryo, Yi.** *New York: The Asia Society, 1968).*

Itoh, Ikutaro and Yutaka Mino, with contributions from Jonathan W. Best and Pamela B. Vandiver, **The Radiance of Jade and the Clarity of Water: Korean Ceramics from the Ataka Collection** *The Art Institute of Chicago, 1991.*

Korea

Choson dynasty (1392-1910)

WINE BOTTLE, *17th century*

Porcelain with underglaze cobalt blue decoration

H: 5 1/2 inches; Dia: 3 3/8 inches

Gift of Mrs. Virginia W. Kettering, 1969.42d

Cobalt is the source for the underglaze blue pigment used in Asian ceramics since the 7th century. Although a few native sources of cobalt were discovered on the Korean peninsula, these failed to yield any sizable quantity of usable ore and finer grades of cobalt continued to be imported from China, which in turn had it imported from Near Eastern sources. The expense of importing this precious commodity not only placed the blue and white wares beyond the reach of the common people, but heightened the social status of those who could afford it. In 1461, a decree was issued to prohibit the use of blue and white porcelains for the common people. Eight years later, another imperial decree encouraged the production of blue and white wares as gifts to the court. This elegant wine vessel is such a piece, probably created and given as a gift for an official associated with the court.

The potter has united successfully two divergent forms in this bottle, the sweep of the neck and everted mouthrim being nicely contrasted against the flat faces of the square body. The sides are decorated in cobalt blue underglaze with plum blossoms, bamboo, chrysanthemums, and banana fronds. Floral motifs such as these are replete with symbolic connotations. The naturally long lifespan of the plum makes it a symbol of longevity. The plum is also a symbol of spring and rebirth, its flowers appearing early in the season on apparently lifeless branches often still covered with snow. Bamboo is a preferred emblem of the *literati* (scholarly gentlemen) class. As bamboo stalks bend before the wind but do not break, so, too, the scholar must bend before adversity without yielding. The chrysanthemum is similarly associated with the literati class and has long been a symbol of retirement from office. It is cherished as an emblem of the life of ease. The prolific and nutritious fruit of the banana plant makes it a symbol of good health and abundance.

CWK

SUGGESTED READINGS:

Gompetz, G.S.G.M. **Korean Pottery and Porcelain of the Yi Period**. *New York and Washington: Frederick A. Praeger, 1968.*

Griffing, Robert P. **The Art of the Korean Potter: Silla, Koryo, Yi**. *New York: The Asia Society, 1968.*

Itoh, Ikutaro, and Yutaka Mino, with contributions from Jonathan W. Best and Pamela B. Vandiver. **The Radiance of Jade and the Clarity of Water: Korean Ceramics from the Ataka Collection**. *Chicago: The Art Institute of Chicago, 1991.*

Korea

Choson dynasty (1392-1910)

BRUSH HOLDER, *18th century*

White porcelain with reticulated decoration

H: 5 1/8 inches; Dia: 5 1/8 inches

Gift of Mrs. Virginia W. Kettering, 1976.193

The Korean peninsula is richly endowed with fine clay (kaolin) deposits suitable for porcelain manufacture. White porcelain wares were among the most-valued ceramics of the early Choson dynasty and were used exclusively in the royal household of King Sejong (1419-1450). In 1466, a prohibition restricted kaolin clay to be reserved for the royal household only. White porcelains were so highly prized that even the use of white porcelains as gifts for the court was prohibited.

However, the regulation was amended in 1469, so that white porcelains with underglaze cobalt blue decoration could be produced. Porcelain brush holders and other objects of the scholar's desk enjoyed a great popularity and were produced in great quantities at the government kiln sites. The Art Institute's piece most likely came from one of these kilns.

Early white Choson porcelains are characterized by the extremely hard clay covered with grayish white glaze. Later examples tend to be either a purer white or bluish-white in tone as seen in this brush holder. The reticulated design of this piece was a popular device for such wares. The bold design and vitality of the interlaced plantain fronds between twisted rope bands seen here is indicative of the 18th century, as is the bluish-white bloom of the glaze.

CWK

SUGGESTED READINGS:

Gompetz, G.St.G.M. **Korean Pottery and Porcelain of the Yi Period**. *New York and Washington: Frederick A. Praeger, 1968.*

Griffing, Robert P. **The Art of the Korean Potter: Silla, Koryo, Yi**. *New York: The Asia Society, 1968.*

Itoh, Ikutaro and Yutaka Mino, with contributions from Jonathan W. Best and Pamela B. Vandiver. **The Radiance of Jade and the Clarity of Water: Korean Ceramics from the Ataka Collection**. *Chicago: The Art Institute of Chicago, 1991.*

Kim, Won-yong. Ahn Hwi-joon, Kim Lena, Han Byong-sam, Chung Yang-mo, and Shin Yong-hoon. **Korean Art Treasures**, *Roderick Whitfield and Pak Young-sook, eds. Seoul: Yekyong Publications, 1986.*

Japan

Kamakura period (1185-1333)

AMIDA BUDDHA, 12th - 13th century

Wood: joined block construction, painted and lacquered with gilt

H: 35 1/2 inches

Gift of Mrs. Harrie G. Carnell, 1935.1

A direct response to the increasing popularity of the "Pure Land" sect of Japanese Buddhism during the Kamakura period was the creation of many images of *Amida Buddha*, the principal deity of the sect. Seated here in the diamond posture of meditation, this statute depicts Amida in the gesture of argumentation that is commonly associated with Amida Raigo images. (See the Art Institute's *Descent of Amida Triad, pg. 186*) This carving could well represent a sculptural interpretation of this theme that is more frequently represented in paintings.

This wooden image has a tightly curled hairstyle with painted eyes and a rock-crystal insert on the forehead to imply the third eye of spiritual wisdom. A second crystal adorns the dome of wisdom on the top of the head. The figure is constructed from several joined blocks of wood and covered with black lacquer and gilt. The tranquility and grace of *Amida Buddha* are eloquently expressed in the downward-looking eyes, long and narrow in design with arched eyebrows. The fullness of the cheeks, expansive chest and stomach, and cascading pleats of the garment folds—sensitively designed with fluidity and undulating rhythms—are reminiscent of the work of the great Buddhist sculptor Kaikei (fl. 1185-1220); and this example is a likely product of his legacy.

CWK

SUGGESTED READINGS:

Koytaro, Nishikawa, and Emily J. Sano. **The Great Age of Japanese Buddhist Sculpture, A.D. 600-1300**. Fort Worth, TX: Kimball Art Museum, 1982.

Mori, Hisashi. **Sculpture of the Kamakura Period**. Katherine Eickmann, trans. **The Heibonsha Survey of the Japanese Art**, Vol. 11. New York and Tokyo: Weatherhill/Heihonsha, 1974.

Pal, Pratapaditya, with essays by Robert L. Brown, Robert E. Fisher, George Kuwayama, and Amy G. Poster. **The Light of Asia: Buddha Sakyamuni in Asian Art**. Los Angeles: Museum Associates, Los Angeles County Museum of Art, 1984.

Japan

Kamakura period (1185-1333)

DESCENT OF AMIDA TRIAD, *14th century*

Hanging scroll: colors and gold on silk

34 x 15 3/4 inches

Gift of Mrs. Harrie G. Carnell, 1938.46

"Blessed art thou! Blessed art thou . . . Therefore thou art now welcome." This jubilation welcomed the faithful into the paradise of the Buddha of the West, Amida—the central figure of the "Pure Land" sect of Japanese Buddhism. In the "Pure Land" sect, it was believed that with sincere devotional worship and faith in Amida, salvation was immediately achieved. For those who were excluded from the darker mysteries of Esoteric Buddhism, this tenet offered a transcendent deliverance. An explicit representation of this concept is the *Amida Sanzon Raigo* as seen in this painting.

The painting depicts the descent of Amida Buddha accompanied by his two principle disciples—Kannon, Lord of Compassion and Mercy, and Seishi, Lord of Might. Kannon leans forward offering a lotus seat on a plate decorated with jeweled pendants to the soul of the faithful while Seishi clasps his hands in prayer and adoration. The figures stand on lotus blossoms amid swirling clouds, indicating their descent, further heightened by their fluttering garments and strands of hair. They emerge out of the darkened void of ignorance, radiant in their brilliant gold attire. The visual effect is stunning and was intended to inspire awe in the supplicant.

Amida, with his left hand down, right hand raised, and both palms exposed, performs the gesture of appeasement with thumb and forefinger touching. The circle formed by this gesture is a symbol of perfection, being complete without a beginning or an end, and represents the law of Buddhism that is both eternal and perfect. In a few wall examples, especially paintings, silken cords were attached to the hands of Amida so that the faithful could literally pull themselves up and therefore ascend to the Western Paradise.

CWK

SUGGESTED READINGS:

Okazaki, J. **Pure Land Buddhist Painting**. Translated and adapted by Elizabeth ten Grotenhuis. Japanese Arts Library. Vol. 4. Tokyo, New York, and San Francisco: Kodansha International Ltd., 1977.

Pilgrim, Richard B. **Buddhism and the Arts of Japan**. Chambersburg, PA: Anima Publications, 1981.

Rosenfield, John M., and Elizabeth ten Grotenhuis. **Journey of the Three Jewels: Japanese Buddhist Paintings from Western Collections**. New York: The Asian Society, 1979.

Japan
Late Muromachi (1333-1568)/early Momoyama period (1568-1615)

MIROKU BOSATSU, 16th century
Wood: hollowed, single-block construction with gilt, gold, indigo, and black paint,
bronze, and beads
17 1/2 x 13 inches
Museum purchase with funds provided by Virginia Rike Haswell, 1979.49

One of the more popular deities in Japanese Buddhist literature is Miroku, the Buddha of the Future, depicted here as a *bosatsu*, (*bodhisattva* in Indian Buddhism), seated in the posture of meditation. *Miroku Bosatsu* is attired in a robe with a multitude of folds and pleats. The fluttering loops of his scarf and the ripples of his robe imply a sense of movement. His hair, colored an indigo blue, is arranged in a high chignon with braided strands flowing down. Originally, there likely was an elaborate crown dressed with a *stupa* (sepulchral monument) and the five Jina Buddhas. Across his chest, he wears a bronze pectoral with bead drops. In his left hand, the figure holds a lotus blossom, while his right hand makes the gesture of the exposition of the law. The facial features are delicately painted in black.

Miroku Bosatsu is shown here as he awaits the moment in the future when he will be reborn as a Buddha. Following an immeasurable period of time after the death of Shaka Buddha, Miroku will be reborn and descend to earth to provide the means of final salvation for mankind. For the present, however, he dwells in Tusita Heaven (the Paradise of the Satisfied), administering the law of Buddha to those who are reborn there.

CWK

Suggested Readings:

Elison, George, and Bardwell L. Smith, eds. **Warlords, Artists and Commoners: Japan in the Sixteenth Century**. Honolulu: University Press of Hawaii, 1981.

Momoyama: Japanese Art in the Age of Grandeur. New York: The Metropolitan Museum of Art, 1975.

Snellgrove, David, ed **The Image of Buddha**. Paris, Tokyo, and New York: UNESCO and Kodansha International, 1978.

Japan

Momoyama period (1568-1615)

FOOTED DISH

Mino ware: E Shino (Painted Shino) stoneware with underglaze iron decoration

H: 9 3/8 x W: 8 x D: 2 1/4 inches

Gift of Mrs. Virginia W. Kettering, 1969.16

Constructed of slabs of clay pressed into a mold design, this square, footed dish shows the evidence of its production. The clay has been painted in underglaze iron with foliage designs and decorative patterns, and then covered with a white glaze. Four clay buttons applied to the under-corners serve as feet.

Used for serving cakes at the tea ceremony, this dish dates to the Momoyama period in response to rising interest in such traditions. Accompanying this interest was an increased demand for appropriate vessels, such as cups, caddies, water pots, and dishes. When imports from China could no longer satisfy the demand, local production developed at several kiln sites, including Seto near present-day Nagoya and Mino in Gifu Prefecture. Tea masters recognized the beauty of this type of pottery and guided potters in matters of form and decoration. Shino ware, named after Shino Shoshin, a well-known tea master, is characterized by painted floral and foliage motifs, as seen here in the center of the dish.

CWK

SUGGESTED READINGS:

Cort, Louise Allison. **Seto and Mino Ceramics: Japanese Collections in the Freer Gallery of Art**. Washington, D.C.: Freer Gallery of Art, Smithsonian Institution, 1992.

Effie, Allison B. "Chinese Ceramics for the Japanese Tea Masters." **Arts of Asia** (1977, Vol. 7, No. 2): 48-56.

Faulkner, R.F.J. and O.R. Impey. **Shino and Oribe Kiln Sites**. Oxford: Robert G. Sawers Publishing/Ashmolean Museum, Oxford University, 1981.

Yoshiharu, Sawada. "A Gallery of Shino Ceramics." **Chanoyu Quarterly** (No. 35): 16-29.

Japan
Edo period (1615-1868)
BOTTLE VASE, *17th century*
Arita ware, Kakiemon style: porcelain with underglaze blue and overglaze blue enamel
H: 9 3/8 inches
Gift of Mrs. Virginia W. Kettering, 1978.124

M ost likely used as a flower vase for the tea ceremony, this enchanting bottle has a chubby bottom and a ridge along its waist, which subtly changes the curve of its silhouette. The upper section of the bottle is painted in an underglaze blue wash with a rich blue enamel overglaze. The intensity of this glossy cobalt contrasts with the starkly white band decorated in pale underglaze blue with three chrysanthemum sprays, an emblem of mid-autumn and a symbol of a life of ease.

This vase is an example of early Arita ware, a blue and white porcelain ware made in the town of Arita in Kyushu in the 17th century. When Arita ware was shipped from Imari, a nearby port, it came to be known as Imari ware. In the 1640s, when the potter Kakiemon I added overglaze enamels to underglaze blue vessels, the ware was distinguished as Kakiemon ware. Traditionally given an Arita designation, the subtle shape of this bottle hints at its construction possibly by a Kakiemon potter. The overlay glaze design is likewise unusual for an Arita ceramic, while the delicate handling of the floral sprays, clarity of the glazing, and fine white quality of the clay points to a Kakiemon kiln.

CWK

Suggested Readings:

Cleveland, Richard S. **200 Years of Japanese Porcelain**. *St. Louis: City Art Museum of Saint Louis, 1970.*

Jenyns, Soame. **Japanese Porcelain**. *London: Frederick A. Praeger, 1965.*

Mikami, Tsugio. "The Art of Japanese Ceramics." Translated by Ann Herring. **The Heibonsha Survey of Japanese Art**. *4th ed. Vol. 29. New York and Tokyo: Weatherhill/Heibonsha, 1979.*

Reichel, Friedrich. **Early Japanese Porcelain; Arita Porcelain in the Dresden Collection**. *Translated by Barbara Beedham. London: Orbis Publishing, 1980.*

Kobayashi Tokuemon
Edo period (1615-1868)

SAKE BOTTLE, *around 1690*
Arita ware, Ko Imari type: porcelain with underglaze blue, overglaze polychrome
enamels and gilt
H: 8 3/4 inches; Dia: 4 7/16 inches
Museum purchase with funds provided in part by an anonymous donor, 1982.37

This finely potted, white porcelain square bottle is lavishly decorated in underglaze blue, overglaze red, green, and yellow enamels, and gold decoration. The borders of the sides are outlined with a deep cobalt band and a variety of floral designs worked in gold. Each of the central panels is decorated with the four-season flowers associated with an auspicious characteristic: plum blossoms (winter, long life), peonies (spring, love and affection), squirrels and grapes (summer, fruitfulness), and chrysanthemums (autumn, joviality). A splayed chrysanthemum, emblematic of the rising sun and symbol of Japan, surrounds the collar of the neck. The underside of the bottle is signed "Toku," the signature of Tokuemon Kobayashi, the second-generation master of the Kobayashi family whose production was centered at Awataguchi, Kyoto.

In the mid-17th century, Japanese potters began the large-scale production of color enamel wares commonly known as Ko Imari or "Old Imari." Best known for their polychrome brocade-like patterns, these brilliantly colored, luxury porcelains of Arita became extremely fashionable for both the domestic and foreign markets. Stupefying numbers were produced to supply the enormous demands of the Dutch East India Company for the European market. Ko Imari porcelain, such as this example, reached its apogee in the Genroku era (1688-1703) of the Edo period. The square shape of this bottle is European in origin and was adapted by Japanese potters in response to Western preferences.

CWK

SUGGESTED READINGS:

Fukugawa, Tadashi. Igaki Hauro, and Tanio Minoru. **Sekai no Koimari meihin ten-aritayaki no furusato o tazunete** *("An Exhibition of Old Imari Masterpieces–In Search of the Birthplace of Aritaware"). Tokyo: Society of the Promotion of Aritaware, 1977.*

Jenyns, Soame. **Japanese Porcelain**. *London: Frederick A. Praeger, 1965.*

Munsterberg, Hugo. **The Ceramic Art of Japan: A Handbook for Collectors**. *Rutland and Tokyo: Charles E. Tuttle Company, 1964.*

Reichel, Friedrich. **Early Japanese Porcelain: Arita Porcelain in the Dresden Collection**. *Translated by Barbara Beedham. London: Orbis Publishing, 1980.*

Japan
Edo period (1615-1868)
FOOTED DISH, *18th century*
Arita ware, Nabeshima type: porcelain with underglaze blue design
Dia: 8 inches
Gift of Mrs. Virginia W. Kettering, 1969.42c

This finely potted dish has a slightly rolled rim and a base decorated with a comb design. The interior well is decorated with a dramatic underglaze blue design of sea swells along the edges that look as if they are about to spill over. The overhanging mist-shroud and stark, white sky provide an excellent visual foil to this turbulence. The exterior has three peony sprays.

This dish is an example of Nabeshima ware, which is named after Nabeshima Naomasa, whose family owned the kiln in Saga Prefecture. Originally founded at Iwayakawachi, the kiln was moved to Nangawarayama and then to Okochiyama in 1675, where the wares were perfected. The kiln was organized as a manorial enterprise, wares being reserved for members of the clan and as gifts to the imperial family, the shogun, and other feudal leaders.

Nabeshima decorations are often derived from textile designs reflecting the tastes of the clan aristocracy. The wares are noted for their highly refined craftsmanship with precise shapes, as seen in this footed dish; and flawed or miscalculated products are virtually unknown. Similar precision is found in design elements. These tend to the fastidious with careful definitions of line and design fields. Such meticulousness is seen in the small circles of spray done in white reserve silhouetted against the pale blue mists. At times, as is not uncommon with official wares, the classical elegance of Nabeshima ceramics appear to be more calculated than vigorous. The heads of the swells, for instance, are copies of each other, each crest designed with little variation or modification. The color of the underglaze blue and the crowdedness of the design elements indicate a late 18th century date.

CWK

SUGGESTED READINGS:

Cleveland, Richard S. **200 Years of Japanese Porcelain**. St. Louis: City Art Museum of St. Louis, 1970.

Jenyns, Soame. **Japanese Porcelain**. London: Frederick A. Praeger, 1965.

Mikami, Tsugio. **The Art of Japanese Ceramics. The Heibonsha Survey of Japanese Art**. Translated by Ann Herring. 4th ed. Vol. 29. New York and Tokyo: Weatherhill/Heibonsha, 1979.

Munsterberg, Hugo. **The Ceramic Art of Japan: A Handbook for Collectors**. Rutland and Tokyo: Charles E. Tuttle Company, 1964.

Attributed to Tosa Mitsuoki

Japanese (1617-1691)

THE POETESS LADY SAGAMI, 17th century

Album leaf mounted as a hanging scroll: ink and colors on silk

13 1/4 x 10 inches

Calligraphy by Asukai Masaaki (1611-1679)

Museum purchase with funds provided by the Associate Board's 1978 Art Ball, 1978.15

Inscription:

Urami wabi	Remorseful over love turned bitter,
Hosanu sodedani	My sleeves remain wet with grief.
Arumono wo	Still worse than
Koi ni kuchinamu	wasting away in passion
Nakoso oshikere	Is having my name maligned.*

Lady Sagami was a famed, 11th century poetess whose works form part of an anthology of famous Japanese poems first collated by Fujiwara no Kinto (966-1041). This painting is from a group of 100 such illustrated poets, as other leaves from the same album set are known. The isolated posture of Lady Sagami, her elegant robes of brilliant colors, and the dramatic curve of her black hair are characteristic of the *yamato-e* (Japanese painting) style. This term was first used in the 10th century to distinguish paintings that were purely Japanese in nature from others more Chinese in theme and subject matter. Although the painting is unsigned, it shares stylisic and design similarities with works by Tosa Mitsuoki.

The accompanying poem, originally composed by Lady Sagami, is written by Asukai Masaaki on paper decorated with gold leaf. Composed in *waka* form of 31 syllables arranged in five lines of 5, 7, 5, 7, 7 syllables, the poem is an ingenious mixture of both Chinese characters and Japanese phonetic symbols (*kana*). The contrast between the slender, fluid *kana* calligraphy and the more formal, heavier Chinese characters produces an appealing visual effect.

CWK

SUGGESTED READINGS:

Fister, Patricia. **Japanese Women Artists, 1600-1900**. *Lawrence, KS: Spencer Museum of Art, University of Kansas, 1988.*

Link, Howard A., *with an abstract from an essay by Sanna Saks Deutsch.* **The Feminine Image: Women of Japan**, *Honolulu: Honolulu Academy of Arts, 1985.*

Terukazu, Akiyama. **Japanese Painting**. *New York: Rizzoli International Publications, Inc., 1977.*

Wheelwright, Carolyn, **ed. Word in Flower: The Visualization of Classical Literature in Seventeenth-Century Japan**. *New Haven: Yale University Art Gallery, 1989.*

*Translation provided by Dr. James Huffman, Wittenberg University (Springfield, Ohio).

Japan

TALES OF ISE, *mid-17th century*

Three volumes: ink, colors, gold, and silver on paper

9 1/4 x 6 3/4 inches (each page)

Gift in honor of Clarence W. Kelley, Curator of Asian Art, from his many Friends and Colleagues, 1994.18.1-3

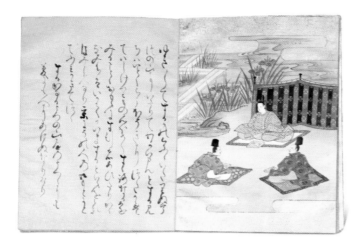

A Japanese classic completed in the 10th century, *Tales of Ise* depicts the life of noblemen and court ladies of the Heian period (794-1185). Based on the activities and adventures of the poet Arihara no Narihira (825-880), *Tales of Ise* consists of more than 100 short stories and poems with classical grace, wit, and sensitivity. For centuries, *Tales of Ise* has served as a handbook to the Japanese and inspired many poets as well.

The set of three volumes in the Art Institute's collection is one of the finest examples of this type, which consists of 48 paintings depicting scenes from *Tales of Ise*. The text is written by a skilled calligrapher on paper decorated with golden foliage motifs. The page illustrated at the upper left is based on the story in Chapter nine that depicts a trip on Tokaido Road. Narihira and his friends left the capital to explore a new life in the East. When they arrived at a river near present-day Aichi Province, they saw the river branched into eight streams, each mounted with a bridge. Not sure which way to go, they dismounted to have their meal. The blooming irises on the swamp inspired them to recite poems on the subject of "A Traveler's Sentiments."

The following poem was composed at the scene, each line beginning with a syllable from the word "iris" (*kakitsubata*):

Karagoromo	I have a beloved wife,
Kitsutsu narenishi	Familiar as the skirt
Tsuma shi areba	Of a well-worn robe,
Harubaru kinuru	And so this distant journeying
Tabi o shi zo omou.	Fills my heart with grief.*

The painting is drawn in Tosa style as seen in the composition and the use of colors. The triangular design for the bridge echoes the decorative style of the 17th century that was also used later by Korin (1658-1716) in his painting, lacquer, and textile designs of bridges and irises. The painting is enriched by the use of brilliant and vivid colors of green, gold, yellow, red, and purple.

This set of *Tales of Ise* is very similar in the style of representation, the use of paper, and the method of binding, to a set of 54 volumes of *Tales of Genji* in the collection of the Chester Beatty Library in Dublin, Ireland. These similarities suggest that the dating of our volumes is of the same period as the mid-17th century date of the Dublin version.

LJ

Suggested Readings:

McCullough, Helen Craig trans. **Tales of Ise: Lyrical Episodes from Tenth-Century Japan**. Stanford, CA: Stanford University Press, 1968.

Rosenfield, John M. **The Courtly Tradition in Japanese Art and Literature: Selections from the Hofer and Hyde Collections**. Cambridge, MA: Fogg Art Museum, 1973.

Ushioda, Yoshiko. **Tales of Japan: Three Centuries of Japanese Painting from the Chester Beatty Library, Dublin**. Alexandria, VA: Art Service International, 1992.

* Helen Craig McCullough, trans. **Tales of Ise: Lyrical Episodes from Tenth-Century Japan**. Stanford, CA: Stanford University, 1969, p. 75.

Japan
Edo period (1615-1868)
***MUSASHI PLAIN**, late 17th - early 18th century*
Pair of six-fold screens: colors and gold on paper
66 1/2 x 24 1/4 inches (each panel)
Museum purchase, 1960.24a-b

The theme of Mount Fuji, Musashi Plain, and the autumnal season has a long tradition in Japanese literature. Musashi Plain lies on the western outskirts of Tokyo. Visible in the distance is Mount Fuji. By the early 10th century, the beauty of this uninterrupted stretch of grasses, the majestic vision of Mount Fuji, and the serenity of autumn was embraced in literary circles as a metaphor for love, the transient nature of life, and the isolation of man. By the end of the 17th century, a distinctive association had developed between classical literature and a type of screen painting known as *byobu-uta* (poems for screens), as seen in this pair of screen paintings.

On the lower screen, a full moon lies low in an expansive blanket of weeds, grasses, and flowers. On the other, Mount Fuji is seen in the distance across the Musashi Plain with its snow-capped peak emerging through the billowing clouds. The triangular form of Mount Fuji with its steep slopes is nicely contrasted with the low, circular form of the moon. In the same manner, the changing nature of the moon is contrasted against the constant qualities of Mount Fuji. A rhythmic wall of the interwoven stalks of green pampas grasses unifies the two screens.

While the screens ostensibly depict Musashi Plain with Mount Fuji in the distance and the silvery moon, they are intended to be more evocative of an emotion, suggestive of a time and place that was more metaphysical and transcendent than a description of a physical reality. The viewer was expected to be familiar with the literary allusions implied in the painting even without a written poem or any inscription.

CWK

SUGGESTED READINGS:

Kelley, Clarence W. "Musashi Plain and The Classical Theme of Mount Fuji, the Moon and Autumn Grasses." **The Dayton Art Institute Bulletin** (December 1985, Vol. 40): 6-10.

Murase, Miyeko. **Masterpieces of Japanese Screen Painting: The American Collection.** New York: George Braziller, 1990.

Wheelwright, Carolyn, ed. **Word in Flower: The Visualization of Classical Literature in Seventeenth Century Japan.** New Haven: Yale University Art Gallery, 1989.

197

Kaiho Yusetsu

(1598-1677) Japanese

CRAFTSMEN AND THEIR STORES, *17th century*

Pair of six-fold screens: ink, colors, and gold on paper

43 x 18 3/4 inches (each panel)

Gift of Mr. Einosuke Yamanouchi, 1938.3-4

Edo, Japan is perhaps best-known for its woodblock prints, popularly called *ukiyo-e*, which means "pictures of the floating world." These prints reflect the everyday life, pleasures, and culture of the Japanese people of the time. Their popularity in the West has tended to overshadow the achievements of *ukiyo-e* painting, also a mirror of the lifestyles of Edo Japan.

With the blooming of craftsmanship in the early Edo period, the depiction of craftsmen at work became highly popular in the 17th century. Illustrated on the six panels on the upper screen are a blacksmith, metal worker, bow maker, fan maker, quiver maker, musical instrument shop, and a sword grinder. The lower screen depicts a paper maker, calligraphic brush store, lacquer store, samurai sword and armor shop, cloth store, and fabric maker. The trades depicted are family-operated ventures with the family quarters attached.

A court painter at Kyoto before moving to Edo, Kaiho Yusetsu is noted primarily for his charming landscapes in the Kano style, in which he was trained in his early years. He also engaged in bird-and-flower paintings and genre scenes as in these screens. The similarity of subject matter and compositional groupings found throughout the craftsmen screens genre, however, suggests a conventional standard which Yusetsu exploited. Few genre screens by Yusetsu are known, and it is uncommon to find a pair such as these that are both signed and marked with Yusetsu's seal.

CWK

SUGGESTED READINGS:

Narazaki, Muneshige. **Masterworks of Ukiyo-e: Early Paintings**. Translated and adapted by Charles A. Pomeroy. Tokyo and Palo Alto: Kodansha International, Ltd., 1967.

Stern, Harold P. **Freer Gallery of Art Fiftieth Anniversary Exhibition, Vol. I: Ukiyo-e Painting**. Washington, D.C.: Smithsonian Institution, 1973.

Till, Barry. **Figure Paintings of the Edo Period (1615-1868) with An Emphasis on Ukiyo-e Painting: The Bunzo Nakanishi Collection**. Victoria, BC: Art Gallery of Greater Victoria, 1987.

Young, Martie W., and Robert J. Smith. **Japanese Painters of the Floating World**. Ithaca, NY: Andrew Dickson White Museum of Art, Cornell University, 1966.

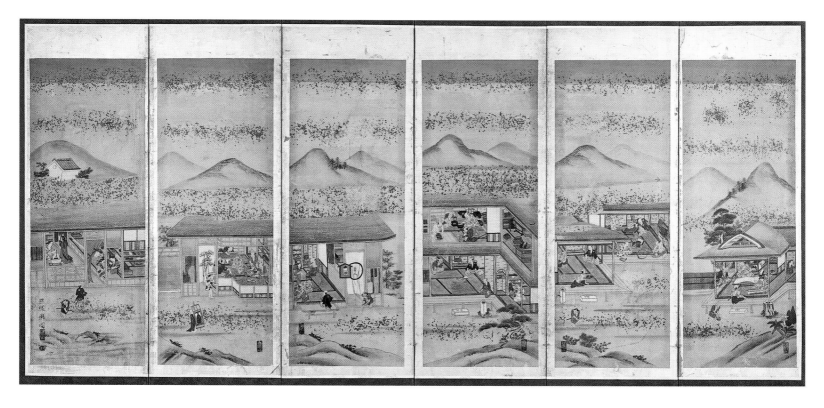

Japan

Edo period (1615-1868)

SCENES IN AND AROUND KYOTO

early 18th century
Four-fold screen: colors and gold on paper
48 x 19 1/4 inches (each panel)
Gift of Mrs. Virginia W. Kettering, 1976.272

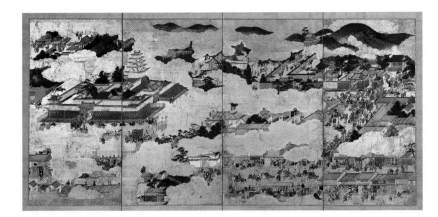

Scenes in and around Kyoto are scenic illustrations of seasonal activities associated with the imperial family and the aristocracy at the imperial capital Kyoto. This type of painting first appeared in the 16th century and was originally commissioned by the nobility and wealthy visitors as their return-home souvenirs. By the Edo period, this type of work was in great demand by the new middle class.

Seen from above in a bird's-eye view, the right screen panel is dominated by the majestic palanquins of the Gion Festival, still celebrated today from July 16 to July 24. It is dedicated to Gozu Tenno, a protector-deity against pestilence and calamity. The festival dates back to 876 when a procession with decorated floats paraded through the streets of Kyoto entreating the gods to intervene against a virulent plague ravaging the city. Participants crowd the streets that are lined with merchants selling their luxury items. The festival brought people and money to the city, increasing the wealth and prestige of the middle class, who underwrote the expensive costs of the floats.

This type of screens could also be propaganda tools in the Shogun's (military ruler) campaign to politically legitimize his rule. Centered on the left two panels is Nijo Castle, built in 1603 as the Kyoto residence of the first Tokugawa Shogun, Ieyasu. The scene likely illustrates the visit of the Emperor Gomizuno-o (reigned 1611-1629) to Nijo Castle in 1626 following its renovations. The imperial procession is few in number and apparently oblivious to the lively Gion celebrations depicted on the right panels. Even the emperor's palanquin is obscured by clouds with only the top and his bearers visible to the small entourage of spectators—a subtle hint of the Shogun's elevated status at the expense of the imperial family.

CWK

SUGGESTED READINGS:

Chapin, Helen B. "The Gion Shrine and the Gion Festival." *Journal of the American Oriental Society* (September 1934, Vol. 54, No. 3): 282-289.

Grilli, Elise. *The Art of the Japanese Screen*. New York and Tokyo: Walker/Weatherhill, 1970.

Jacobson, Robert D. *The Art of Japanese Screen Painting: Selections from the Minneapolis Institute of Arts*. Minneapolis: The Minneapolis Institute of Arts, 1985.

Murase, Miyeko. *Masterpieces of Japanese Screen Painting: The American Collections*. New York: George Braziller, 1990.

Okada Koku (Beisanjin)
(1744-1820) Japanese
LANDSCAPE, *18th-19th century*
Hanging scroll: ink on silk
52 x 6 1/4 inches
Museum purchase with funds provided by the Honorable Jefferson Patterson, 1969.47

Inscription:
> With white mists following its winding banks,
> A sea of dew, the spirit-river flows.
> The clouds descend until one can grasp them with his hands;
> Incantations echo from the cliffs above.

Artist's Seals: "Den Koku no in, Shigen."*

One of the leading artists of the Osaka school was Okada Koku, otherwise known as Beisanjin. Although he made his living as a rice merchant, at an early age he had studied Chinese literature and history and served the Lord of Tsu as a Confucian scholar. He studied painting later in life and all of his paintings date from his latter years. Among the Chinese artists he admired was Mi Fu (1051-1107), a Song dynasty *literati* painter, whose name Mi in Japanese is pronounced "bei," and to which Okada's pseudonym alludes.

Beisanjin belongs to the Nanga School of painting, essentially the Japanese version of the Chinese *literati* or scholarly-gentleman school of painting. The repeated, horizontal brush strokes seen in the distant trees, the whimsically domed mountain peaks, and the fungus-shaped clouds all point to Chinese conventions. Yet Beisanjin has exploited these elements in the narrow format of this work. The intensely dense lower portion with its strong brush strokes, dark applications of ink, and exacting details is a remarkable contrast to the upper section. Here, the hilltops are painted in lighter washes and a repeated series of rough lines are accented only with dark peaks. The low-hanging clouds painted as a negative space opens the composition even more, and the effect is one of soaring heights dwarfing the babbling brook and the cottage below.

CWK

SUGGESTED READINGS:

Addiss, Stephen. **Zenga and Nanga: Paintings by Japanese Monks and Scholars: Selections from the Kurt and Millie Gitter Collection**. *New Orleans: New Orleans Museum of Art, 1976.*

Cahill, James. **Scholar Painters of Japan: The Nanga School**. *New York: New York Graphic Society, 1972.*

Cahill, James. "Three Japanese Paintings." **The Dayton Art Institute Bulletin** *(September 1970, Vol. 29, No. 1): 6.*

Graham, Patricia J. "Lifestyles of Scholar-Painters in Edo Japan." **The Bulletin of The Cleveland Museum of Art** *(September 1990, Vol. 77, No. 7): 262-283.*

Yonezawa, Yoshiho, and Chu Yoshizawa. "Japanese Painting in the Literati Style. Translated and adapted by Betty Iverson Monroe. **The Heibonsha Survey of Japanese Art**, Vol. 23. New York and Tokyo: Weatherhill/Heibonsha, 1974.*

Translations of the seals provided by Fumiko Togasaki, Wittenberg University (Springfield, Ohio).

Bunrin Shiokawa

(1808-1877) Japanese

NANIWA BAY IN SNOW, ARASHIYAMA UNDER A SUMMER'S MOON, AND CHERRY BLOSSOMS AT ASUKAYAMA, *19th century*

Triptych: hanging scrolls; ink, colors and gold washes on silk

43 3/8 x 13 15/16 inches (each)

Museum purchase with funds provided by the 1986 Associate Board, 1986.24.1-3

Signature: "Bunrin"

Artist's Seals: "Shio Bunrin" and "Shion"

The subjects of snow, moon, and flowers depicted in this triptych have a tradition dating back to the 18th century. Most commonly seen in works of the Maruyama-Shijo school, scenes of famous places and specific sites are metaphors for the beauty of Japan.

The old name for Osaka is Naniwa, which means "Rapid Waves." In this Naniwa painting, a fishing boat lies at anchor in the quiet of a snow-covered winter's day, gently tossed by nearly imperceptible "rapid waves."

Arashiyama, famous for its scenic beauty, is situated on the outskirts of Kyoto. Along the bottom of the hill flows the Omi River, seen here along the forefront of the scroll. Arashiyama is especially acclaimed for its majestic pines and maple and cherry trees that were first planted there by imperial order in the 13th century. Illuminated by the summer's moon with enshrouding mists, the painting is an evocation of quiet serenity.

In the early 18th century, Asukayama Park in Edo, present-day Tokyo, was planted with cherry trees under the auspices of the eighth Tokugawa Shogun. The park is one of the oldest flower resorts in the city, famous for its single-petaled cherry blossoms, seen here in full bloom. It is a popular picnic site even today.

Bunrin Shiokawa was an important Shijo School painter in Kyoto during the late Edo and the early Meiji periods. He specialized in landscape painting of the Shijo School, which was influenced by both Nanga School painting in Chinese *literati* tradition, and Western-style painting, which became increasingly popular from the early 19th century through the Meiji period (1868-1912) when Japan opened its doors to the West. The triptych in the Art Institute's collection demonstrates Bunrin's distinguished style in his use of linear technique, broad brush washes, and golden highlights. A sense of a real space and romantic warmth evoked in his painting mark the Shijo-style painting of the late Edo and the early Meiji periods.

CWK

SUGGESTED READINGS:

Cunningham, Louise. **The Spirit of Place: Japanese Paintings and Prints of the Sixteenth through Nineteenth Century**. New Haven: Yale University Art Gallery, 1984.

Hillier, Jack. **The Uninhibited Brush: Japanese Art in the Shijo Style**. London: Hugh M. Moss, Ltd., 1974.

Okyo and the Maruyama-Shijo School of Japanese Painting. St. Louis: The St. Louis Art Museum and Seattle Art Museum, 1980.

Myanmar (Burma)
VOTIVE TABLET, *around 12th century*
Molded clay
8 1/2 x 5 1/2 inches
Gift of Miss Louise Mellinger, 1955.54

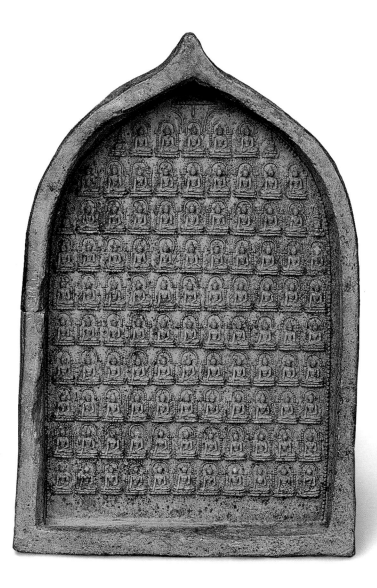

This deeply recessed, rimmed plaque in the form of a pointed *stele* contains 100 identical images of the Buddha. The tablet depicts the Buddha-to-be seated beneath the *bodhi* tree after his defeat of the evil forces of Mara. All the Buddhas sit on double-lotus pedestals within beaded and arched niches. The uppermost and third row of Buddhas are flanked by *stupas* or burial mounds. The central Buddha at the pinnacle is shaded by a parasol and sprays of leaves from the *bodhi* tree, beneath which this episode of the Buddha's life occurred. Small beads line the perimeter of the recessed tablet, except along the bottom where an area has been left blank for an inscription. Found throughout the Buddhist world, these votive tablets were devotional memorabilia, souvenirs usually obtained at pilgrimage sites. Easily transportable, they assisted in spreading the Law of the Buddha throughout Southeast Asia.

The shape of this votive plaque is typical of those of early Pagán. The "hundred Buddhas" imagery, a visual expression of the universal and omnipresent nature of the Buddha and his law, is closely related to those associated with King Alaungsithu of Pagán whose royal title, Sri Tribhuvanadityapavara, is found inscribed on many of these plaques. The *stele*-shaped design, however, is also similar to that found in late Pala period stone *stelae* and may indicate an Indian influence.

CWK

SUGGESTED READINGS:

Aung-Thwin, Michael. **Pagán: The Origins of Modern Burma**. Honolulu: University of Hawaii Press, 1985.

Huntington, Susan L. and John C. Huntington. **Leaves from the Bodhi Tree: The Art of Pala India (8th-12th centuries) and Its International Legacy**. Dayton: OH: The Dayton Art Institute, 1989.

Luce, Gordon H. "Old Burma-Early Pagán," **Artibus Asiae Supplementum 25**, 3 vols. Locut Valley, NY: J.J. Augustin, 1969-70.

Thailand

PLATE, *14th century*

Kalong ware: porcellaneous stoneware with painted decoration

H: 1 3/4 inches; Dia: 8 5/8 inches

Museum purchase with funds provided by an anonymous donor, 1989.5

L ocated atop a mountain ridge in northern Thailand is the unassuming village of Kalong, once a prosperous community of ceramic production. The clay at Kalong is extremely fine. During their peak, the kilns produced well-potted, high-fired stonewares in a wide variety of shapes including dishes, jars, oil lamps, bowls, and toys. The kilns were not on any major trade route and most Kalong wares were made for the local market.

The largest group of Kalong ceramics is black-and-white decorated ware, especially the finely potted, thin plates such as this one in the Art Institute's collection. The bold underglaze designs are characteristically energetic and assured, and were applied spontaneously by brush with no preliminary sketch design. Distinctive to the wares are its floral designs that, at times, are so highly stylized that they are mistaken as images of birds in flight. Other decorative styles include incised decorations of combed lines, floral medallions, and radiating petals.

CWK

Suggested Readings:

Asian Art Museum of San Francisco. **Thai Ceramics; The James and Elaine Connell Collection**. Kuala Lumpur, Oxford, Singapore, and New York: Oxford University Press, 1993.

Brown, Roxanna M. **The Ceramics of South-East Asia: Their Dating and Identification**. 2d ed. Singapore, Oxford, and New York: Oxford University Press, 1988.

Kelley, Clarence W. "Recent Acquisition: Kalong-ware Plate in The Dayton Art Institute," **Orientations** (March 1990, Vol. 21, No. 3): 54-55.

Shaw, J.C. **Introducing Thai Ceramics; Also Burmese and Khmer**. 2d ed. Bangkok: J.C. Shaw, 1988.

Annam (Vietnam)
JARLET, *15th century*
Stoneware with underglaze blue decoration
H: 3 inches
Gift of Mrs. Virginia W. Kettering, 1978.116

This small jar has been given a squarish character by the use of eight alternating broad and narrow facets and a flat, circular shoulder. The underglaze blue decorations on the larger panels are small sprays from a long-leafed plant. The alternating narrower panels all have the same design of a triple-lined, zigzag motif with scattered dots. On the shoulder surrounding the wide mouth with its short, slightly flaring neck and rolled lip, is a double band of lotus leaves. The pale blue color is likely derived from imported Near Eastern cobalt. The underside is unglazed.

Jarlets, such as this sample, were used for a variety of purposes, including oil bottles and condiment containers. Made for export to Philippine, Indonesian, Thai, and Near Eastern markets, the shape and design reflect Chinese influence and Annamese innovation. This vessel was excavated on the island of Luzon in the Philippines.

CWK

Suggested Readings:

Brown, Roxanna M. **The Ceramics of South-East Asia: Their Dating and Identification**. *2d ed. Singapore, Oxford, and New York: Oxford University Press, 1988.*

Brown, Roxanna M. ed. **Guangdong Ceramics from Butuan and other Philippine Sites**. *Manila: The Oriental Ceramic Society of the Philippines, 1989.*

FraschÈ, Dean F. **Southeast Asian Ceramics: Ninth through Seventeenth Centuries**. *New York: The Asia Society, 1976.*

Spinks, Charles Nelson. "Siam and the Pottery Trade of Asia." **Journal of the Siam Society** *(August 1956, Vol. 44, No. 2): 61-111.*

Annam (Vietnam)

WATER DROPPER IN THE FORM OF TWO DUCKS, *early 16th century*

Stoneware with underglaze blue decoration

H: 3 3/4 inches

Gift of Mrs. Virginia W. Kettering, 1978.125

Vessels of this shape have been identified as wine vessels, but this one was probably used as a water dropper at a scholar's desk. There is a spout in the open beak of one of the ducks that is unobtrusive to the design of the vessel. The whimsical design, plastic qualities of the ducks, and the well-defined and freely drawn markings in underglaze blue hint of Chinese antecedents and influences that permeated Southeast Asia, especially along the coastal areas. Today this area is Vietnam, but it was known as Annam or "Pacified South," to the Chinese overlords of the Ming dynasty (1368-1644).

As ducks mate for life, the depiction of pairs is often understood as a measure of matrimonial bliss, and by extension abundant progeny and prosperity.

CWK

Suggested Readings:

Brown, Roxanna M. **The Ceramics of South-East Asia: Their Dating and Identification.** 2d ed. Singapore, Oxford, and New York: Oxford University Press, 1988.

Frasché, Dean F. **Southeast Asian Ceramics: Ninth through Seventeenth Centuries.** New York: The Asia Society, 1976.

Young, Carol M., Marie-France Dupoizat, and Elizabeth W. Lane, eds. **Vietnamese Ceramics.** Singapore: Southeast Asian Ceramic Society, 1982.

Annam (Vietnam)

PLATE, *15th - 16th century*
Stoneware with iron red and green overglaze decorations
H: 3 inches; Dia: 13 1/2 inches
Gift of Mrs. Virginia W. Kettering, 1976.209

Large portions of the northern regions of Vietnam were once controlled by China during the Han dynasty (206 B.C.-A.D. 220). Through centuries of intermediate and often close contacts, this area of Southeast Asia has strong cultural and economic affinities to China. The semblances are especially strong in the ceramic wares of what is known as Annam, the Chinese term meaning "Pacified South," for today's Vietnam.

A wide range of stoneware, including large plates like this, were produced in northern Vietnam during the 14th through 17th centuries. The fine crackle and red and green overglaze enamel decoration are typical of these wares. On the steeply sloping sides of the vessel are four panels with floral pattern designs, separated by large, red dots outlined in green among a field of small, red, budlike designs. Characteristic of the motifs of the period is the peony sprig in the well, ringed by a thin, double band reminiscent of Chinese designs from the Yuan and early Ming dynasties from the 14th through the 15th centuries.

The peony motifs seen in this plate have deteriorated slightly because Annamese overglazes were usually applied in thin layers. In addition, due to their chemical properties, they tend to erode easily.

CWK

SUGGESTED READINGS:

Brown, Roxanna M. **The Ceramics of South-East Asia: Their Dating and Identification**. 2d ed.. Singapore, Oxford, and New York: Oxford University Press, 1988.

FraschÈ, Dean F. **Southeast Asian Ceramics: Ninth through Seventeenth Centuries**. New York: The Asia Society, 1976.

Iraq

Abbasid period (750-1258)

DISH WITH DESIGN OF BIRDS AND ANIMALS, *9th - 10th century*

Earthenware in luster painting in yellow on white ground

H: 2 1/4 inches; Dia: 9 1/4 inches

Museum purchased with funds provided by the Associate Board's 1968 Art Ball, 1968.74

The luster painting evident in this bowl was a technique first used on glass by Egyptians as early as the 4th or 5th centuries, and then adapted to ceramics by Islamic potters of the 9th century. In this technique, compounds of silver and copper were applied to a glazed vessel, which was then fired a second time to achieve a glossy surface resembling more expensive copper vessels. The early luster pottery was rare and seems to have been made as wine vessels for the Abbasid court in the capital Baghdad and Samarra, 100 miles north of Baghdad.

Decorated with bold silhouettes of animal forms against a background of tiny arabesques, the bowl appears dramatic and mysterious. A pictorial representation with animal images, similar to those seen in this bowl, is found in a wall painting in the residential complex in Samarra, a city built in the first part of the 9th century. It is assumed that this painting, which depicts a human figure and a dog fighting with a goat-like animal, was derived from some unknown ancient legend. The similarity between the painting and this bowl may suggest that figurative representations applied are not simply decorative, but address a mythical or even social message.

A comparison to an early illustration suggests that the bowl, now heavily restored, most likely is the same bowl excavated early in this century in the ancient city of Rayy, present-day Rhages, Iraq. Previously in the collection of Charles Vignier, this bowl was first documented by Maurice Pezard in 1920 and presented in 1940 at the Iranian Institute, New York, and at the Johns Hopkins University (Baltimore, Maryland).

LJ

Suggested Readings:

Ackerman, Phyllis. **Guide to the Exhibition of Persian Art**. New York: The Iranian Institute, 1940.

Atil, Esin. **Islamic Art Patronage: Treasures from Kuwait**. New York: Rizzoli International Publications, Inc., 1990.

Caiger-Smith, Alan. **Lustre Pottery: Technique, Tradition and Innovation in Islam and the Western World**. London: Faber & Faber, 1985.

Pezard, Maurice. **La Ceramique Archaique de l'Islam et ses Origines**. Paris: Editions Ernest Leroux, 1920.

Iran

BOWL WITH DESIGN OF HUMAN FIGURE, 12th - 13th century

Earthenware with polychrome slip painting
H: 4 1/4 inches; Dia: 8 7/8 inches
Museum purchase with funds provided by the Honorable Jefferson Patterson, 1968.65

Islamic art is distinguished by its use of overall surface decoration and the use of stylized foliated motifs, called arabesques, as the background. This bowl has a deep body decorated with foliated Arabic inscriptions that serve as background for images of birds, deer, and a cross-legged figure, probably a ruler, conveying the message of good fortune. The exterior of the bowl is decorated with simple leaf motifs, a strong contrast to the sophisticated interior design.

Decorated by the slip-painting technique, the bowl was first painted with polychrome slips, water-based mixtures of pigment and clay, and then covered with a clear glaze to provide a smooth surface and also protect the polychrome painting from flaking. The slip-painting pottery was produced mostly in Nishapur and Samarkand, two of the largest cities in northeastern Islam in the 10th century.

The origin of the slip-painting technique is unclear. One explanation suggests that it was influenced by Chinese Changsha ware, characterized by its distinctive underglaze painting, produced in the Changsha area in central China during the 9th century and exported in large scale to Islamic countries. An opposing theory suggests that Changsha ware was influenced by Islamic pottery. The geographic sites may support the connection between the ceramic production of Islam and that of China. Both Nishapur and Samarkand, where numerous vessels and shards were discovered, were located at the intersections that link Islam to China. Further archaeological discovery and research related to these two types of wares will certainly shed new light on this subject.

LJ

SUGGESTED READINGS:

Atil, Esin. **Ceramics from the World of Islam**. *Washington, D.C.: Freer Gallery of Art, 1973.*

Changsha Ceramics: featuring gifts from Dr. and Mrs. Wally Zollman and Keith Uhl Clary. *Indianapolis: Indianapolis Museum of Art, 1993.*

Fehervari, Geza. "Islamic Pottery in the Tareq Rajab Museum, Kuwait." **Arts of Asia 6** *(1994): no pp.*

Lam, Timothy S.Y. **Tang Ceramics–Changsha Kilns**. *Hong Kong: Lammett Arts, 1990.*

Selected
Works from
EUROPEAN ART
The Dayton Art
Institute Permanent
Collection

Italian (Venetian)

MADONNA AND CHILD WITH FOUR EVANGELISTS, mid-14th century

Tempera and gold leaf on wood panel

14 1/2 x 11 inches

Anonymous gift, 1949.30

SUGGESTED READING:

White, John. **Art and Architecture in Italy, 1250-1400.** 3d ed. New Haven: Yale University Press, 1993.

At its center, this work depicts a Madonna with the Christ Child in her arms. Positioned within the large, central medallion, the Madonna and Child are surrounded by representations of the four evangelists enframed in smaller medallions. The evangelists, whose names are inscribed in the gold, hold copies of their gospels. From right to left, they are Saints John and Mark above and Luke and Matthew below. In the central medallion, the letters MR (an abbreviation of *mater*, Latin for mother) and QV (for the Greek *Theos* or God) declares the holy relationship between the Madonna and Child.

In addition to the spatial separation from the evangelists, the Madonna and Child are further removed by their physical and emotional concentration upon each other. Their eyes meet with unalterable focus, and their closeness is further stressed by the intersection of their halos and the actions of their hands. The Madonna's hands firmly hold and respectfully touch the Child, as he in turn raises a hand to bless his mother. A connection more symbolic than physical exists between the evangelists and the central pair by virtue of the open gospel books that, in their entirety, chronicle the life and death of Christ. The eventual crucifixion of Christ is foreshadowed by the cruciform pattern of the infant's halo; it is also anticipated in the arrangement of the incised vegetal motifs that spread outward from the central medallion in a cruciform pattern.

This work is painted on wood with tempera pigments and gold leaf. In general, a medieval artist would apply several thin layers of plaster to the wood as a hard surface on which to paint. Using a sharp instrument and in some cases a compass, the artist would inscribe lines into the plaster to delineate areas to be painted and those to receive gold leaf. For the latter, the artist would also apply layers of red clay as a soft, tacky surface to receive the thin sheets of gold. After painting the figures, the artist would punch and incise halos and other areas of the gold where ornamentation was desired. In this *Madonna and Child*, incision lines are evident around the figures and in the demarcations of the halos. A delicate ornamentation of the gold characterizes the entire surface, and where the gold has worn away, the underlying clay layer is exposed. Hinge marks along the right side of the panel suggest that it once formed part of a *diptych*. Such small, two-paneled objects were commonly produced by late medieval painters as private devotional works.

Despite slight abrasion to the gilding and the detachment of its companion panel, the *Madonna and Child with Four Evangelists* is an excellently preserved example of 14th century Venetian painting. Like many late medieval paintings produced in Venice, a strong Byzantine influence is evident in the richly ornamented surface, stylized abstraction of anatomy, and crisp linearity of the drapery folds.

RJC

Giovanni di Francesco Toscani
(1370-1430) Italian

MADONNA OF HUMILITY, *around 1410*

Tempera and gold leaf on wood panel
26 3/4 x 18 1/4 inches
Gift of Mr. and Mrs. Elton F. MacDonald, 1957.142

Like the Venetian *Madonna and Child with Four Evangelists*, Giovanni di Francesco Toscani's *Madonna of Humility* is painted on wood with tempera pigments and gold leaf. Toscani's *Madonna* is seated on a pillow with the Christ Child in her arms. From the inclination of the Madonna's head, the direction of her glance, and the action of her hands, it is clear that she devotes absolute psychological and physical attention to her son. As for Christ, he reaches for his mother's breast and points toward his mouth, as he looks out of the picture in address to the ostensible worshipper.

Toscani's *Madonna of Humility* is a typical example of late Gothic painting in Florence. Compared to the linear crispness and angularity of the Venetian *Madonna and Child with Four Evangelists*, this painting is characterized by a gentle, even playful, fluidity of line. This is particularly noticeable in the looping folds of the pinkish-orange cloth and in the near mimicking of these folds in Christ's diaphanous skirt.

Although the gilded background eliminates any sense of three-dimensional space and focuses attention on the outlines of forms, the painter endeavored to suggest the figures' physicality. For example, the Madonna weights down the pillow on which she sits, and her twisting torso and protruding knees suggest the presence of a living form with potential for movement. The Christ Child is no less believable as a representation of a physical being. Together, the Madonna and Child approximate the appearance of a real woman and baby. Only the almond-shaped eyes of the two figures and the unnaturally long fingers of the Madonna's hands recall the anatomical abstractions of an earlier, more abstract tradition.

This Madonna and Child could have served as a small altarpiece for a church, but it is more probable that it functioned as a private devotional object. The accessibility of the holy figures was the main emphasis of the *Madonna of Humility* as a devotional subject; indeed, Christ's outward gaze invites the worshipper to approach. Derived from narrative scenes such as the Nativity, this subject seems to have originated in Sienese art in the early 14th century. From Siena, Italy, the popularity of the *Madonna of Humility* spread to other sites in Italy, Spain, France, and Germany.

RJC

Suggested Readings:

Cole, Bruce. **Masaccio and the Art of Early Renaissance Florence**. Bloomington: The University of Indiana Press, 1980.

Meiss, Millard. **Painting in Florence and Siena after the Black Death**. Princeton: The University of Princeton Press, 1951.

German (Middle Rhennish)
Early 15th century

PIETÀ, *around 1430*
Carved alabaster
H: 12 7/8 inches
Museum purchase with funds provided by the Associate Board's 1970 Art Ball, 1969.33

The relatively small scale and contemplative nature of this carved alabaster *Pietà* point to its intended use as an object of private devotion. Made in the first half of the 15th century and probably in the region of the Middle Rhine, this sculpture depicts the Virgin Mary holding the dead Christ, her son, following the Crucifixion. Although there is no biblical source for the *Pietà*, its popularity as a theme for religious devotion increased greatly during the 14th and 15th centuries. Some religious historians believe the theme of the *Pietà* grew out of depictions of the Virgin holding the infant Christ Child on her lap, foreseeing his death as a young man. One of the most unusual features of this particularly fine sculpture is Christ's crossed hands and feet, a reference to his death and preparation for his entombment.

Yet unlike earlier Medieval versions of the same theme, this work has no overtly gory reminders of Christ's passion and death. Rather, the sculpture embodies sentiments of intense human loss and grief coupled with a quiet humility. No longer evident are the Gothic conventions of rigid angularity and disproportionate scale. Both figures are carved with a high degree of naturalism and clothed with draperies that reveal and enhance the underlying musculature of the bodies rather than obscuring it. Along with the sensitive carving, the alabaster shows minute traces of four pigments which would have been used to paint this work: gold along Christ's loincloth, blue and red on the Virgin's cloak, and green on the base.

DHV

SUGGESTED READINGS:

van Nuis Cahill, Jane. "Two Franco-Flemish Sculptures." **The Dayton Art Institute Bulletin** *(March 1971, Vol. 29): 2-7.*

Salvini, Roberto. **Medieval Sculpture**. *Greenwich, CT: New York Graphic Society, 1969.*

Master of Marradi

Italian

THE STORY OF JUDITH AND HOLOFERNES, 15th century

Tempera on wood panel

15 3/4 x 58 1/2 inches

Museum purchase with funds provided by Mr. and Mrs. Ralf Kircher, 1964.10

This panel is the earlier of two paintings in the Art Institute's collection that depicts the subject of Judith and Holofernes. Compared to the psychological concentration and pictorial economy of the Art Institute's Baroque example by Carlo Saraceni, this Renaissance work is characterized by a less analytical approach to mood and a more discursive telling of the biblical story. The story comes from the apocryphal Book of Judith in the Old Testament. The Jewish town of Bethulia was under siege by the Assyrian army and its general, Holofernes. When the residents were at the brink of capitulation, a beautiful widow, Judith devised a scheme for their deliverance. Dressing in her finest clothes, Judith left Bethulia with her maid and entered the Assyrian camp as an ostensible deserter. Holofernes found her a welcome addition to his camp, as much for her beauty as for her veiled promise to assist in the defeat of the Jews. After a banquet, at which Holofernes became drunk, the general lured the beautiful widow into his tent. He quickly fell asleep, however, and Judith seized the opportunity to cut off his head with his own sword. Together with her maid, who stuffed Holofernes' head into a bag, Judith stole back to Bethulia. Once apprised of Judith's heroic act, the Bethulian soldiers charged from the city and defeated the Assyrian army.

With Bethulia in the distance, Holofernes' camp to the right, and the climactic battle to the left, this panel provides a summary of the major localities and moments of the Judith story. The story proceeds from right to left, foreground to background, as Judith decapitates Holofernes, flees with her maid, and enters the city in the distance. In the background to the left, the Bethulian soldiers emerge from the city and advance to engage the Assyrian army. This "comic strip" manner of narration is typical of Florentine 15th century painting. Also typical are the balletic figures, their representation in contemporary dress, and the depiction of Bethulia as a walled, Italian town. The town actually resembles Florence, a city that often regarded the biblical Judith as a protector figure.

Although this work may originally have functioned as an independent painting, it is more likely that it formed one side of a decorated *cassone* (chest). In the 15th century, a pair of *cassoni* was traditionally given to brides. They were often adorned with scenes depicting the deeds of virtuous women from classical history and mythology, the Bible, or medieval literature; the story of Judith's heroic deliverance of Bethulia is a typical example. While the primary motivation of this practice was to enhance the aesthetic appeal of these chests, there must also have been an instructional aim in furnishing the domestic environment with representations of virtuous conduct. In later centuries, *cassoni* were often dismantled and their various panels sold separately on the art market. Such is probably the origin of this work as an independent painting.

RJC

SUGGESTED READING:

Thornton, Peter. *The Italian Renaissance Interior, 1400-1600.* New York: Harry N. Abrams, Inc., 1991.

Attributed to Cristoforo Solari

(active 1489-1520) Italian

THE DEAD CHRIST, *around 1500*

Carved marble

H: 27 inches

Museum purchase with funds provided by the Associate Board's 1971 Art Ball and the Blakeney Endowment, 1970.29

Devotional works, both paintings and sculptures such as this fragmentary sculpture of *The Dead Christ*, played an important part in the decoration of churches, cathedrals, and chapels throughout Medieval and Renaissance Europe. Here, the crucified Christ, with bleeding wound at his side, is shown frontally, his head bowed and eyes almost closed in death. Attendant angels, now missing, in all probability would have supported his arms. That this high-relief sculpture is best seen from beneath suggests it was originally placed above eye level, requiring the faithful to raise one's eyes to view it. It may, therefore, have graced an altar or tomb or have been placed over a doorway.

The identity of the sculptor of this unsigned and undocumented work is not entirely certain. One sculptor has been suggested, the Milanese Cristoforo Solari, who worked in the northern Italian cities of Venice, Padua, and Milan, where he died in 1527. Architect and sculptor to the Milanese duke Lodovico il Moro in the 1490s, Solari was commissioned to produce several important works following his return from Venice and Pavia. These include the carved marble tombs of Lodovico il Moro and his wife, Beatrice d'Este (in the Carthusian Monastery at Pavia), marble statues of Adam and Eve placed on the facade of the Duomo of Milan, and a marble Christ at the Column inside the same cathedral. Each of these works bears similarities to the Art Institute sculpture, including many qualities that are characteristic of Lombard art—a softened classicism, a subtle elegance, and a strong interest in patterning—very unlike the robust art of Florence. Especially notable in this sculpture is the sensitively carved face of Christ, the handsome carving of the torso, details such as the beard, hair, and parted lips, and the overall excellent state of preservation.

DHV

Suggested Readings:

Leonardo & Venice. *Exhibition catalogue, Palazzo Grassi. Milan: Gruppo Editoriale Fabbri, Bompiani, Sonzogno, 1992.*

van Huis Cahill, Jane. "A Lombard Sculpture of about 1500." **The Dayton Art Institute Bulletin** *(November 1971, Vol. 30): 2-5.*

Valentiner, Wilhelm R. "A Madonna by Cristoforo Solari." **Bulletin of the Detroit Institute of Arts** *(December 1941, Vol. XXI, No. 3): 18-20.*

Pier Francesco Bissolo

Italian (active 1492-1554)

THE HOLY FAMILY WITH A DONOR IN A LANDSCAPE, *early 1520s*

Oil on wood panel

Signed lower right: Franciscus Bisolus

3 11/2 x 39 3/4 inches

Museum purchase with funds provided by the John Berry Family, the James F. Dicke Family, and the Deaccessioned Works of Art Fund, 1998.41

Local tradition holds that Pier Francesco Bissolo was born in Treviso, a town located to the northwest of Venice. He is documented in Venice in 1492 when he was employed as a gilder. Later as a student of painting, he rose among the ranks to become one of the better pupils of Giovanni Bellini, the greatest master of the High Renaissance in Venice. Bellini exerted a great force upon Bissolo's generation of painters. By the 1520s, Bissolo had skillfully assimilated many lessons from Bellini, but his work also shows the further influence of Palma Vecchio, another respected Venetian painter. This painting, probably dating to this period, demonstrates Bissolo's soft and sensitive style filtered through the lessons learned from his teachers.

Painted for an as-yet unidentified donor, kneeling with hands folded in adoration in front of the Madonna and Child, this work is characteristic of the Italian High Renaissance in its careful realism, its harmony of composition and color, and in its attention to real human emotion. Mary's poignant, almost apprehensive gaze at her son, the infant Jesus, seems to foreshadow her later inconsolable grief at Christ's Crucifixion. The Christ Child, as the literal focal point of this work, seems alert and confident as if to reassure his mother. Joseph, the ever-dutiful husband, stands respectfully to the right ready to assist in whatever way possible. The fact that the Holy Family is depicted in the out-of-doors would seem to indicate the popular story of the "Rest of the Flight into Egypt." The cool-blue mountainous landscape in the background is characteristic of northern Italy and helps to bring this religious moment into the concrete reality and "present" of the 16th century.

The creation of religious pictures such as this during the Renaissance was an important livelihood for many painters, who often apprenticed to a given master or succession of mentors. Bissolo's reputation grew during the 1520s and 1530s, and he received commissions from the Bishop of Padua and an important printer and canon of the cathedral of Treviso. Although his style evolved as evidence of his awareness of the work of younger contemporaries, essentially Bissolo remained true to the general form and demeanor of Giovanni Bellini.

DHV

Suggested Readings:

Berenson, Bernard. **Italian Pictures of the Renaissance: Venetian School.** Vol.1, The Phaidon Press, 1957.

Crowe, J.A. and G.B. Cavalcaselle. **A History of Painting in North Italy.** London:1871.

217

Attributed to the Támara Master

Spanish

THE LAMENTATION OVER THE DEAD CHRIST, *around 1520*

Oil on wood panel

50 1/2 x 45 3/4 inches

Gift of Dr. and Mrs. Hans Schaeffer, 1965.109

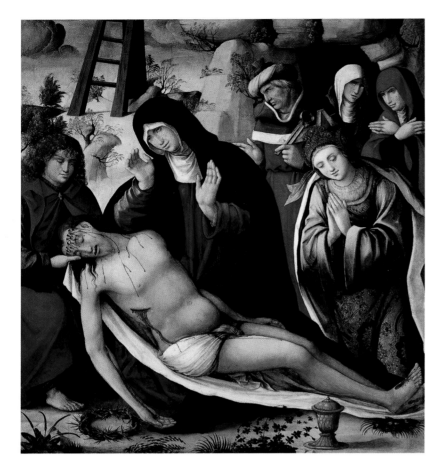

Although there exists a number of uncertainties about the authorship and provenance of this painting, the emotional impact of the grieving Virgin Mary over her crucified son points to an artist of considerable talent. Traditionally considered to have come from the 13th century Church of St. Michel (San Miguel) of Támara in the province of Palencia, Spain, this panel painting would probably have been part of the *predella* (paintings beneath the main painting) of an altar. The anonymous artist's amazing sensitivity to individual expression and emotion are evident in the outward swoon of the Virgin Mary, the inwardly focused contemplation and prayer of Sts. John, holding Christ's bloody head, and Mary Magdalen as she prepares to anoint the holy body with unguent from the pyxis near Christ's feet.

Religious imagery during the Middle Ages often dwelt on the terrible suffering of Christ, and images such as this—with its horrific wounds issuing blood—point not to Christ's glorious Resurrection and establishment of the Church but rather to his passion, suffering, and death—grim reminders to the faithful of the hardship of life and the final suffering that awaited many. Medieval artists, therefore, exaggerated such important aspects of these images, thereby calling the viewer's attention to the principle message to be conveyed.

By the 16th century, however, and with the advent of the Italian Renaissance, artists working in the service of the Roman Catholic Church began to demonstrate a greater interest in the reality of the human figure. Although this work remains linked to the Gothic tradition of Flemish painters working in Spain—especially evident in the stylized landscape, still-life elements, and "frozen" quality of the individual figures—one senses the beginnings of new breath of life in the figure of Christ and in the individuality of human emotion embodied by these figures.

DHV

SUGGESTED READING:

Shrader, J.L. *The Waning Middle Ages*. Exhibition catalogue. Lawrence, KS: The University of Kansas Museum of Art, 1969.

Giovanni-Battista Franco
(around 1510-1561) Italian
NOLI ME TANGERE, *around 1537*
Oil on wood panel
67 1/2 x 52 1/2 inches
Museum purchase with funds provided by Mr. Robert Badenhop, 1980.11

SUGGESTED READINGS:

Sobotik, Kent. "Michelangelo's Lost 'Noli Me Tangere.'" **The Dayton Art Instiiute Bulletin** *(XXXVIII, 1982): 5-8.*

Wallace, William E. "Il 'Noli Me Tangere' di Michelangelo: tra sacro e profano." **Arte Cristiana** *(LXXVI, 1988): 443-450.*

According to the Gospel of John, Mary Magdalen weeps beside Christ's empty tomb after the moment of Resurrection. When the risen Christ appears, the Magdalen first mistakes him for a gardener who may have knowledge of the whereabouts of Christ's body. But soon she recognizes the man as Christ himself and makes a joyous attempt to embrace him. Christ deflects this advance with the instruction that Mary Magdalen is not to touch him since he has not yet ascended to heaven.

This painting is entitled *Noli Me Tangere*, which corresponds to the words of Christ meaning "touch me not" that are recorded in the Latin Bible. While Christ holds a hoe under his left arm, suggestive of the gardener's guise, the focus of the painting is clearly on the awkward meeting of these biblical characters. Characterized by contrary and almost balletic movements of advance and retreat, of joy and reluctance, the engaging drama between these two perfumed and powdery figures takes place on a shallow, natural stage of equal theatricality. This stage is defined by a mountainous outcrop, a loosely rendered landscape, and a hill town in the distance, painted in muted earth tones that provide neutral and natural contrast to the coloristic brilliance of the robes worn by the protagonists. A stormy, grayish-green sky underscores the tension of the moment, which is further enhanced by the closeness of the figures and by the ambiguous force and position of Christ's gesture, which seems both to resist and seek physical contact with the Magdalen and her breasts.

Sexual nuance, rarified figure types, and extraordinary coloration are common characteristics of 16th century Italian Mannerism, the art historical classification to which Giovanni-Battista Franco's *Noli Me Tangere* squarely belongs. Franco was a Venetian who left home as a young painter to pursue his craft in Rome, Florence, and Urbino; by 1554 he returned to Venice, where he died in 1561. Throughout his career, Franco was strongly influenced by the famed Michelangelo Buonarroti, and the figure types and exotic colors in his *Noli Me Tangere* bear witness to a study of Michelangelo's *Risen Christ* and the Sistine Chapel frescoes. More directly, it is known that Franco produced another painting of Christ's meeting with the Magdalen that was based on a drawing by Michelangelo. That painting, to which the Art Institute's *Noli Me Tangere* is clearly related, is now in the Casa Buonaroti in Florence. Despite their religious subject, both paintings could well have been produced more as collectors' items than as altarpieces.

RJC

Attributed to Francesco Salviati

(1510-1553) Italian

PORTRAIT OF A MAN WITH A LETTER, *around 1530-1540*

Oil on wood panel

30 5/16 x 21 5/8 inches

Museum purchase with funds provided by the 1982 and 1983 Associate Boards, 1983.20

P resented in three-quarter length and with eyes cast toward the observer, this man supports himself against a draped table and holds a folded letter in his right hand. Whether he is seated or standing is both unclear and unimportant. Leaving the evidence cast in shadow, the painter chose to emphasize the sitter's clothes, the arrangement of his hands, and the expression of his face. The sitter's apparel is comprised of a black garment with slit shoulders, ruffled, crimson sleeves, and a white, lace collar and cuffs; a black cape is draped about his shoulders. Together with a small ring and a belt buckle ornamented with two river gods and a standing figure in between, the reserved elegance of this apparel subtly attracts attention. Ultimately, however, the observer's attention is captivated by the delicate construction and artful placement of the man's hands and by the enigmatic expression on his face. Lit from a source in the upper-left corner that casts an ominous shadow in the background, this face shines forth from a mass of curly, red hair and beard. A protruding temple and forehead vein communicate a sense of the sitter's vitality, but the expression of the eyes, lost somewhere in sadness, apprehension, or perhaps fear, confound a sure interpretation of this portrait.

Attributed to the Florentine artist Francesco Salviati, this work is a good example of the "stylish style" in Italian portraiture of the 16th century. The painter's delight in the sitter's rich apparel and elegant bearing are typical of the portraiture of this period. Common also are the painter's explorations of the man's ambiguous, distant expression, and the related inclusion of a letter tantalizingly concealed. Since these portraits were often commissioned in pairs, the possible existence of a pendant representing either a lover or spouse may have lent valuable meaning to this inviting though difficult work.

RJC

SUGGESTED READING:

Pope-Hennessy, John. **The Portrait in the Renaissance**. Princeton, NJ: The University of Princeton Press, 1966.

Frans Geubels

(1535-1590) Flemish

***KING ABIMELECH RESTORES SARAH TO
HER HUSBAND, ABRAHAM**, around 1560-1570*

Tapestry: dyed wool and silk

166 x 185 inches

Gift of Mr. Robert Badenhop, 1952.10

The subject of this very fine example of 16th century Flemish tapestry weaving appears to be an episode from the life of Abraham. The Old Testament (Genesis 20:1-16) reads that while Abraham and his people were in the land of Gerar, he feared that he might lose his beautiful wife Sarah to Gerar's king, Abimelech. Hoping to protect Sarah, Abraham introduced her to Abimilech as his sister, but his plans backfired and Abimelech abducted Sarah to his palace where she entered his harem. However, when Abimelech learned of Sarah's true identity through a dream, being an honorable man, he returned her to Abraham and offered gifts of servants, sheep, and oxen to atone for his near transgression.

The central scene of the tapestry depicts the resolution of the tale. Just left of center, Abimelech, wearing a crown and holding a scepter, gestures to Abraham at the right. Sarah turns toward her husband, as if to say that she is his spouse and is grateful for being returned to him. To the left of Abimelech, a general of the king approaches humbly bearing a sack of money that represents the peace offering of the honorable king to Abraham. In the background, various aspects of the story are told and unfold in time, from Sarah appearing before the king at the far upper left, to Abraham and Sarah's joyful reunion and the eventual departure of the Israelites from the land of Gerar. Surrounding the central panel is a border of exquisite flower garlands of flowers entwined with mythological female figures on chariots and cartouches enclosing figural scenes.

Elegant tapestries, such as this one, were usually woven in series by ateliers (studios) headed by a master weaver or family of weavers. The Geubels atelier in Brussels is identified by a cipher in the selvage (or border) at the lower right. It was probably separated from its series through a sale or natural disaster. Essential throughout the Middle Ages and the Renaissance as decoration for reception halls and public and private rooms, tapestries were elegant examples of functional room insulation, providing both protection from the cold, damp climate of northern Europe and sound insulation in large, echoing spaces.

DHV

SUGGESTED READINGS:

Standen, Edith Appleton. **European Post-Medieval Tapestries and Related Hangings in the Metropolitan Museum of Art**. New York: The Metropolitan Museum of Art, 1985.

Abraham Janssens
(around 1575-1632) Flemish

THE LAMENTATION OF CHRIST, *around 1600-1604*

Oil on wood panel
37 1/4 x 47 3/4 inches
Gift of Mr. Robert Badenhop, 1956.23

This scene of mourning over the crucified Christ offers an excellent example of the manner in which prints influenced artists. Furthermore, they provided painters with visual points of departure for other works of art or, as in this case, for nearly direct interpretations. This composition by the Flemish painter, Abraham Janssens, is a near-literal copy of a print by Annibale Carracci, a work known as the *Christ of Caprarola*, that shows the Virgin Mary holding her dead son, Jesus, while John the Evangelist and two Marys grieve at the foot of the cross.

Carracci was one of the most famous early Baroque Italian artists whose paintings and prints attempted to revive the aspirations of the High Renaissance, coupling them with a new interest in naturalism. His *Christ of Caprarola* was one of his most famous etchings done around 1597, after a lengthy hiatus from printmaking, and was undoubtedly one of his most successful as witnessed by the fact that it was copied by numerous Italian and Dutch artists, among them Abraham Janssens.

Janssens was in Rome in 1598, the year after Carracci probably made his famous etching. Soon after his Italian visit, Janssens settled in the Catholic city of Antwerp, where his early paintings exhibited a decidedly Mannerist bent—the late 16th century, fashionable style known for its sinuous line, unnaturalistic anatomy, and interesting colors. This early trend toward the elegant and precious was to give way to a preference for rather stiff classical forms modeled in a cold, northern light. The Art Institute's *Lamentation* probably falls between these periods at the early part of the 17th century, possibly during another trip to Rome around 1604.

DHV

SUGGESTED READING:

Gerson, H., and E. H. Ter Kuile. **Art and Architecture in Belgium, 1600-1800**. Baltimore: Penguin Books, 1960.

Ludovico Carracci

(1555-1619) Italian

PORTRAIT OF A WOMAN, *1589-1590*

Oil on canvas

39 1/4 x 30 1/2 inches

Museum purchase with funds provided by Dr. and Mrs. E. R. Arn and the Junior League of Dayton, Ohio, Inc., 1958.15

Dressed in dark-gray attire often associated with mourning, this woman is perhaps a widow. Yet, her dress and the obvious piety of her actions may suggest that she is a nun. Whether she is a widow or nun, the rich quality of her clothing and the sharpness of her aquiline facial features certainly distinguish her as a woman of aristocratic birth. Ultimately, the identity and station of this woman may never be determined, but her strong individuality is unmistakably preserved in this profile portrait.

The woman is largely contained within the right-half of the composition where the chestnut-colored expanse of background offers little competition for the viewer's attention. Through the extension of an arm, the upward turn of a hand, and the direction of the eyes, the viewer slowly begins to assemble the whole of this portrait and to decipher its narrative. Occupying the left half of the picture is a table on which rests a prayer book, rosary, and a standing crucifix. A swag of drapery, richly painted with varied folds, hangs from the upper left, where it shelters the body of Christ and provides a visual counterweight to the woman's form.

In some ways, this work seems less a formal portrait than a portrayal of a private moment of prayer and revelation. The possibility of revelation is suggested in the image of Christ who is not painted in simulation of a sculpted figure, but rather as the man himself crucified on the cross. In the presence of Christ, the woman stands transfixed and seems instinctively to draw one hand in piety toward her breast and extend the other below Christ to catch a drop of blood from his wounds, that Ludorico Carracci intended for the figure of Christ to be understood as the result of visualized meditation is perhaps indicated by the seemingly haphazard manner in which the rosary and prayer book have been set aside. In fact, the prayer book appears still partially open from recent use.

Carracci was a Bolognese painter of the late 16th and early 17th centuries. Together with his cousins, Annibale and Agostino, Carracci helped organize the Carracci Academy that served as an informal school for artists in Bologna. The Carracci and their pupils responded to the call for a powerful new religious art that had been issued by the Counter-Reformation Church at the Council of Trent (1545-1563). With its strong emphasis on unmitigated piety, the Art Institute's *Portrait of a Woman* fully shares in the spirit of that age.

RJC

SUGGESTED READING:

The Age of Correggio and Carracci. Exhibition catalogue. Washington, D.C.: The National Gallery of Art, 1986.

Flemish

Late 16th century

AN ALLEGORY OF FORTUNE (FORTUNA), *around 1590*

Oil on canvas

75 1/4 x 47 inches

Museum purchase, 1962.13

In this painting, an allegorical figure of Fortune, the mythological goddess of Fate stands balanced upon her wheel and catches the ever-changing winds of chance with her extended scarf. Behind her are scenes of safety and chaos: at the left, a boat heads for safe harbor under the legs of the famed Colossus of Rhodes (one of the Seven Wonders of the classical world); at the right, a town burns, perhaps the aftermath of a raiding party, civil strife, or some natural disaster. To 16th century European artists, the allegory was a powerful vehicle of communication. By using classical or mythological figures, such as Fortune, artists could try to explain the vicissitudes, glories, and foibles of life. Life has always been and will always be full of change and uncertainty, and above life's drama, Fortune is balanced precariously.

The painter of this imposing canvas is not known. When acquired by the Art Institute in the early 1960s, the painting was attributed to the German Hans van Aachen (1552-1615), a leading painter at the Prague court of the Holy Roman Emperor, Rudolf II. Rudolf's court especially favored the elegantly elongated and antinatural figural types now called Mannerist (from the Italian word *Maniera*), a style developed in Italy and taken up by northern Europeans who visited Florence and Rome during the 16th century. The painting was later attributed to the Dutch artist Bartholomeus Spranger (1546-1611); however, recently, this attribution has been felt to be unsatisfactory. Hans Speckaert (died around 1577) and Hendrick Goltzius (1558-1617), both Mannerist painters in Rome, have also been suggested. Incidentally, the painting has been X-rayed and shows the underdrawing of a full-length male portrait, demonstration that the artist changed his mind and used the canvas for an allegorical composition instead.

The figure of Fortune is a type found in other 16th century works, most notably a bronze sculpture by Flemish-born Italian Giambologna (Giovanni da Bologna or Jean de Boulogne, 1529-1608), sculptor to the famous Medici family. Dating prior to Giambologna's famous sculpture, a drawing in the Louvre (Paris) by the Florentine sculptor and painter, Baccio Bandinelli (1493-1560) of around 1529, also depicts a sea battle presided-over by Fortune holding up a sail and standing upon a wheel. An engraving by the Flemish Mannerist printmaker Aegidius Sadeler (around 1570-1629) also attests to the contemporary popularity of this allegorical theme.

DHV

SUGGESTED READING:

Kaufmann, Thomas DaCosta. **The School of Prague: Painting at the Court of Rudolph II**.Chicago: University of Chicago Press, 1988.

Bohemian (Prague)
Early 17th century

SPOON, *around 1600*
Jasper mounted in painted and enameled gold
L: 6 inches
Museum purchase, 1980.31

This elegantly crafted spoon was probably never intended to be used. Its purpose was, no doubt, to amuse and intrigue its likely owner, Holy Roman Emperor Rudolf II of Bohemia (reigned 1578-1612). The spoon's decorative gold mounts, with their red, white, blue, and green enamels, are characteristic of the Rudolfine Court workshop after the arrival in Prague of Hans Karl, a master Nuremberg goldsmith. Prior to Karl's tenure, the Prague workshop—renowned for exquisitely crafted objects—produced works characterized by linear scrollwork or strapwork executed solely in black enamel. In addition to its decoration of multicolored *champlevé* enamel (colored enamels fused in gouged channels), the spoon is crowned by the bust of a helmeted harpy, a mythological figure composed of half-woman, half-bird. Beads of red enamel on the C-scroll beneath the harpy simulate real garnets, the use of which would later come to characterize the Baroque style in Bohemia.

Rudolf, like many German princes of his time, created *Kunst-und-Wunderkammern*, collections of art objects, scientific materials, and all sorts of unusual natural phenomena. The *Kunstkammer* was meant to express the personality of its creator, demonstrating those attributes befitting an emperor whose court artists eventually included famous painters, sculptors and goldsmiths from Italy, Germany, and the Netherlands.

Rudolf's own particular fondness for precious and semi-precious stones is demonstrated by the handsomely patterned, green-brown jasper that comprises the bowl and stem of this delicate object. Yet, the emperor's attraction to these stones may well have been motivated by more than simply visual enjoyment. From times of antiquity, stones were thought to possess special powers that could be transferred to their owners by touch and possession. Jasper was widely held to improve one's vision and to protect against unseen dangers during the night. Nevertheless, Rudolf's personal physician, Boethius de Boodt, held that the emperor's own importance and majesty was already so great that his interest in such minerals was solely to help him understand the grandeur and infinite power of God.

DHV

SUGGESTED READINGS:

Hayward, J.F. **Virtuoso Goldsmiths and the Triumph of Mannerism, 1540-1620**. London and Totowa, NJ: Sotheby Parke Bernet Publishers, 1976.

Trevor-Roper, Hugh. **Princes and Artists, Patronage and Ideology at Four Habsburg Courts, 1517-1633**. London: Thames and Hudson, 1976.

Italian (possibly Venetian)

CHASUBLE WITH ORPHREY BAND, *16th -17th century*

Silk embroidered with gold thread

45 x 26 inches

Gift of Mrs. A. Siegel, 1960.30

This handsomely decorated chasuble was meant to be worn by a Roman Catholic priest over other liturgical vestments during the celebration of the Liturgy (the Mass). The green silk brocade of this vestment indicates that it was worn during ferial times, weekdays of the liturgical calendar when no religious feasts are celebrated. Of particular note is the heavily embroidered *orphrey* band—an ornamented band originally intended to cover the garment's seams—depicting God the Father, Sts. Peter and John the Evangelist on the front, and the Blessed Virgin, Paul, and John the Baptist on the back. The fact that the lower figures of John the Evangelist and John the Baptist are truncated indicate either that this chasuble was shortened at some time or that the *orphrey* band may have originally come from another vestment and was later adapted for use in the present one.

As with most liturgical vestments of the Roman Catholic Church, the often richly decorated chasuble has its origins in the most humble of garments. The Roman *casula* ("little house" or "little cottage"), from which the chasuble took its form, was originally a circular cloth with a head opening in the center worn in rainy or cold weather by field workers, peasants, travelers, and monks. It was during the 8th century, at the Council of Ratisbon, that a decree formalized the use of the chasuble as a vestment for the clergy. With its official adoption by the Church, the chasuble became increasingly decorated with religious symbols, scenes, and figures. Those of this chasuble may be copied from paintings or tapestries of the High Renaissance or Baroque periods. Originally conical in shape during the Middle Ages, the chasuble was reduced in both length and width during the Renaissance and Baroque periods so that its function became religiously symbolic rather than practical.

DHV

SUGGESTED READINGS:

Gilfoy, Peggy Stolz. **Fabrics in Celebration from the Collection**. *Exhibition catalogue. Indianapolis: Indianapolis Museum of Art, 1983.*

Mayer-Thurman, Christa C. **Raiment for the Lord's Service: A Thousand Years of Western Vestments**. *Exhibition catalogue. Chicago: The Art Institute of Chicago, 1975.*

Giuseppe Cesari, called "Il Cavalier d'Arpino"

(1568-1640) Italian

ADORATION OF THE MAGI, *around 1600-1610*

Oil on wood panel

17 1/4 x 14 1/4 inches

Gift of Mr. Robert Badenhop, 1956.21

I n the Gospel of Matthew, the story is told of three Magi, or kings, who followed a star from the east that led them to the city of Bethlehem. There they found and presented gifts to the Christ Child who some days earlier had been born in a manger. In this depiction of the story, the three Magi are recognizable by their exotic dress and golden vessels. Arranged before a rustic manger set within an atmospheric landscape, the Magi and their equally exotic entourage encounter the Holy Family. The presentation of gifts, however, is suspended in a moment of hushed adoration. Seated on his mother's lap and reaching for the elderly Magus' beard, the Christ Child is clearly the focal point. As the Christ Child and elderly Magus engage one another eye to eye, the attention of all others—even the horses—focuses on them. The concentration of the Magi and their retinue is so intense that no one seems aware of the small, mysterious figure, perhaps identifiable as Lucifer or a close associate, who peers out from an opening in the manger. According to the medieval *Golden Legend*, Lucifer witnessed the Nativity that was staged to confuse him and enable man to "obtain pardon from sins, cure his weaknesses, and humble his pride."

The subject of the *Adoration of the Magi* often provided painters and their patrons with an excused opportunity to indulge in exoticism and regal finery. That is particularly true of this 16th century representation by Giuseppe Cesari in which little differentiation is made between the Magi and the Holy Family. Cesari, who is also known by his papal title, "Cavalier d'Arpino," was among the most prolific painters in Rome during the late 16th century. Although he lived until 1640, and was in contact with the young realist painter Michelangelo Merisi da Caravaggio in the early 1590s, Cesari adhered to a Mannerist style throughout his career. He may have produced the Art Institute's *Adoration* as a private devotional work or, perhaps, simply as a work of fine art.

RJC

SUGGESTED READINGS:

The Age of Caravaggio. Keith Christiansen ed. Exhibition catalogue. New York: The Metropolitan Museum of Art, 1985.

Röttgen, Herwarth. **Il Cavalier d'Arpino**. Exhibition catalogue. Rome: Palazzo Venezia, 1974.

Bartolomeo Manfredi
(around 1580-1621) Italian

ALLEGORY OF THE FOUR SEASONS, *around 1610*

Oil on canvas

53 x 36 inches

Gift of Mr. and Mrs. Elton F. MacDonald, 1960.27

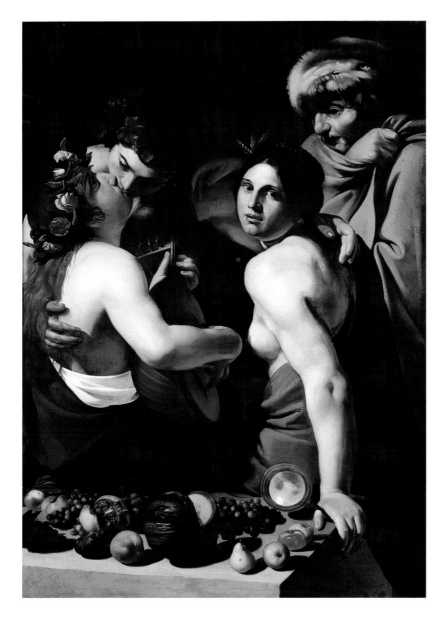

Bartolomeo Manfredi was a possible apprentice to and devoted follower of Michelangelo Merisi da Caravaggio (known as Caravaggio), arguably one of the most highly influential artists of the early Italian Baroque. Although his influence upon a whole generation of European artists was relatively short lived, it was, nonetheless, irresistible and highly powerful. While Caravaggio's temperament did not lend itself easily to the conventional teacher-apprentice mode, Manfredi may have been employed by the master as early as 1602. Of all the *Caravaggisti* (painters influenced by Caravaggio), Manfredi appears to have most faithfully assimilated the spirit of the famous rebel artist.

Nowhere is the influence of Caravaggio's naturalism more evident than in the works such as this *Allegory of the Four Seasons*. Manfredi places the large, half-figures prominently in the foreground of the picture plane and lights them dramatically. A realistically painted still-life of various seasonal fruits and vegetables on the stone ledge invites the viewer's gaze and reinforces the painting's theme. Spring, with her crown of roses, is embraced by Autumn with his wreath of grape vine; Summer with wheat in her hair and magnifying glass in hand turns to the viewer, while the bearded, "old man" Winter, wrapped in furs, seems excluded from the group by his advanced age and his position in the picture. Unlike a scene in which we are merely observers, Manfredi's figures seem to include us by their gesture and their accessibility.

The allegorical meaning of this painting may, in fact, reach further than a simple depiction of personifications of the seasons. European painters and writers often alluded to the five human senses: taste, sight, hearing, smell, and touch all of which are represented in this work. Manfredi carried on this style of painting after Caravaggio's death in 1610 and was no doubt responsible for its dissemination to other Caravaggisti artists from Italy and northern Europe.

DHV

Suggested Readings:

Brejon de Lavergnée, Arnauld, et al. **Dopo Caravaggio: Bartolomeo Manfredi e la Manfrediana Methodus**. *Milan: Arnold Mondadori Editore, 1988.*

Moir, Alfred. **The Italian Followers of Caravaggio**. *Cambridge: Harvard University Press, 1967.*

Peter Paul Rubens
(1577-1640) Flemish
STUDY HEADS OF AN OLD MAN, *around 1612*
Oil on wood panel
26 1/2 x 19 3/4 inches
Gift of Mr. and Mrs. Carlton W. Smith, 1960.82

When it was first acquired by the Art Institute in 1960, this work showed only one, central study of the old man's head, nearly frontal, looking to the left. The other study, behind and to the left, had no doubt been overpainted sometime in the early 20th century. The intent was probably to lessen the effect of a sketch and create the appearance of a finished portrait thereby enhancing the work's marketability and price. In 1991, while the painting was being cleaned and treated at a conservation facility, the decision was made to have the overpaint removed from the second study head, thus restoring the panel to the artist's original intent.

Peter Paul Rubens—artist, diplomat, friend of kings—is without a doubt one of the most well-appreciated and successful painters of all time, perhaps the perfect embodiment of the Baroque-age artist. Like his early works executed after he returned to Antwerp, Holland following a lengthy trip to Italy and Spain (1600-1608), this sketch shows how Rubens synthesized a great number of contemporary artistic styles into a highly vigorous, personal, artistic vocabulary. His use of naturalism and dramatic lighting derives from his interest in the very influential works of Michelangelo Merisi da Caravaggio (called Caravaggio). Rubens' bold, robust forms, seen in the confident modeling of the heads, demonstrate his study of the great High Renaissance painter and sculptor Michelangelo Buonarroti, while his preference for strong, saturated color result from his exposure to such Venetian Renaissance painters as Titian.

Rubens' brilliant handling of the paint and his ability to capture the color and texture of aged flesh and silky white hair contribute to the freshness and immediacy of this preliminary study sketch. The model who sat for these studies appears in a number of Rubens' finished paintings, most notably in *Christ and the Woman taken in Adultery* in the Royal Museum in Brussels; another version of the same painting is owned by the Toledo Museum of Art in Ohio.

DHV

Suggested Readings:

Cahan, Claudia Lyn. **Rubens**. *New York: Avenel Books (Crown Publishers), 1980.*

Held, Julius S. **The Oil Sketches of Peter Paul Rubens**. *Princeton: Princeton University Press, 1980.*

Bernardo Strozzi
(1581-1644) Italian
ST. FRANCIS IN ECSTASY, *around 1615-1618*
Oil on canvas
46 1/2 x 35 1/2 inches
Gift of Mr. and Mrs. Harry S. Price, Jr., 1966.1

This selfless 13th century saint has been one of the most revered and frequently depicted of all Christendom. The Genoese artist Bernardo Strozzi painted St. Francis nearly 40 times. Here, Strozzi depicts a moment of great spiritual importance in St. Francis' life. The saint, born the son of a wealthy merchant from Assisi in Umbria, rejected his family's wealth and turned to a life of devoted faith, founding an order of brothers known as the Franciscans. After a life of great piety and charitable works, he withdrew to the mountains in 1224 and after years of meditation, self-denial, and prayer, experienced a miraculous vision that left his body marked with Christ's five sacred wounds, the *stigmata*.

The luscious, thickly applied paint, or *impasto*, is a typical Genoese characteristic. The corpus of the crucifix is created by what would seem to be several ribbons of white paint, quickly applied to the canvas—a marvelous example of virtuoso painting. The emotional intensity conveyed by this painting, both through its subject and painterly execution, would most assuredly have met with the approval of the Counter-Reformation Church that espoused art works that were meant to uplift the thoughts and actions of the faithful, while bringing them back to the Roman Catholic Church.

The spiritual intensity that is evident in this Counter-Reformation painting may be due in part to Strozzi's personal religious experience. Strozzi had belonged to a Capuchin (a branch of the Franciscan order) monastery for just more than ten years when he took leave in order to care for his mother and sister. He supported his family in Genoa as an artist until his mother's death in 1630, at which time he refused to return to the monastery. Rather, he fled to Venice where he continued his highly successful career as a painter.

DHV

SUGGESTED READINGS:

Manning, Robert, and Bertina Suida Manning. **Genoese Masters: Cambiaso to Magnasco, 1550-1750**. Exhibition catalogue. Dayton, OH: The Dayton Art Institute, 1962.

Milkovich, Michael. **Bernardo Strozzi**. Exhibition catalogue, University Art Gallery. Binghampton, NY: State University of New York at Binghamton, 1967.

Mortari, Luisa. **Bernardo Strozzi**. Rome: De Luca Editore, 1995.

Claude Vignon
(1593-1670) French

THE ADORATION OF THE MAGI, *around 1619*

Oil on canvas

76 1/2 x 54 1/4 inches

Museum purchase in honor and in memory of Miss Virginia V. Blakeney, 1963.110

Painted in Rome, this large and imposing canvas combines typical 17th century Roman Baroque grandeur with a French quietude and nobility befitting this scene taken from the Gospel according to Saint Matthew. Monumental, yet at the same time imbued with a mood of tender religious devotion, Claude Vignon's *The Adoration of the Magi* is composed of rich colors and solidly painted forms that emerge from the darkness into a silvery starlight. A masterful and moving scene, this altarpiece is undoubtedly one of Vignon's most important works outside any European collection.

Due to its shimmering light effects that are typical of the art of Venice, this unsigned picture was once attributed to the Italian painter Domenico Fetti. It was later correctly attributed and dated by the discovery of an etching of the identical composition, signed by Vignon, inscribed "Roma, 1619." A painting of this scale and subject must have been commissioned from Vignon as an altarpiece intended for a Roman church or noble family's private chapel, although no supporting documents are yet known.

Vignon's long career was marked by travel and abundant productivity. Following his early training in Paris, he went to Rome in 1617, as did many artists of his time. There, he encountered the dramatically lit compositions of the iconoclastic Michelangelo Merisi da Caravaggio, whose influence can be seen in the use of large and naturalistically conceived figures sculpted and modeled by an external, diagonally directed light source. Likewise, Vignon admired and was influenced by the small and exquisitely painted nocturnal scenes of the German landscape artist, Adam Elsheimer, who was in Rome from around 1600 until 1610. Though Vignon's paintings are flavored by the drama of the new Italian Baroque style, more importantly they also demonstrate a sense of calm and propriety which can be seen as a hallmark of French 17th century art.

DHV

SUGGESTED READINGS:

Brejon de Lavergnée, Arnauld, and Jean-Pierre Cuzin. **Valentin et les Caravagesques Francais**. Exhibition catalogue, Grand Palais. Paris: Editions des Musèes Nationaux, 1974.

Vasseur, Dominique H. "Two Recent Acquisitions in the Graphic Arts." **The Dayton Art Institute Bulletin** (December 1986, Vol. 41): 18-23.

Wright, Christopher. **French Painters of the Seventeenth Century** . Boston: Little, Brown and Co., 1985.

Frans Francken the Younger
(1581-1642) Flemish

THE CRUCIFIED CHRIST ENFRAMED WITH SCENES OF THE MARTRYDOMS OF THE APOSTLES, *after 1605*

Oil on wood panel

34 1/2 x 27 3/4 inches (outside dimensions)

Gift of Mr. Robert Badenhop, 1954.15

This particularly fine representation of the Crucifixion of Christ is all the more interesting for its framework of smaller scenes depicting martyrdoms of various apostles. These are painted in *grisaille* and *brunaille*, that is, in a monochromatic palette of grays and browns respectively, rather than with a usual full range of color. The various apostles depicted here appear to be, starting in the upper-left corner and proceeding clockwise: Sts. Peter, Matthew, Andrew, James the Major, John the Evangelist, Thomas, James the Minor, Philip, Bartholomew, Simon, Mark, and Paul. Although the martyrdoms appear somewhat lugubrious and ghostly in their monochromatic tints, the central image of Christ, alone and near death, is one that the artist intended to inspire devotion and promote contemplation by its viewer.

The convention of surrounding a central religious image with smaller scenes may stem from the Italian convention of placing smaller scenes, or *predella* panels, below the principle painting of an altarpiece. Johan Sadeler, a 16th century Flemish artist and engraver, produced a very similar image to this one by Francken: a crucifixion with surrounding scenes of martyrdom. Francken may have taken his composition, and others like it, directly from the Sadeler engraving of the late 16th century.

Francken came from a line of important artists from Antwerp, a predominantly Roman Catholic city. He was a prolific artist who painted many small pictures used to decorate elaborate cabinets or to serve as private devotional paintings as was, no doubt, this painting. Francken often collaborated successfully with other Flemish painters, contributing the figures to landscapes scenes, as was frequently the convention of the time.

DHV

SUGGESTED READING:

Gerson, H., and E.H. Ter Kuile. **Art and Architecture in Belgium, 1600 to 1800**. Baltimore: Penguin Books, 1960.

Giovanni Francesco Barbieri (Il Guercino)
(1591-1666) Italian
CHRISTIAN CHARITY, *around 1625-1626*
Oil on canvas
34 3/4 x 43 1/4 inches
Museum purchase with funds provided by Miss Anne Chapman and the Junior League of Dayton, Ohio, Inc., 1958.99

The theme of this painting, *Christian Charity*, belongs to the repertory of Christian iconography, at least since the Renaissance. At the root of this allegory are the contrasting aspects of human love versus divine love, the former intended to illustrate human love's fragility and the latter the immortal love of the human soul. During the Counter Reformation, the theme of a beautiful woman nursing her young undoubtedly would have been recognized as an allegory for Charity or Love. The woman might also represent a personification of the Roman Catholic Church, her children representing the human soul hungry for spiritual nourishment provided through the Church's sacraments—a decidedly Catholic doctrine rejected by most Protestant denominations.

Born at Cento, near Bologna, Barbieri, known as *Il Guercino* (i.e., "Squint-Eye"), studied at the famous Bolognese Academy founded by the Carracci family. Guercino's early trips to Ferrara and Venice helped form his sense of color and composition, while the lessons he learned from the Carracci were the basis of his artistic style favoring a more naturalistic rendering of the human figure.

Unlike this painting, much of Guercino's early work tended to be highly emotional, following the dramatic Baroque spirit. This painting echoes the art of Caravaggio fashionable in Rome in the first and second decades of the 16th century. The large allegorical figure of Charity suckling her children looms large within the picture plane, while a sharply raking light sculpts the group of figures, giving them form and a certain quiet monumentality. Several *pentimenti*—or changes in the painting that with time become visible—can be seen, especially in tha head shape of the child touching his finger to his mouth.

DHV

Suggested Readings:

Grimaldi, Nefta. **Il Guercino**. *Bologna: Tamari Editori, 1957.*

Guercino, Master Painter of the Baroque. *Washington, D.C.: National Gallery of Art, 1992.*

Wittkower, Rudolf. **Art and Architecture in Italy**, *1600-1750. Baltimore: Penguin Books, 1958.*

Hendrick Terbrugghen
(1588-1629) Dutch

A BOY VIOLINIST, *1626*

Oil on canvas
41 3/4 x 31 1/4 inches
Gift of Mr. and Mrs. Elton F. MacDonald, 1960.7

After returning to Utrecht in 1614, Hendrick Terbrugghen took with him Michelangelo Merisi da Caravaggio's characteristic use of naturalism, oblique, raking light, and a propensity for exotically clothed figures. Unlike Caravaggio's *bravo* figures (lowlife dandies and young thugs who frequented taverns), this youthful violinist seems less a true musician than a poor country bumpkin dressed up in fancy clothes posing as a musician. The wide-open toothy smile and happy, distracted gaze would seem to indicate a lad whose concentration is hardly upon the music he is supposedly playing.

This engaging painting clearly demonstrates the strong, stylistic influence of Caravaggio upon Terbrugghen, a Dutch contemporary of the Italian revolutionary painter. Terbrugghen had first studied with the Dutch Mannerist artist, Abraham Bloemaert, in the Catholic city of Utrecht. Then, from 1604 to 1614, like many of his northern European compatriots, Terbrugghen traveled to Rome where he experienced and was strongly influenced by the dramatic and highly realistic works of Caravaggio and his followers.

Whether or not this painting was intended to have meaning beyond its obvious subject is debatable. Paintings such as this may have been part of a series of the five senses, this example representing hearing. Since depictions of music and singing were sometimes used as a metaphor for the brevity of human pleasure and life, it may be a *vanitas*, that is, a reminder of man's mortality. On the other hand and perhaps more likely, the painting may have been merely intended to amuse and delight its viewer without such morose hidden meanings or warnings about the fleeting nature of human life.

DHV

Suggested Readings:

Nicholson, Benedict. **Hendrick Terbrugghen**. *London: Lund Humphries & Co., 1958.*

Slatkes, Leonard J., and Wolfgang Stechow (essayist). **Hendrick Terbrugghen in America**. *Exhibition catalogue. Dayton, OH: The Dayton Art Institute, 1965.*

Gerrit van Honthorst
(1590-1656) Dutch
THE FLEA HUNT, *1628*
Oil on canvas
52 1/4 x 78 1/2 inches
Museum purchase with funds provided in part by the Associate Board's 1980 Art Ball,
1980.2

At first glance, the Art Institute's painting seems to be an innocent, even humorous, genre scene. As most 20th century viewers are unfamiliar with the very real annoyance of fleas, bedbugs, and the like, it may be surprising for the casual visitor to learn that the old crone who points at the young beauty's bedclothes is, in fact, helping her kill fleas. Paintings of this mundane activity were relatively common in the 17th and 18th centuries and important artists like Georges de La Tour, Dirck Hals, and Giovanni Maria Crespi chronicled commonplace people engaged in this necessary "sport."

However, this seemingly simple record of a normal 17th century bedtime ritual takes on a different meaning when we notice the two young men—without doubt clients in a brothel—who peer over the bed curtains secretly enjoying the lovely courtesan who is assisted by the old procuress. In fact, the lowly flea was elegized by some great writers throughout history as a "nocturnal visitor" that, according to Christopher Marlowe, "can creep into every corner of a wench." Clearly the bawdy reference to the brothel, another common aspect of 17th century life, would not have been lost on a knowing eye. Whether the depiction of catching fleas was intended to serve as a visual metaphor for another human activity is debatable, although it was sometimes used as an analogy for touch, one of the five senses.

Like other European painters, Gerrit van Honthorst had gone to Rome in the early decades of the 17th century where he was influenced by the dramatic and radically new art of Caravaggio and his most important follower, Bartolomeo Manfredi. It was during his Caravaggesque phase that Honthorst frequently employed a northern European convention of an internal light source, a shielded single candle, such as he used in *The Flea Hunt* to illuminate the scene. So successful was he with these works that Honthorst earned the Italian nickname "Gherardo delle notte" (Gerard of the night scenes).

DHV

Suggested Readings:

Held, Julius, and Donald Posner. **17th and 18th Century Art: Baroque Painting, Sculpture and Architecture.** *New Jersey and New York: Prentice-Hall, Inc. and Harry N. Abrams, 1972.*

Moffitt, John. "La Femme á la Puce: The Textual Background of 17th century Painted 'Flea Hunts.'" **Gazette des Beaux-Arts.** *(October 1987, Vol. CX): 99-103.*

Gioacchino Assereto
(1600-1639) Italian

CIRCE MULLING WINE, *around 1630*

Oil on canvas
29 3/4 x 35 inches
Gift of Mr. and Mrs. Elton F. MacDonald, 1965.117

The subject of this painting is taken from the rich, classical epic, *The Odyssey*, which recounts the journey of the Greek hero Odysseus and his men back from the Trojan War to their homeland in Ithaca. Near the end of their long sea voyage, Odysseus and his crew chanced to land on the island of Aeaea, ruled by the beautiful witch, Circe. As she had done with many an unfortunate sailor, Circe planned to change Odysseus and his men into swine by giving them a magic potion mixed in wine. Here, the enchantress is shown mulling the wine with a hot poker as she waves her left hand and recites an incantation.

Gioacchino Assereto, a Genoese painter, imbues this scene with a sense of impending drama. Any Baroque viewer familiar with the story of Odysseus would be able to imagine the misfortune about to befall the crew and Circe's own fate. The tale, by the way, ends happily: Circe falls hopelessly in love with the Greek hero, who has been made impervious to her potion by an herb given him by the god, Hermes.

A native and lifelong resident of the seaport city Genoa, Assereto was strongly influenced by his Genoese colleague, Bernardo Strozzi, by whom the Art Institute owns a handsome painting depicting St. Francis. Both painters employed certain stylistic characteristics that, at times, make their works indistinguishable. Thickly applied paint and the construction of forms with almost faceted planes are characteristics of Strozzi's style also seen here in Assereto's work. This painting was, in fact, at one time attributed to Strozzi. Nevertheless, the proportions of the figure, the highly expressive hands—large and prominently placed—along with a scheme of deeply saturated colors point rather to Assereto.

DHV

Suggested Readings:

Suida Manning, Robert, and Bertina Suida Manning. **Genoese Masters: Cambiaso to Magnasco, 1550-1750**. *Exhibition catalogue, The Dayton Art Institute, 1962.*

Wittkower, Rudolph. **Art and Architecture in Italy, 1600-1750**. *Baltimore: Penguin Books, 1958.*

German

17th century

APOSTLE GLASS (HUMPEN), 1631

Gray-green handblown glass with colored enamel decoration

H: 16 inches

Gift of the Honorable Jefferson Patterson, 1959.11

The shape and enameled decoration of this *humpen*, or tall beaker used for drinking beer or wine, is completely in keeping with its function and 1631 date. From the middle of the 16th century, German glassmakers and enamelers imitated Venetian glassware, technically and stylistically the highest standard for European glassmaking at the time. As indigenous glass studios arose outside Venice, objects like this handsome covered glass were produced in relatively large numbers throughout Germany, Bohemia, and Austria. This glass was fully intended for use, not merely as a decorative work.

The tall, vertical sides of *humpen* were ideal surfaces for painted enamel decoration, an art that flourished during the 16th and 17th centuries. Often coat of arms of the families for which glassware was produced embellished these *humpen* along with allegorical representations of the Emperor, scenes commemorating famous battles or peace treaties, hunting scenes, and views of local towns. In the 17th century, however, religious subject matter was used with increasing regularity, such as the Art Institute's beaker with its two painted registers of representations of Christ (holding a banner, his hand held in benediction) and the 12 Apostles. Examples of this type can be found in major collections the world over. The highly schematized, heavily outlined images of Christ and the Apostles were taken from woodcuts of the period, an example of the exchange of visual information among the arts during the Renaissance and Baroque periods.

DHV

SUGGESTED READINGS:

Kampfer, Fritz, and Klaus G. Beyer. Dr. Edmund Launert trans. **Glass: A World History**. Greenwich: New York Graphic Society, 1967.

von Saldern, Axel. **German Enameled Glass: The Edwin J. Beinecke Collection and Related Pieces**. Corning: The Corning Museum of Glass, 1965.

Ferdinand Bol

(1616-1680) Dutch

PORTRAIT OF A YOUNG MAN WITH A SWORD, *around 1635-1640*

Oil on canvas

81 x 51 1/2 inches

Gift of Mr. and Mrs. Elton F. MacDonald, 1962.18

This full-length and larger-than-life-sized portrait of a young dandy, once thought to be a self-portrait, most certainly dates from Ferdinand Bol's years in Rembrandt van Rijn's studio. It would seem to be inspired by several of Rembrandt's self-portraits and other works of the same period. Rembrandt's *Reconciliation of David and Absalom* of 1642, in the collection of the Hermitage in St. Petersburg, uses almost identical objects to the ones found in Bol's portrait. In the aforementioned Rembrandt and in Bol's portrait, a quiver of arrows, a heavily embroidered velvet tunic, and a velvet scabbarded sword are the studio props evidently shared by master and pupil.

Bol also shared Rembrandt's fascination with unusual costumes and gear. The great sword, fashionable high-heeled leather boots, the richly embroidered clothes, velvet cloak, and plumed cap are far removed from the sober, black garb of most Dutch citizens. Rather, they have more in common with the brightly colored costumes of the subjects favored by Michelangelo Merisi da Caravaggio (1573-1610), a revolutionary and controversial Italian artist whose paintings influenced a generation of artists across Europe. Although grounded in a keen observation of detail, the sensuously depicted, exotic finery lends an air of fantasy to this portrait of an unknown friend or artist colleague of Bol's.

Bol was one of Rembrandt's most talented students and shared his master's interest in complex textures, dramatic use of light and shade, and richly applied paint. After a decade of apprenticeship with the master, Bol opened his own painting studio and began a successful career as a history scene painter and, ultimately, a painter of portraits. Wealthy 17th century Dutch merchants and civil officials all sought to have their portraits painted by famous contemporary painters, and Bol's career, which lasted until 1669, the year of his retirement and—ironically, the death of his teacher, Rembrandt—was based largely on such commissions.

DHV

SUGGESTED READINGS:

Blankert, Albert. **Ferdinand Bol, Rembrandt's Pupil**. *Doornspijk, Netherlands: DAVACO Publishers, 1982.*

Broos, Ben, et al. **Great Dutch Paintings from America**. *Exhibition catalogue, Mauritshuis, The Hague. Zwolle: Waanden Publishers, 1991.*

Adriaen van Nieulandt

(1587-1658) Flemish

MOSES AND THE BRAZEN SERPENT, *1640*

Oil on wood panel

39 x 48 1/2 inches

Gift of Mr. Robert Badenhop, 1957.135

The theme of this Old Testament story tells of the Israelites' journey from captivity in Egypt though the desert and mountains on their way back to the Promised Land. Many of the party, tired by this journey, complained bitterly that they should have never left Egypt. In anger, God sent poisonous snakes into the Israelite camp where hundreds were bitten and died.

Wishing to appease God's wrath, Moses, their leader, prayed and received instruction to fashion a serpent made of brass and affix it to a pole; anyone who looked upon this serpent would be saved by their faith in God. Consequently, the Israelites learned not to despair but, rather, to place their confidence in God. Here, Moses and his brother Aaron, wearing the jeweled breastplate and crown of the High Priest, point to the metal serpent while the Israelite camp responds with praise and exclamation although some writhe in pain or are already gray with death.

Nieulandt was a Protestant painter who had been taken from Antwerp to Amsterdam by his parents around 1588. He was known primarily as a painter of landscapes with figures, such as this Old Testament story, portraits, and still-lifes. While a painting such as this probably did not refer to any specific contemporary event, its message, confidence in God, was certainly quite plain. War, famine, and pestilence were rampant in 16th and 17th century Europe and one's faith might indeed serve to alleviate the sufferings of a painful world.

DHV

SUGGESTED READING:

Gerson, H., and E.H. Ter Kuile. **Art and Architecture in Belgium, 1600 to 1800**. *Baltimore: Penguin Books, 1960.*

Mattia Preti

(1613-1699) Italian

THE ROMAN EMPRESS FAUSTINA VISITING ST. CATHERINE OF ALEXANDRIA IN PRISON, *around 1640-1643*

Oil on canvas

167 1/2 x 100 inches

Gift of Mr. and Mrs. Elton F. MacDonald, 1961.108

A quiet yet powerful drama unfolds in this scene from St. Catherine's life. After Roman Emperor Maxentius imprisoned Catherine for spreading the Gospel and converting many of his pagan philosophers, Faustina Maxentius' wife decides to visit the learned and holy woman. Upon their meeting, Faustina is immediately converted to Christianity. With its emphasis upon conversion, this painting is the perfect example of a Counter Reformation plea for the return of the faithful to the Roman Catholic Church. Much like a scene from a grand Baroque opera, this life-sized composition is staged in swirling, upwardly progressing levels, from the burly jailers in the lower right to the angelic spectator above. The painting anticipates Catherine's torturous ordeal on the wheel from which she was miraculously released while it simulianeously hints at Catherine's ultimate martyrdom for her faith.

Bearing an inventory number of the Roman Barberini family collection, this large and impressive altarpiece painted for a Roman church or private chapel, is one of Mattia Preti's masterworks. Originally from Calabria and knighted by Pope Urban VIII in 1641 (hence his nickname "Il Cavaliere Calabrese"), Preti's early works show the inevitable influence of the important painter Michelangelo Merisi da Caravaggio. However, Preti's later style demonstrates a tempering of Caravaggio's dramatic realism with an increased admiration for the illusionism of Giovanni Lanfranco. Preti's style was well suited to such contemporary trends in Baroque Rome and Naples for ecclesiastical paintings that directed the attention of the faithful to pious thoughts of Christ, the Virgin Mary, and the saints.

Throughout its history, the Roman Catholic Church had long placed great importance in the veneration of the saints, and images such as this served to demonstrate the endurance and power of the Christian faith—especially in times of great adversity. Although little fact is known of St. Catherine of Alexandria, popular devotion to her throughout the Middle Ages to the Baroque period is testimony to the power of her traditionally held wisdom and holiness.

DHV

SUGGESTED READINGS:

Spear, Richard E. **Caravaggio and His Followers**. Cleveland Museum of Art, 1971.

Waterhouse, Ellis. **Italian Baroque Painting**. London: Phaidon Publishers and the New York Graphic Society, 1962.

Eustache LeSueur

(1617-1655) French

ALLEGORY OF MAGNIFICENCE, *around 1654*

Oil on canvas

39 x 50 1/2 inches

Gift of Mr. and Mrs. Harry S. Price, Jr., 1961.88

The grandeur and solemnity of the French royal court in the mid-17th century is accurately reflected in this classically conceived allegory. Each figure in the painting makes a symbolic reference to the renewed vigor and strength of the French monarchy under the young Louis XIV. Like many allegorical works of his age, Eustache LeSueur's symbolic language was undoubtedly based on Cesare Ripa's *Iconologia*, a compendium of attributes of various virtues, vices, times of the day, seasons of the year, and human emotions. A pupil of Simon Vouet and an admirer of the great Nicolas Poussin, LeSueur painted primarily in Paris for the monarchy and aristocracy in a style characterized by classicism, extreme decorum, and a certain sweetness.

Winged Time holds a book in which a Muse inscribes the great deeds of the monarchy, personified by a crowned and seated female figure. She, in turn, holds a cornucopia of riches and the plans for a palace, either real or imaginary. Two putti bridle a lion, itself a symbol of force, while a third holds aloft a wreath of laurel leaves, a traditional symbol of victory perhaps over rebellious French nobles, the *Fronde*. The sphinx in the background may well refer to the silent power of Louis' mother, Anne of Austria, who acted as regent during his youth, or to Cardinal Mazarin who helped quell the French nobility's rebellion.

This painting was probably painted as part of the decorations for the bedroom antechamber of the young Louis XIV in the Parisian palace of the Louvre, now the world-famous art museum. Its cool and balanced classicism, harmonious colors, and evenly lit, solidly constructed compositions are derived from principles of Italian Renaissance art, while its message is one of royal propaganda extolling the grandeur and stability of the French monarchy under the youthful Louis XIV.

DHV

SUGGESTED READINGS:

Henderson, Natalie Rosenberg. "LeSueur's Allegory of Magnificence." **Burlington Magazine** (April 1970): 213-217.

Rosenberg, Pierre. **France in the Golden Age: Seventeenth Century French Paintings in American Collections**. Exhibition catalogue. New York: The Metropolitan Museum of Art, 1982.

Jan de Bray

(1627-1697) Dutch

PORTRAIT OF DAMMAS GULDEWAGEN, *around 1657*

Oil on canvas

44 x 37 inches

Gift of Mr. Carlton W. Smith, 1969.32

This *Portrait of Dammas Guldewagen*, secretary to the Town Council of Haarlem, is typical of the "classical style" in 17th century Dutch portraiture. Like many of the portraits of the period, this work by Jan de Bray exhibits an insistence upon stability, a lack of violent diagonal recession or deep space, a cool, neutral setting, and a certain idealization of the sitter. The relaxed, seated pose of the figure lends an informal air to the work while the sitter's typically dark, Dutch clothing and the neutral, gray background draw attention to his face and hands.

This painting was possibly created with the aid of a *camera obscura*, a painter's tool for help in creating the proper perspective and forerunner of the modern camera. Handsome in its restraint, this work presents an approachable image of a solid Dutch citizen, much as he would wish to be remembered by his family and community.

Jan de Bray was one of the few 17th century Dutch portrait painters whose works can rival those of his more famous contemporaries, Frans Hals and Rembrandt van Rijn. In contrast, however, to Hals' expressionistic and virtuoso brushwork or Rembrandt's psychological insight and brilliant chiaroscuro effects, de Bray adopted a more traditional, classical manner seen in the evenly modulated colors and smooth brushwork. Yet to avoid a formulaic solution, de Bray places the chair diagonally to the picture plane, forcing the sitter to turn slightly to face the viewer and thereby lending a subtle and interesting asymmetry to the composition.

DHV

SUGGESTED READINGS:

Broos, Ben, et al. **Great Dutch Paintings from America**. *Exhibition catalogue, Mauritshuis, The Hague. Zwolle: Waanden Publishers, 1991.*

Leymarie, Jean. **Dutch Painting**. *New York: Editions d'Art Albert Skira, 1956.*

Wilson, William H. **Dutch Seventeenth Century Portraiture**. *Exhibition catalogue. Sarasota: John & Mable Ringling Museum of Art, 1980.*

Jacob van Ruisdael
(1628/29-1682) Dutch
LANDSCAPE WITH A WATERFALL AND CASTLE, *around 1670s*
Oil on canvas
27 3/4 x 21 3/4 inches
Gift of the Arkaydia Foundation of the Rike-Kumler Company, 1953.1

This small, handsome landscape painting stands as a testament to the prevailing view that Jacob van Ruisdael was the greatest Dutch landscape painter of his century. With its depiction of heavily clouded sky, a quickly rushing stream, and a country manor house, this is typical of Ruisdael's later landscapes, underscoring what was said of him, "he never painted a hot day." Certainly the Art Institute's landscape seems to suggest a brisk, country outing in early autumn. Subtle and contrasting tensions are set up by the action of the waterfall in the foreground and the isolated manor in the middle ground that alone receives the oblique rays of late afternoon sun through the clouds that dominate the sky. Ruisdael's masterful handling of the deep forest greens, sandwiched between monochromatic bands of rocks and clouds, make this painting a small gem of the Dutch 17th century landscape genre.

Although Ruisdael was perhaps the greatest Dutch landscape painter of the 17th century, he has been appreciated far more during the modern age than during his own lifetime largely because of his stylistic, Romantic affinities. French painters of the 19th century Barbizon school—along with the English landscapist, John Constable—admired Ruisdael's handsome works. Ruisdael was born in the lowlands of Holland, the son of the painter, framer, and dealer Isaac and nephew of the well-known landscape artist Salomon van Ruysadael. In the early 1650s, he traveled to western Germany where he may have seen mountains for the first time; the rushing stream and mountainous background visible in the Art Institute's painting may well have stemmed from this experience outside Holland. Thought by his contemporaries to have died tragically insane, the artist's somewhat grave and melancholy temperament shows through in this small, dramatic landscape, typically Dutch in flavor despite its unusual vertical format.

DHV

SUGGESTED READINGS:

Rosenberg, Jakob, Semous Slive, and E.H. Ter Kuile. **Dutch Art and Architecture, 1600-1800**. *Baltimore: Penguin Books, 1966.*

Stechow, Wolfgang. **Dutch Landscape Painting of the Seventeenth Century**. *London: Phaidon Press, Ltd., 1966.*

Gaspard Marsy
(1624-1681) French

LATONA AND HER CHILDREN, APOLLO AND DIANA, *after 1671*

Bronze with brown-black lacquer patina
H: 19 3/8 inches
Museum purchase, 1981.15

This handsome, table-sized bronze is a scale reduction of the white marble sculpture by Gaspard Marsy still situated in the gardens of Versailles. The same sculpture originally sat in the center of a low, circular pool, surrounded by gilt-lead statues of the Lycian peasants while the ensemble was finished off by cattails and water reeds executed in copper by the master tinsmith, Adrien Gascoin. In 1689, the marble sculpture was raised upon an imposing, three-level, marble pedestal where it stands today. Works of art, like the fountain of Latona, commissioned for the gardens of Louis XIV's palaces, were frequently laden with allegorical meanings that extolled the king's virtues and power (see, for example, the Art Institute's *Allegory of Magnificence* by Eustache LeSueur pg. 242).

Classical mythology provided the theme for the Latona fountain. Considered to be either the first wife of Jupiter before his marriage to Juno, or his mistress, Latona was the mother of Jupiter's most famous children, Apollo and Diana. Driven from Mount Olympus by the jealous Juno and pursued by a serpent from country to country, Latona finally came to Lycia in Asia Minor, where she paused to quench her thirst at a clear pool. Hostile, jeering peasants waded into the pool to muddy its waters and the exhausted Latona implored Jupiter to take pity on her and his children. This is the dramatic moment Marsy depicts in sculpture. Hearing Latona's cries, Jupiter changed the Lycian peasants into frogs, thereby assuring they would never leave the pool.

The fact that Louis XIV, self-styled Sun King, identified himself with Apollo, mythological god of the sun, may be ample justification for his selection of this theme to grace the gardens at Versailles. However, a more subtle reference may be noteworthy. Only a year before Marsy began work on this fountain, Louis XIV, although already married to Maria-Theresa of Spain, had taken Madame de Montespan as his mistress, a fact well known at court and beyond even the queen's power to repudiate. The Latona fountain might have suggested to courtiers and visitors that vengeance could be wrought upon any or all who dared to insult a divine—or in this instance, royal—mistress.

DHV

Suggested Readings:

Hedin, Thomas. **The Sculpture of Gaspard and Balthasard Marsy: Art and Patronage in the Early Reign of Louis XIV**. *Scranton: University of Missouri Press, Harper & Row, 1983.*

Rosasco, Betty. "Masquerade and Engima at the Court of Louis XIV." **Art Journal** (Summer 1989, Vol. 48, No. 2): 144-149.

Vasseur, Dominique H. "A Latona and Her Children, Apollo and Diana by Gaspard Marsy". **The Dayton Art Institute Bulletin**, Vol. 38, Dec. 1982, pp. 9-14.

Flemish (Brussels)

Late 17th century

BENEDICTION VEIL, *around 1690-1700*

Linen, bobbin lace

24 x 28 inches

Gift of Mrs. Harrie G. Carnell, 1944.110

This superb example of ecclesiastical lace exhibits many characteristics of Baroque style: a dynamic pattern of symmetrically opposed curves, C-scrolls, stylized flowers, foliage, and butterflies. The central scene of the Holy Family depicts the Flight into Egypt recounted in the Gospel of St. Matthew. The infant Jesus flees to Egypt with his parents, Mary and Joseph, and eludes slaughter by King Herod's troops—a parallel to the Old Testament journey of the Israelites out of Egypt centuries before.

Produced around 1690 to 1700, this veil was made with a noncontinuous-thread bobbin lace, a type known as "Flanders" or "Angleterre" (England), although ironically it was never made in England. Its function would have been to veil a *monstrance*, an elegant vessel used to hold a consecrated Host—worshipped by the Church as the real presence of Christ—sometimes placed on the altar during Benediction or 40 Hours Devotion, both special liturgical devotions of the Roman Catholic Church celebrating the Eucharist.

For more than 400 years, lace was one of the most precious commodities made in Europe; its price could surpass even that of gold and precious gems. Painstaking to produce, lace was so highly valued by the nobility and Church that sumptuary laws were regularly passed in most European countries (e.g., 1643 in Denmark; 1463, 1554, 1573 in England; 1594, 1600, 1606, 1613 in France; 1623 in Spain) to restrict or forbid its wearing by members of the lower social classes. Lace played an integral part in European fashion and was extensively used in churches for vestments, altar frontals, liturgical cloths, and garments for processional statues. Although to modern eyes its pattern of elegant floral garlands, swags, and butterflies may seem much too secular, this veil would have been entirely appropriate for use in a solemn liturgical ceremony, such as Benediction. In this modestly sized exquisite textile, one can easily see the sheer exuberance and elegance of the European Baroque style.

DHV

Suggested Readings:

Kraatz, Anne. **Lace: History and Fashion**. *New York: Rizzoli, 1989.*

Levey, Santina M. **Lace: A History**. *London: W.S. Maney & Son Ltd., 1983.*

Alessandro Magnasco

(1667-1749) Italian

A WOODED LANDSCAPE WITH MONKS, around 1710

Oil on canvas

37 x 48 1/4 inches

Gift of Mr. and Mrs. Elton F. MacDonald, 1962.57

So overpowering is his view of a mountainous landscape that one might easily look at it for a few moments before noticing the group of monks resting in the lower foreground. Indeed, Alessandro Magnasco seems to point out mankind's insignificance in the midst of nature, just as these monks are dwarfed by a huge tree that extends from their resting place near a rushing stream to the top of the canvas.

Magnasco often primed his canvases with a dark color, as in this work. The effect of time upon the overlaying white of the clouds often produces the appearance of a sky about to turn stormy. To heighten the effect of wind and atmospheric movement, Magnasco employed a highly activated brushstroke and some thickly applied areas of paint (*impasto*) that enliven the paint surface and gives it an expressive character especially appealing to modern eyes.

Magnasco, called "Il Lissandrino" (Little Alexander) because of his small stature, was an unusual painter, and difficult to categorize. The Genoese-born Magnasco spent a large part of his life in Milan, although his artistic formation was largely that of Genoa with added Venetian and Lombardesque elements. He was, in some respects, the spiritual heir to Salvator Rosa (1615-1673) whose work a century before heralded the Romantic movement of the 19th century. Likewise, Magnasco's work seems charged with an energy not typical of other landscape painters of his time. As in this fine example, Magnasco tended to paint large, expressive landscapes or turbulent seascapes peopled with small travelers, often monks, nuns, beggars, and gypsies.

DHV

Suggested Readings:

Geiger, Benno. **Magnasco**. Bergamo: Isituto Italiano d'Arti Grafiche, 1949.

Wittkower, Rudolph. **Art and Architecture in Italy, 1600-1750**. Baltimore: Penguin Books, 1958.

Bernardino Cametti
(1669-1736) Italian
THE VIRGIN ANNUNCIATE, *around 1730*
Terra-cotta modello
H: 10 5/8 inches
Museum purchase, 1982.19

Just as Baroque painters often produced oil sketches in preparation for larger, more finished works, sculptors made studies in wax, plaster or terra-cotta (fired clay). These studies, whether for two-dimensional paintings or three-dimensional sculptures, were known in Italian as *bozzetti*. A more finished study presented to a patron or commission panel is usually called a *modello* or, in French, a *maquette*.

This study by Bernardino Cametti is probably his *modello* for a marble relief of *Annunciation to the Virgin*. Cametti is a sculptor who began his career executing decorative stucco work in the famous Jesuit Church of San Ignazio in Rome. Commissioned by King Vittorio Amadeus II of Savoy to commemorate the French victory at the Battle of Turin in 1706, the marble relief for which this is a study is nearly 15-feet high and is in the famous Basilica di Superga in Turin. Although the Art Institute's terra-cotta study and Cametti's marble relief in Turin cannot be connected by specific documentation, the general pose and attitude of the Virgin kneeling at her *prie dieu* is sufficiently similar to suggest a relationship with the finished sculpture.

Visible in *modello* and finished relief are those characteristics that mark Cametti's work as belonging to the Baroque period. The modeling of his figures is naturalistic and concerned with conveying a sense of physical fullness, spiritual dynamism, and drama. Much of this sense of energy and spring-like tension is created by the curling, billowing draperies that wind around the figure, lending a feeling of emotional headiness and otherworldliness befitting a moment of such religious importance as the Annunciation by the Archangel Gabriel to Mary of her chosen role in the birth of the Messiah.

DHV

SUGGESTED READINGS:

Enggass, Robert. **Early Eighteenth-Century Sculpture in Rome: An Illustrated Catalogue Raisonné**. *University Park, Pennsylvania and London: The Pennsylvania State University Press, 1990.*

Keutner, Herbert, and consultant ed. John Pope-Hennessy. **A History of Western Sculpture: Renaissance to Rococo**. *Greenwich: New York Graphic Society, 1969.*

Jean-Baptiste Oudry
(1686-1755) French
STILL LIFE WITH GAME IN A LANDSCAPE, *around 1730s*
Oil on canvas
84 1/16 x 63 5/8 inches
Museum purchase with funds provided by the 1983 Associate Board, 1983.48

Although he studied with the famous French portraitist, Nicolas Largillière, Jean Baptiste Oudry's real skill lay in depicting animals. For his talent, he was honored by being named the official painter of King Louis XV's royal hunting dogs. In the Art Institute's large painting, seasonal summer fruits and a selection of wild game—a young stag, a duck, and a pheasant—are arranged in a casual manner.

The arched top of this painting would indicate that it was once part of a decorative scheme in a French *château*, a country estate often surrounded by forests well stocked with game. The painting's effect in an elegant 18th century dining room would be that of a window into a garden where the fruits of the estate and the rewards of the hunt were being gathered in preparation for the next meal.

While Oudry's still-lifes are frequently large in scale, this slightly over-life-sized canvas is particularly impressive as it combines elements of both still-life and landscape in one illustionistic setting. Rarely do Oudry's still-lifes have such an implied depth of space or a sense of atmosphere. While the viewer's attention is immediately focused upon the handsomely painted game, plump fruits, and ripe vegetables in the foreground, instinctively one looks beyond and over the tree tops to the distant roofs and church spire of a typical French village illuminated in the silvery rose of twilight, a scene of pre-Revolutionary tranquility and prosperity.

DHV

Suggested Readings:

Oppermann, Hal. **J.B. Oudry**. *Exhibition catalogue. Forth Worth, TX: Kimbell Art Museum, 1983.*

Rosenberg, Pierre. **The Age of Louis XV, French Painting, 1710-1774**. *Exhibition catalogue. Toledo, OH: The Toldeo Museum of Art, 1975.*

Ayme Videau
(active 1730-1770) English
COVERED CUP, *around 1752-1753*
Sterling silver (weight 124 oz.)
H: 15 11/16 inches
Gift of Mr. I. Austin Kelly III, in memory of his great-great-grandfather,
Ironton Austin Kelly, founder of Ironton, Ohio, 1973.80

This splendid covered cup—the shape of which today would be called a trophy cup—was created in London around the mid-18th century and reflects the expansive late Baroque style prevalent in Europe at the time. The solid, high-relief decoration of masks, caryatid figure handles, and grape clusters gives way to a fully conceived piece of sculpture serving as the finial for the cover. Unfortunately, the identity of the classical figure holding a staff is unknown to us today. His Roman helmet and armor would suggest a hero from classical mythology or one of Ovid's literary works.

Elaborate drinking cups have existed since ancient times; the Greek *kantharos* (or footed, two-handled cup) was one of the four main types of such terra-cotta vessels. While functional, these Greek vessels were typically decorated with painted scenes of heroic deeds or mythological events thereby providing an antecedent for later trophy cups. Ancient Greeks and Romans also made drinking cups from precious metals, yet while the two-handled cup was originally functional in form, it later evolved into an object of more symbolic than functional nature. From a purely practical point of view, objects of precious metal could be melted down to provide liquid assets if the need arose—a practice that frequently happened during times of war or family financial ruin.

In late 17th century France, the revocation of the Edict of Nantes, which granted freedom of worship to French Protestants, led to an exodus of Huguenot craftsmen, including goldsmiths, to neighboring England and Flanders. Ayme Videau, like his more famous contemporary, Paul de Lamerie, belongs to the second generation of Huguenot goldsmiths who found new fame and fortune across the English Channel. Parenthetically, de Lamerie became so well-known as to be named the King's goldsmith, but Videau did not achieve such a level of fame. This splendid cast and chased cup by Videau bears an engraved crest that appears to be that of the Radcliffe Family.

DHV

SUGGESTED READING:

Wenham, Edward. **Domestic Silver of Great Britain and Ireland**. *New York, London, Toronto: Oxford University Press, 1931.*

Francesco Guardi
(1712-1793) Italian

THE TORRE DELL'OROLOGIO, VENICE, *around 1760*

Oil on wood panel
20 x 24 3/4 inches
Bequest of Susanne Rike Kircher, 1977.171

Although unsigned, this work was probably painted by Francesco Guardi, a leading Venetian painter of *vedute*, or scenic city views. This painting depicts the *Torre dell'Orologio*, the clock tower that stands to the left of the famous Venetian St. Mark basilica, the facade and portals of which are shown at the right of this composition. Since the clock tower was restored in 1760 and this picture records those restorations, it would seem likely that this would provide an approximate date for the work. Here, Guardi records the canvas tents set up in the Piazza di San Marco to shelter merchants from the summer sun. He also shows Venetians strolling about through the famous square that remains an important tourist site in Italy today.

Francesco Guardi was born into a family of scene painters and often collaborated on the same paintings with his brother, Gian-Antonio. Around the 1750s, Guardi began to specialize in views of his native Venice in the manner of his older contemporary, Giovanni Antonio Canal, called "Il Canaletto." Stylistically, the Art Institute's small panel painting shows some of the hallmarks of Canaletto's influence upon Guardi. Although in his time Guardi never attained the same fame as Canaletto, he was far-better appreciated in the 19th century, when interest in atmospheric effects was favored over photographic truthfulness.

DHV

Suggested Readings:

Levey, Michael. **Painting in XVIII Century Venice**. *Garden City, New York: Phaidon Publishers, Inc., and Doubleday and Company, Inc., 1959.*

Zampetti, Pietro. **Mostra dei Guardi**. *Exhibition catalogue, Palazzo Grassi. Venice: Edizione Alfieri, 1965.*

Austrian (Vienna)

18th century

ST. TERESA, *around 1760-1765*

Carved lindenwood with polychromy

H: 50 3/8 inches

Museum purchase, 1981.11

St. Teresa of Avila (1515-1582) was one of the most beloved saints of the Baroque age and, as such, was often portrayed in painting and sculpture. The vivacious, Spanish-born saint is best known as the reformer of the Carmelite order of nuns. She was, however, also a mystic whose life devoted to prayer and meditation allowed her to experience visions of great spiritual and physical intensity that she recorded in several important books (e.g., *Interior Castle*). In this wood sculpture, Teresa is shown kneeling, holding the crucifix, absorbed in a state of prayer. Characteristic of the Baroque style, the seemingly windswept robes of her Carmelite habit enforce the spiritual intensity of this sculpture.

Unlike many undocumented sculptures whose artist or original site will no doubt remain unknown for posterity, this anonymously sculpted work was created as part of a large decorative scheme for the Ursuline Convent in Vienna, a religious building that was secularized in the 20th century and its contents subsequently dispersed. Each figure or group of figures, which represented saints or scenes from the lives of Christ and the Virgin Mary, were installed in glass-covered niches around a three-story cloister in the Ursuline Convent; the roughly-chiseled, unfinished back of this *St. Teresa* demonstrates that the back was never intended to be seen. Each niche was in essence a three-dimensional tableau with illusionistically painted backgrounds, a type of religious decoration not uncommon to parts of Austria, Italy, and Spain. As such, this work carries on a centuries-old tradition of polychromed sculpture found in European churches, monasteries, and convents.

Not a great deal is known about the artists and the genesis of this once impressive decorative cycle. Other sculptures from the convent have been acquired by the Cleveland Museum of Art, the The Nelson-Atkins Museum of Art (Kansas City, Missouri), the National Gallery of Canada (Ottawa), and the Montreal Museum of Fine Arts. While the figures generally share the same scale, technical elements, and dramatic style, it is quite evident that several artists were employed by the Ursuline sisters to execute this large series comprised of 40-plus individual statues or groups. Though the identities of the sculptors of these works remain obscured by time, two artists have been associated with this project: Franz Anton Danne (active 1726-1764) and Josef Peer (active 1760).

DHV

SUGGESTED READINGS:

Keutner, Herbert. **Sculpture: Renaissance to Rococo**. *Greenwich: New York Graphic Society, 1969.*

Stech, V.V. **Baroque Sculpture**. *London: Springs Books, 1959.*

Sir Joshua Reynolds
(1723-1792) English

HENRY, EIGHTH LORD ARUNDELL OF WARDOUR, *around 1764-1767*

Oil on canvas

94 x 58 inches

Gift of Mr. and Mrs. Harry S. Price, Jr., 1969.52

The act of having one's portrait painted must be nearly as old as human vanity itself, and the desire to be remembered and immortalized, especially in a life-sized portrait, follows the Roman epigram, "Life is brief, art is long." Indeed, art can extend the fame of the famous or, in some rare cases, even create fame for an otherwise "ordinary" individual.

Just such a case is that of Henry, Eighth Lord Arundell of Wardour (1740-1808), who has the dubious distinction of having done little to earn a place in England's history, other than in 1764 having commissioned Sir Joshua Reynolds to paint his and his wife's portraits. Henry was of English Catholic nobility, eighth heir to a title created by King James I in 1605, which became extinct in 1944 at the death of the 15th Lord Arundell.

Sitter and artist could not have been less similar. Sir Joshua Reynolds was a very different sort of man, undoubtedly the most famous English painter of his age. Although called "Sir Sploshua" by some of his contemporary detractors for his generous, Rubenesque handling of large, painted surfaces, Reynolds drastically changed the look of English portraiture and helped to transform the sociology of English art. Before him, most important English portraits were painted by imported European masters—Dutch, Germans, and Italians. Reynolds was the first to establish himself as a master portraitist at home. He did this by assimilating the traditions of the Baroque era's "Grand Manner" and further enriched his compositions with references from Roman portraiture to stylistic elements of the Italian High Renaissance.

The Art Institute's portrait of *Henry* is typical of Reynold's work, full of bravura and aristocratic elegance. In his own day, Reynolds' critics lampooned his lofty artistic sentiments and his elegant snobbery, yet few could argue with the painter's importance, however much they disdained the society that patronized him.

DHV

Suggested Readings:

Reynolds. *Nicholas Penny ed. New York: Harry N. Abrams, Inc., 1986.*

Waterhouse, Ellis K. **Painting in Britain, 1530-1790**. *Baltimore: Penguin Books, 1953.*

French

STILL LIFE WITH ONIONS AND A TRUFFLE, *18th century*

Oil on wood panel

9 1/4 x 12 inches

Gift of Mr. and Mrs. Elton F. MacDonald, 1962.56

Although once thought to be painted by the great 18th century French still-life painter, Jean Baptiste Siméon Chardin, this small still-life has for many years been without an attribution. The reasons for its connection with Chardin are not difficult to explain. The work has a straightforward approach, a simplicity both of subject matter and artistic vision coupled with a great sophistication and technical perfection that is worthy of the great master. Still, no painting like this was ever recorded in Chardin's work, therefore in the future, one must hope for a correct attribution. Numerous suggestions have been made during the years, including 18th century French still-life painters Dominique Pergaut (1729-1808), Anne Vallayer-Coster (1744-1818), Jean-Etienne Liotard (1702-1789), and Henri-Horace Roland de la Porte (1725-1793).

The great charm of this little painting depends upon the talent of its unknown maker to portray common objects not only with verisimilitude, but with a certain personal flair. Likewise, the painter's choice of two earth-grown foods, one common, the other a culinary rarity, makes for an interesting comparison. The light that falls across the small, but open picture plane sculpts the simple forms, heightening a sense of reality of these humble onions and highly prized fungus. The straightforward and unpretentious manner of presentation imparts an accessibility that is appropriate and believable. Whoever painted this work was certainly a highly capable still-life painter.

DHV

SUGGESTED READINGS:

Fare, Michel, and Pierre Cailler ed. **La Nature Morte en France: son historie et son évolution du XVIIe au XXe siécle**. *Geneva: P. Cailler, 1962.*

Rosenberg, Pierre. **The Age of Louis XV, French Painting 1710-1774**. *Exhibition catalogue. Toledo, OH: The Toledo Museum of Art, 1975.*

Baron François-Xavier Fabre
(1766-1837) French

ROMAN CHARITY: CIMON AND PERA, 1800

Oil on canvas

39 3/4 x 58 inches

Museum purchase with funds provided by Mr. and Mrs. Henry G. Schneider in memory of Theodore Cole Dye, 1965.114

In *Roman Charity*, the classically draped figures are depicted in profile with their dramatic gestures set against a stark, dimly lit, stage-like setting. The absence of extraneous detail serves to heighten the central action and the moral message of charity that the painting conveys. The work depicts the classical theme of Cimon, an old man condemned to starve to death in prison. Only the heroic actions of his daughter Pera, who sustained him from her breast, kept her father alive. Such a Roman "example of virtue", or *exemplum virtutis*, was a favorite theme with Jacques-Louis David and his followers, including Baron François-Xavier Fabre.

Although this work was painted in Florence, Italy, where Fabre lived much of his life, *Roman Charity* is a particularly fine example of the French Neoclassical idiom in painting. Neoclassicism first developed as a style of painting and decoration in response to the light-hearted, curving sensuality and feminine sentimentality of the Rococo, the dominant style of the French 18th century associated with the court and nobility. Inspired in part by the discovery of Roman ruins at Herculaneum in 1738 and at Pompeii in 1749, Neoclassicism emphasized Greek and Roman subjects, settings, and details.

As led by David, Fabre's one-time teacher, Neoclassicism became the heroic style associated with the political aims of Republicanism and the French Revolution. Largely through the impact of David's *The Oath of the Horatii* (1784), *The Death of Socrates* (1787), and *Brutus and his Dead Sons* (1789), paintings that depict Greek and Roman subject matter extolling personal honor and virtue even in the face of great adversity, Neoclassicism influenced an entire generation of French painters, including Fabre.

A native of Montpellier, a city in the south of France, Fabre was a student of David's before entering the school of the Royal Academy in 1783 and winning the coveted *Grand Prix de Rome* in 1787. Unlike many of the other French artists working in Rome, Fabre did not hold revolutionary political views and as a consequence, he left Rome in 1793 for the safer atmosphere of Florence. There he painted subjects from history or Roman legend, such as the Art Institute's *Roman Charity*, along with numerous portraits, often commissions from visiting foreign noblemen and dignitaries. Fabre enjoyed a long and successful career, returning to Montpellier in 1825.

DHV

SUGGESTED READINGS:

Bordes, Philippe. "Francois-Xavier Fabre, 'Peintre d'Histoire,'" **Burlington Magazine** (March 1975): 155-162.

Rosenberg, Pierre, and Robert Rosenblum, et. al. **French Painting 1774-1830: The Age of Revolution**. Exhibition catalogue, Detroit Institute of Arts and The Metropolitan Museum of Art, 1975.

Rosenblum, Robert. "Caritas Romana after 1760: Some Romantic Lactations," **Art News Annual** (XXXVIII, 1972): 43-63.

Pierre-Nolasque Bergeret

(1782-1863) French

MARIUS MEDITATING ON THE RUINS OF CARTHAGE, *1807*

Oil on canvas

51 x 39 inches

Museum purchase with funds provided by the Berry and Dicke Families, 1997.20

Bordeaux-born artist and designer Pierre-Nolasque Bergeret is one of the more interesting, but less studied, artists of early 19th century France. A pupil of Jacques-Louis David, Bergeret was one of the first painters whose work begins to bridge the gap between Neoclassicism and Romanticism. Likewise, he was the first to make artistic lithographs at a time when the medium was thought to be suited for commercial purposes only. Bergeret also designed the *bas-reliefs* (shallow relief) for the column in the Place Vendome in Paris, as well as medals to commemorate Napoleon's victories and generals.

In this work, Bergeret focuses on a scene from the life of the Roman general Caius Marius, taken from Plutarch—a suitable source for an artist well-versed in Neoclassicism. Forced to flee Rome by his enemy Sulla, Marius was first taken prisoner at Minturnae, where he narrowly escaped assassination. Then after taking refuge in the ruined city of Carthage, Marius is told by a messenger of the governor that he must leave or be considered an enemy. It is at this point that the once-great general reflects upon how his own fate parallels Carthage, a city destroyed by Rome. Bergeret's masterful depiction of Marius' psychological struggle between disillusionment and pent-up fury characterizes the beginnings of Romanticism.

One fascinating aspect of this painting is its similarity to, as well as its difference from, a painting of the same subject by the American painter John Vanderlyn, now in the collection of the Fine Arts Museum of San Francisco. Vanderlyn is documented to have painted his Marius in Rome during 1807. In the following year, Vanderlyn moved to Paris and entered it in the annual Salon where, legend has it, the painting caught the eye of the emperor Napoleon and consequently was awarded a gold medal. While Bergeret's painting appears to be dated 1807, one cannot help question the date and genesis of his work. Bergeret frequently was "inspired" by the works of other artists; therefore, the possibility exists that the Art Institute's painting is in reaction to Vanderlyn's prize-winning work. Time and further research may help illuminate this interesting relationship.

DHV

SUGGESTED READINGS:

Levitine, George. **The Dawn of Bohemianism: The "Barbus" Rebellion and Primitivism in Neoclassical France**. *University Park and London: The Pennsylvania State University, 1978.*

Rosenblum, Robert. **Transformations in Late Eighteenth-Century Art**. *Princeton: Princeton University Press, 1967.*

Vasseur, Dominique H. **The Lithographys of Pierre-Nolasque Bergeret**, *exhibition catalogue, Dayton: The Dayton Art Institute, 1982.*

Antoine-Louis Barye
(1795-1875) French

THESEUS FIGHTING THE MINOTAUR, *around 1840*

Bronze with dark brown patina

H: 24 inches

Museum purchase with funds provided by the James F. Dicke Family in memory of Timothy M. Webster, 1998.17

The story of the Athenian prince Theseus and the ferocious Minotaur is one of the most interesting of the Greek myths. Born of the unnatural passion of Queen Pasiphae for a bull, the Minotaur was kept in the famous Labyrinth in the palace of King Minos on the island of Crete. For years, Athenian youths and maidens were sacrificed to this bloodthirsty monster until Theseus was sent to slay it. Unwinding a ball of twine so as to find his way out of the deep recesses of the labyrinth, Theseus finally meets up with the Minotaur and successfully kills it, thereby freeing Athens from its annual sacrifices. The myth's story, the triumph of virtue and bravery over abnormal passions is perfectly caught in Antoine-Louis Barye's depiction of the upright and heroic Theseus and the nearly coiling, contorted Minotaur. Barye probably relied upon a number of Renaissance and more contemporary Neoclassical sources for the attitudes of Theseus and the man-bull. Theseus's stance is comparable to a drawing by Henry Fuseli after Andrea del Sarto as well as Jacques-Louis David's famous *Oath of the Horatii* and Théodore Géricault's *Grappling Boxers*.

Antoine-Louis Barye is one of the best known sculptors of Europe's Romantic era. His works of animals parallel to some degree the paintings of his contemporary, the great Eugène Delacroix. Barye was in his 20s when he began studying animals in the Jardin des Plantes, a Parisian zoo. He carefully recorded his anatomical observations in sketchbooks that he consulted for his sculptural models. Barye's career grew after he successfully entered a sculpture of a tiger on the attack in the Salon of 1831. While Barye worked for the French court of King Louis-Philippe, producing numerous large-scale public commissions, he also produced works in series destined for the wealthy middle class. As his royal commissions declined, Barye turned to the *bourgeoisie* for a new source of patronage, and Barye's bronzes, identically cast in limited series at the Barbedienne foundry, provided a new market that endures today.

DHV

Suggested Readings:

Benge, Glenn F. **Antoine Louis Barye, Sculptor of Romantic Realism**. *University Park, PA: Pennsylvania State University Press, 1984.*

Pivar, Stuart. **The Barye Bronzes: A Catalogue Raisonné**. *Woodbridge, England: Antiques Collectors' Club, 1990.*

French
19th century

ROMEO AND JULIET, *around 1860-1870*

Oil on canvas
33 1/2 x 27 inches
Gift of Mr. Robert Badenhop, 1954.13

This fascinating, unsigned painting, traditionally called *Romeo and Juliet*, first came to the attention of the art world in 1942 when art historian and critic Walter Pach wrote about it in the October issue of *Art in America* calling it a "Newly Discovered Ingres." As art historians scrutinized the work, however, it became increasingly evident, stylistically and technically, that it was not the work of the great 19th century painter, Jean Auguste Dominique Ingres. Only superficial parallels could be made between this work and Ingres' early historical paintings with analogous themes of famous lovers such as that of *Paolo and Francesca*.

Around 1978, research turned up a photograph that demonstrated conclusively that the chapel depicted here is not merely the product of an artist's imaginative invention, but in fact, the Chapel of St. John the Baptist at the Collegio del Cambio in Perugia, Italy, decorated with paintings by Giannicola di Paolo. Although the setting is Perugia and not Verona, which would seem to discount the identity of the lovers as Romeo and Juliet of Verona, artistic license might be sufficient justification for this inconsistency.

Although the chapel setting is now known, the artist of this intriguing work remains a mystery. Various 19th century artists have been suggested: the French painter James Jacques Tissot, and the Belgian Baron Hendrik Leys, among others. Recently paintings by Jules Arsène Garnier (1847-1889), a French pupil of the great Academic artist, Jean Léon Gérôme, have provided interesting comparisons to this work. The skillful representation of the two Renaissance-style costumed lovers, the careful depiction of the chapel setting, and the bright, clear colors certainly point to a follower of Gérôme and an academic painter of considerable talent. In time, perhaps Garnier will prove to be the right artist.

DHV

SUGGESTED READINGS:

Foley, Kathy K. *"A Problematic Setting Identified: Report on Research on Progress."* **The Dayton Art Institute Bulletin** *(December 1978, Vol. 37): 19-21.*

Sloane, Joseph C. **French Painting Between Past and Present: Artists, Critics and Tradition from 1848 to 1870**. *Princeton: Princeton University Press, 1973.*

Jean-Léon Gérôme
(1824-1904) French
DANCE OF THE ALMEH, 1863
Oil on wood panel
19 3/4 x 32 inches
Gift of Mr. Robert Badenhop, 1951.15

A polished and meticulously painted work, Jean-Léon Gérôme's *Dance of the Almeh* is representative of a type of painting now referred to as Academic. It also illustrates the European 19th century fascination and taste for scenes of the exotic Near East and North Africa. The clearly lit scene, with its sharply focused and almost photographic style of painting, conforms to the standards of the official Academy of France, the country's most prestigious and powerful artistic institution.

Previously thought to represent an Egyptian coffeehouse, the exotic setting of this painting is undoubtedly the Turkish port city of Smyrna, a fact known from an inscription on two pencil studies by Gérôme that the Art Institute purchased in 1983. One study shows the *almeh*, or dancing girl, the other the seated *Bashi-Bazouk*, or Albanian mercenary soldier whose attention the *almeh* has assuredly captured.

This painting was exhibited at the French Academy's 1864 Salon, the official vehicle for artists to show their work and the means by which many furthered their reputations. Gérôme was one of France's most popular and successful artists of the time. As a member of the Academy, he garnered every honor the French government could bestow upon an artist. Gérôme was particularly admired for his exquisite sense of color and his impeccable drawing style, yet his typically small paintings fell out of favor in the early 20th century as French Impressionism gained in popular acceptance. Today, however, Gérôme's works are highly valued by critics and laypersons alike, enjoyed alongside works by his more unorthodox contemporaries, the Impressionists.

DHV

SUGGESTED READINGS:

Ackerman, Gerald M. **The Life and Work of Jean-Léon Gérôme with Catalogue Raisonné**. New York: Sotheby Publications (Harper and Row), 1986.

Ackerman, Gerald M., Richard Ettinghausen, and Bruce Evans. **Jean-Léon Gérôme**. Exhibition catalogue. Dayton, OH: The Dayton Art Institute, 1972.

Boime, Albert. **The Academy and French Painting in the Nineteenth Century**. London: Phaidon Press, Ltd., 1971.

Charles-François Daubigny
(1817-1878) French

A LAKE IN THE WOODS AT DUSK, *around 1865-1875*

Oil on canvas
25 x 32 1/4 inches
Museum purchase with funds provided by the Associate Board's 1997 Art Ball, 1997.34

Charles-François Daubigny was part of the group of artists known as the Barbizon School. They took this name from a town southeast of Paris on the outskirts of the Fontainebleau Forest. Daubigny and his colleagues were some of the earliest proponents of *plein air* (open air) painting, and they prepared the way for the younger Impressionists. Unlike the Impressionists, the Barbizon artists painted studies in the out-of-doors, then created finished works in the studio.

Daubigny distinguished himself by working almost entirely out-of-doors and he helped to break down the rigid distinction between a sketch and finished work. As in this work from the 1860s to 1870s, Daubigny shares the Impressionists' rapid, broken brush strokes and interest in the effect of evening light upon a lake. The Academic art community severely criticized him for passing off "working sketches" as completed paintings.

Many of Daubigny's paintings, like the Art Institute's, demonstrate his love of the waterways, canals, and lakes around Paris that he would paint from a specially fitted studio-boat. One of his favorite sites to paint was the river Oise located north of Paris. It is little wonder that the young Claude Monet, whom Daubigny had befriended and championed, emulated his older mentor by painting numerous scenes of the Seine River. Likewise, Daubigny painted alongside Gustave Courbet, Eugène Boudin, and Monet at Trouville on France's northern seacoast. Daubigny's importance as a precursor and advocate of Impressionism, as well has his own considerable talent, have earned him a significant place in the history of late 19th century French painting.

DHV

Suggested Readings:

Herbert, Robert L., **Barbizon Revisited**, *exhibition catalogue, Museum of Fine Art, Boston, 1962.*

Hoeber, Arthur, **The Barbizon Painters**, *New York: Frederick A. Stokes Co., 1909.*

Mihaly von Munkacsy
(1844-1900) Hungarian

THE VILLAGE BLACKSMITH, *around 1875*

Oil on canvas

30 x 25 inches

Gift of Mr. Robert Badenhop, 1956.26

This painting by the late 19th century Hungarian artist, Mihaly von Munkacsy appears to be almost portrait-like in its close observation of a village blacksmith. The man's bearded face is ruddy and his features are strong and full of character. His muscular arms and upper torso underscore his occupation and give the man a heroic quality, not unlike a modern Hercules. The neutral, gray room behind the blacksmith provides an interesting foil, contrasting the man's pale shoulder and arm against a darker background. At the same time, his darkened left profile stands out against a brighter patch of wall. This clever convention helps to enliven what might otherwise have been a fairly straightforward depiction of a hard-laboring man.

Munkacsy, like many artists of the second half of the 19th century, was influenced by the French Realist artist Gustave Courbet (1819-1877) whose paintings of everyday people and events provided a revolutionary break from the exotic and erotic allegories and historical paintings of the Parisian art establishment. Likewise, Munkacsy, who spent much of his career in Paris, adopted a technique similar to Courbet's, constructing his figures and compositions with solidity and confidence.

Unlike most of the German artists with whom Munkacsy studied or was associated, his paintings avoid the anecdotal, moralizing, or humorous. Rather, Munkacsy's brand of Realism tended to take a middle-road between complete objectivity and overt subjectivity, and his critical success was rewarded with a number of medals (1870 and 1874) from exhibitions in Paris, then the world's art center. Incidently, Cincinnati-born painter Henry Farny studied with Munkacsy in Düsseldorf as part of his artistic formation.

DHV

SUGGESTED READINGS:

Novotny, Fritz. **Painting and Sculpture in Europe, 1780 to 1880**. Baltimore: Penguin Books, 1960.

Rosenblum, Robert, and H. W. Janson. **19th-Century Art**. New York: Harry N. Abrams, Inc., 1984.

René Lalique
(1860-1945) French

SWALLOWS AND MAIDENS BROOCH, *1889-1900*

Gold, enamel, plique-a-jour enamel, large baroque pearl
2 5/8 x 23 /4 inches
Stamped "LALIQUE"
Museum purchase with funds provided by the James F. Dicke Family,1998.36

René Lalique's exquisite jewelry and art glass are important not only as finely crafted objects, but as expressions of late 19th and early 20th century ideas about the role of the decorative arts in our lives. The Art Institute's brooch, with its undulating lines, whiplash curves, and maidens deep in reverie, is an excellent example of French Art Nouveau translated into the medium of enamel and gold. It epitomizes the Art Nouveau interest in natural forms rendered in the flat, abstract manner of Japanese prints. The two maidens' eyes are half-closed and they seem to be harmoniously and spiritually in tune with the birds that swoop over and under them.

Prior to designing this brooch, Lalique had lent items to the inaugural exhibition at Samuel Bing's Paris shop, "La Maison de L'Art Nouveau," which gave the movement its name. Bing was an importer of Oriental objects and was instrumental in introducing Europe to the aesthetics of Japanese art. Lalique, who was always interested in portraying nature in his glass and jewelry, responded to the Japanese sensitivity to nature and the rendering of nature's forces through sinuous curves, rich design, and startlingly atmospheric settings.

Lalique's family moved from their native town of Ay, in the Marne region of France, to the suburbs of Paris in 1862. They vacationed in the country and the young Lalique was able to observe closely the flowers and insects that dominate his jewelry. In 1876, after the death of his father, Lalique left school and apprenticed himself to the Paris jeweler, Louis Aucoc. He then went to study in London, where he was exposed to the active Arts and Craft movement. Upon his return to Paris in 1880, he began working for numerous jewelry manufacturers as a freelance designer until opening his own studio in 1885. From then on, his designs became increasingly popular and he had many high-profile clients, including Sarah Bernhardt and the Portuguese collector Calouste Gulbenkian.

MAL

Suggested Readings:

Becker, Vivienne. **The Jewellery of René Lalique**. Exhibition catalogue. London: Goldsmiths' Company, 1987.

Brunhammer, Yvonne, ed. **The Jewels of Lalique**. Paris: Flammarion, 1998.

Lionel Noël Royer

(1852-1926) French

PORTRAIT OF FRANCOIS JEAN BAPTISTE EMMANUEL GUSTAVE, COMTE D'ADHEMAR DE CRANSAC, *1890*

Oil on canvas, in original period frame

79 x 38 inches

Museum purchase with funds provided by the James F. Dicke Family in memory of Ben H. Campbell, 1998.18

Lionel Noël Royer was a student of the well-known Academic painters Alexandre Cabanel and William Adolphe Bouguereau, the latter of whom is represented in the Art Institute's collection by *The Song of the Nightingale* of 1895 (see pg. 267). Royer first exhibited at the Paris Salon of 1874 and was awarded a second prize medal at the Salon of 1896. This work is a handsome depiction of a member of the French aristocracy, Count Adhémar de Cransac, who lived from 1836 to 1905. Cransac married Marie Charlotte Alice de Mory de Neuflieux in 1871, and the arms of the Adhémar of Longuedoc of Mory of Lorraine are carved into the shields on the frame. A *fleur-de-lis*, symbol of the French monarchy, is found in each of the frame's corners.

Royer's portrayal of this nobleman carries on a great European portrait tradition, the roots of which can be traced back to Italian Renaissance artists such as Titian. One can immediately tell the man's aristocratic bearing by his elegant evening clothes as well as the calm and sure manner with which he stops and turns as if to address the viewer. Royer heightens the elegance of this portrait through his use of an understated palette limited to white, black, and shades of gray and pink. Royer also takes great delight in depicting the likewise subtle yet rich textures of the count's clothing: the soft fur of his coat collar, the crisp starched white of his shirt, and the touches of gold at the handle of his cane, his monocle, and fob. The count appears to be arriving at or possibly leaving the famed Paris Opera house, an institution on whose board he may have served. Future research should shed light on his relationship with this Paris landmark.

DHV

SUGGESTED READINGS:

Bénézit, E. **Dictionnaire critique et documentaire des Peintres, Sculpteurs, Dessinateurs et Graveurs...**, IX volume, Paris: Libraire Gründ, 1976.

Edgar Degas
(1834-1917) French

AFTER THE BATH*, around 1895*

Pastel on paper

18 x 23 1/4 inches

Gift of Mr. and Mrs. Anthony Haswell, 1952.33

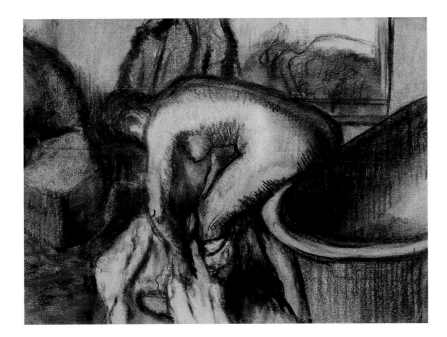

I n this pastel drawing by late 19th century French artist Edgar Degas, one senses a fleeting important moment in a seemingly unimportant activity. For Degas, no human activity or action was unworthy of being observed and recorded. He learned this from one of his elder contemporaries, Realist and social artist Honoré Daumier. Degas explores just such a moment as a woman dries herself after a bath, seemingly unaware of the artist who records her movements. Although the viewer intrudes upon this intimate scene, one senses no embarrassment, but rather the natural feeling of a woman who stoops to dry her feet and ankles. The mirror on the wall at the right captures and from another angle the graceful, yet imperfect curve of the woman's back.

Degas was an unusual, prolific, and extremely complex artist whose personality is still difficult to determine. He was intensely intrigued, obsessed perhaps, with depicting the female body. The women he encountered in late 19th century Paris–ballet dancers, entertainers, laundresses, salesgirls, and models (such as the one depicted in this pastel)–provided Degas with a seemingly endless array of poses and attitudes. Nearly all of the other Impressionist artists preferred landscapes, cityscapes, and the out-of-doors; Degas favored the indoors, the intimate, and the urbane.

Although Degas pushed his artistic explorations into the realm of the third dimension by creating sculptures of ballet dancers and bathing women, his greatest talent and strength remained the art of drawing, of which he said, "it is a way of thinking, and it is not form, but the manner of seeing form." In this pastel, Degas strongly delineates the central form of the stooping woman and the tub. He emphasizes these with parallel lines and reinforced contours. Color, which is generally thought to be of primary importance for Impressionist artists, in this drawing is secondary to line, which for Degas is paramount for the success of his work. As with most of his depictions of women, Degas conveys a sense of the universal beauty and grace that he experienced in the most commonplace.

DHV

Suggested Readings:

Boggs, Jean Sutherland, et al. **Degas**. *Exhibition catalogue, The Metropolitan Museum of Art and The National Gallery of Canada, 1988.*

Brettell, Richard, and Suzanne Folds McCullagh. **Degas in the Art Institute of Chicago**. *New York: Harry N. Abrams, Inc., 1984.*

Vasseur, Dominique (introduction), and Karen Wilkin (essay). **Edgar Degas: The Many Dimensions of a Master French Impressionist**. *Exhibition catalogue. Dayton, OH: The Dayton Art Institute, 1994.*

William Adolphe Bouguereau
(1825-1905) French

THE SONG OF THE NIGHTINGALE, *1895*

Oil on canvas

55 x 35 inches

Gift of Mr. Robert Badenhop, 1954.12

I t is easy to understand why, in his day, William Adolphe Bouguereau's art was so appealing and popular. There can be no denying the artist's consummate skill as a painter; Bouguereau's Academic style favors care and perfection in drawing, anatomy, and execution. His colors are usually cool and soothing, his lighting is soft yet clear, and the surface of his paintings are flawlessly smooth. Like the Art Institute's painting, Bouguereau's most popular works are of humble people, especially women and children, caught in moments of quiet reflection or casual, innocent diversion. Here a simple peasant girl—a personification of innocence itself—presumably lost deep in thought, listens to the song of a nightingale perched upon a branch over her shoulder. Her eyes are diverted from the viewer and her thoughts, perhaps of a loved-one not present, are equally hidden.

In 1895, the year Bouguereau painted this work, Claude Monet was obsessively involved in his famous series of facades of the Rouen Cathedral, Paul Gauguin was painting the exotic women of Tahiti in bright, shocking colors and a purposefully "primitive" style, and Vincent van Gogh had been deceased for five years. Compared with paintings of these moderns, until only recently many 20th century art critics found Bouguereau's paintings staid, somewhat artificial, and to the taste of some, saccharin. In our own time, as a broader-based and more fully developed view of 19th century art is formed, we are able to appreciate such seemingly antithetical artistic styles as Academism and Impressionism. Bouguereau, however, scorned the avant-garde, remaining steadfast to, in his words, "the sincere study of nature, the search for the true and the beautiful."

In 1850, four years after he arrived in Paris, Bouguereau won the coveted first prize of the *Prix de Rome* and was set on course for an extremely successful career. From 1849 until his death, he exhibited regularly at the official Salons, garnering many honors and prizes in Paris and his native city of La Rochelle. In 1876 Bouguereau was a member of the Legion of Honor; that same year he was made a member of the revered and very conservative *Institut de France*, later serving as its president.

DHV

Suggested Readings:

d'Argencourt, Louise, et al. **William Bouguereau**. *Exhibition catalogue. Montreal: The Montreal Museum of Fine Art, 1984.*

Rosenblum, Robert and H.W. Janson. **19th Century Art**. *New York: Harry N. Abrams, Inc., 1984.*

François-Raoul Larche

(1860-1912) French

LOIE FULLER, *around 1896*

Gilt bronze with electric lamps and cord

Signed on front of base and marked: "Siot-Decauville/Fondeur/Paris"

H: 18 1/8 inches

Gift of the James F. Dicke Family, 1998.27

Born in Fullersburg, Illinois, Mary Louise (Loie) Fuller (1862-1928) achieved international success as a theatrical dancer in Paris, where she first appeared at the Folies-Bergère in 1892. Although Fuller's act was amazingly simple in its concept—dancing in voluminous silk garments under the play of colored lights—the American dancer became an overnight sensation and received the attention of a devoted public and admiring and enthusiastic artistic community. Fuller's performances were captured in two and three dimensions by dozens of artists, among whom some of the most important were Henri de Toulouse-Lautrec, Jules Cheret, Georges de Feure, Will Bradley, and François-Raoul Larche, the sculptor of this particular table-sculpture, which doubles as an electric lamp.

Fuller's success in Paris was due in large part to the juncture of two seemingly unrelated factors. The first was the introduction of electric lights into the theaters of Paris, a sign of scientific technological progress. Indeed, Paris was to become known as the "city of light" due to the widespread use of electric light. Second, however, was the prevailing artistic climate of late 19th century Paris: Symbolism. Faced with the growing materialism and rationalism of modern life expressed in both Realism and Impressionism, artists who gathered around the poet Stéphane Mallarmé searched anew for life's mystery. To pursue this goal, poets and painters alike found the dreamlike more real than reality itself. The combined effect of the human senses as filtered through the artistic soul expressed a vision of this new, desired internal reality of Symbolism. It is not surprising then that Fuller's performance, which combined movement, color, and sound, was highly applauded by Mallarmé and other Symbolist artists. Likewise, Fuller's undulating and swirling draperies prefigure the sinuous lines and forms of the Art Nouveau ("New Art"), an international style that developed in Paris at the very end of the 19th century.

DHV

Suggested Reading:

Harris, Margaret Haile. **Loie Fuller: Magician of Light**. *Exhibition catalogue. Richmond: The Virginia Museum, 1979.*

Léon Augustin Lhermitte
(1844-1925) French

SUNDOWN: RETURN OF THE CATTLE, 1897

Oil on canvas
38 3/4 x 31 1/4 inches
Gift of Mr. and Mrs. Irvin G. Bieser, Sr., 1962.67

Here, after a tiring day in the fields, a young peasant woman returning to the farm with the herd of cattle stops to exchange a few words with two field hands resting after a long day, perhaps, cutting wheat. Léon Augustin Lhermitte evokes a quiet mood, the soft shuffling of the cattle as they return home and the drone of cicadas or grasshoppers in the late afternoon air. Although the subjects of this work are tired, a slight tension exists between the resting men and the standing woman: Are the men flirting with the lovely young woman? Is the woman the lover of one of the workmen, or is her interest merely passing?

Throughout the latter-half of the 19th century, rural and rustic life provided interesting subjects to Realist artists like Lhermitte, a painter eclipsed by his avant-garde contemporaries, the Impressionists. Yet, like Jean-François Millet and other Barbizon School painters, Lhermitte's depiction of peasants and farm workers are not merely slices of life. Rather, they belong to a type of art that portrayed the nobility of rural life and the honesty of hard work. Unlike Millet's generalized depictions of the noble peasantry, Lhermitte's canvases are peopled with portrait-like representations of laborious and serious peasants he would have known from his native town, Mont-Saint-Père.

As Lhermitte was born in a tiny village of sturdy, peasant stock, the lives and toils of such people that fill his oil paintings and pastels were not merely fictional to him but very real. Lhermitte, devoutly religious and committed to the virtues of a solid family, led a quiet, undramatic yet, nonetheless, successful life. As a student in Paris, Lhermitte variously studied Millet, Corot, Daubigny, and Legros, creating a style and technique that was pleasing to the eye. The somewhat broken brushstrokes of *Sundown: Return of the Cattle* show his study and adoption of Impressionist principles later in his career. Regrettably, while Lhermitte continued to glorify the life of rural France, growing mechanization, industrialization, and a shift to the life and pleasures of the city irrevocably changed the taste of the times away from subjects of rural life. Lhermitte, however, remained true to his favorite subjects—washerwomen, harvesters, and gleaners—supplementing these with evocations of the French landscape.

DHV

SUGGESTED READINGS:

Hamel, Mary Michele. **Léon Lhermitte**. *Exhibition catalogue, The Paine Art Center & Arboretum, 1974.*

Rosenblum, Robert, and H.W. Janson. **19th-Century Art**. *New York: Harry N. Abrams, Inc., 1984.*

Edward Colonna
(1862-1948) French
MUSIC CABINET, 1899-1900
Walnut, cherry, and fruitwood inlay
H: 62 3/4 (to top of crest) x W: 25 1/2 x D: 17 1/8 inches
Museum purchase with funds provided by the 1981 and 1982 Associate Boards, 1982.2

The 1900 World's Fair in Paris offered Samuel Bing and his studio of craftsmen (among them Edward Colonna, Eugène Gaillard and Georges de Feure) the opportunity to exhibit their splendid new creations to the world in a series of furnished display rooms. Bing was an art dealer and entrepreneur whose Paris shop, La Maison de L'Art Nouveau, promoted beautifully crafted works all done in the current style of the times. This *Music Cabinet*, a unique piece intended to hold sheet music albums, was placed in the corner of a reception room along with a piano, chairs, rugs, and vases, all designed by Colonna. This work's elegant proportions, energetic yet lyrical sense of decoration, and use of handsome, exotic materials won Colonna considerable attention and critical acclaim—as well as a silver medal from the World's Fair Committee.

Colonna (originally Klönne) was born in Germany, but emigrated to the United States in 1882. He found employment in New York with the famous American decorator, Louis Comfort Tiffany, and the fashionable architect, Bruce Price. Colonna's early works as a designer favored motifs derived from historical styles, such as English Tudor, French Romanesque, and the Italian and French Renaissance. In 1885, Colonna left New York for Dayton, Ohio, where he began work as a designer of railway car interiors for the Barney & Smith Manufacturing Company. While in Dayton, he published a small, but highly interesting booklet *Essay on Broom-Corn* (1887) of designs based on the lowly plant from which brooms are made. Due greatly to this small booklet, Colonna is now credited as one of the earliest Art Nouveau ("New Art") designers.

Colonna left Dayton in 1888, spent several years working in Canada, and eventually returned to Europe, where he found work with Bing. This modern "New Art" owed little stylistically to previous historical periods; rather, it was typified by luxurious materials, exquisite craftsmanship, sinuously curving lines, and decorations derived from nature, such as vines, flowers, and insects. Many art critics heralded Art Nouveau as the elegant new style of the modern age.

DHV

Suggested Readings:

*Julian, Philippe. **The Triumph of Art Nouveau, Paris Exhibition 1900**. New York: Larousse and Co., Inc., 1974.*

*Eidelberg, Dr. Martin (essayist). **E. Colonna**. Exhibition catalogue. Dayton, OH: The Dayton Art Institute, 1983.*

Claude Monet
(1840-1926) French
WATERLILIES, 1903
Oil on canvas
32 x 40 inches
Gift of Mr. Joseph Rubin, 1953.11

In this work, one of Claude Monet's quintessential waterlily paintings, the picture plane is completely filled with an impression of light and color reflected from the surface of a lily pond. Neither people, land, nor horizon line break our focused, hypnotic gaze into this cool and soothing scene of a pond on a warm summer's day. Cut off from an exact sense of place or narrative theme, this painting seems amazingly modern for its nearly abstract qualities, even more so considering its date of execution.

Like *Waterlilies*, some of Monet's most important explorations in color and composition were made in the gardens of his home at Giverny, some 30 miles west of Paris. He had installed an ornamental water garden that proved to be the focal point for dozens of his explorations of color and light. Monet began painting his waterlily scenes as a nonintentional series of color and light studies. His repetitive studies of various features of the French countryside around him—poplar trees, haystacks, snowbound villages, and even the facade of the Rouen Cathedral—show an artist whose keen eye and searching intellect were not content to rest after capturing the effects of light, shade, and color only once.

By 1903, the date of this work, this style of painting, Impressionism, had become widely accepted in the art world and highly influential with collectors and young artists alike. Monet was a traditionally trained artist who had become dissatisfied with the somewhat dry and predictable painting produced by artists of the French Academy. Unlike them, Monet favored painting directly from nature (*en plein air*), setting up his canvases in the outdoors to capture his fleeting "impressions" of a scene as it appeared to him under different conditions of weather or lighting.

DHV

SUGGESTED READINGS:

Monet's Years at Giverny: Beyond Impressionism. *Exhibition catalogue, The Metropolitan Museum of Art, New York: Harry N. Abrams, Inc., 1978.*

Rewald, John. **The History of Impressionism**. *New York: The Museum of Modern Art, 1961.*

Daum Glassworks (Nancy, France)

GEOLOGIA VASE, *1905*

Clear glass with variously colored glass overlays and applied shells

H: 12 7/8 inches

Gift of the James F. Dicke Family, 1998.29

The Daum Glassworks, founded in Nancy, France in 1878, is renowned for its creative use of motifs from nature. Daum vases, lamps, and pitchers, are replete with references to trees, flowers, butterflies, dragonflies, and frogs. Use of such decorative motifs is typical of Art Nouveau artists working around the turn-of-the-century, and the Art Institute's *Geologia Vase* can be best understood in terms of French Art Nouveau and Symbolist thought and art. Another source for this vase can be found in the scientific interests and discoveries of the *fin de siècle* (end of the 19th century).

Albert Aurier, French Symbolism's major theorist, asserted that an art of suggestion, rather than one of realist definition, was most capable of expressing the spiritual world of the artist. In this formulation, nature becomes a mysterious, ambiguous realm through which ineffable truths and spiritual longings can be expressed. The French Symbolist Odilon Redon began doing oil and pastel canvases that were dreamlike evocations of primordial worlds around 1895. These works resemble, in subject and style, the *Geologia Vase*.

The late 19th century was also a time of an increasing interest in the natural and human sciences. The new discoveries taking place in natural science and the proliferation of museums devoted to scientific and natural phenomena were augmented by widespread dissemination of new ideas in illustrated magazines and journals. The artists working at the Daum factory were undoubtedly aware not only of Redon's work, which was exhibited regularly in Paris and elsewhere, but of the advances in the natural sciences as well.

Through the use of vitrified powders that create a lavalike, irregular surface and hand-carved shells and ammonites, the artist of this vase has sought to recreate the Earth's prehistoric geologic beauty and mystery. This geologic era is presented not as a physical or visual fact, but is rather suggested, in the same way Redon's paintings and pastels suggest rather than define. This vase is a firm testament to the interrelationship and mutual influences between the fine and decorative arts at the turn-of-the-century.

MAL

Suggested Readings:

Bacri, Clotide. **Daum**. *William Wheeler, trans. New York: Rizzoli International, Inc., 1993.*

Druick, Douglas, et al. **Odilon Redon: Prince of Dreams 1840-1916**. *New York: The Art Institute of Chicago in association with Harry N. Abrams, Inc., 1994.*

Théodore van Rysselberghe
(1862-1926) Belgian

RECLINING WOMAN WITH RED HAIR, 1906

Oil on canvas
21 3/4 x 25 7/8 inches
Gift of Mrs. Erwin D. Swann, 1960.93

The short, neatly applied brushstrokes that Théodore van Rysselberghe employed in creating this painting signal that he was greatly influenced by the Pointillist technique developed by the French artist Georges Seurat. With the use of bright, high-keyed colors, one of Impressionism's great contributions to late 19th century art was the fractured, accentuated brush stroke. Post-Impressionist artists, like Seurat, pushed these qualities to their furthest expression. Here van Rysselberghe uses these accented brush strokes and Impressionistic color to create a scene of repose and calm that is, at the same time, enlivened by the painting's decorative surface and bright, pleasing color.

Born in Ghent, van Rysselberghe was one of the founding members of a group of Belgian artists called *Les XX* (The Twenty). Beginning in 1884, these artists arranged exhibitions of European contemporary artists, especially French Impressionists and Post-Impressionists. Van Rysselberghe found a spiritual kinship in the works of Seurat and followed a similar path for a number of years. The attraction of Paris with its vital art scene was inevitably strong for a young, inquisitive artist. Like many others, van Rysselberghe moved there in 1898 and exhibited with the Neo-Impressionists at the *Salon des Indépendents*. After 1900, van Rysselberghe's works focus less stringently on precise brushwork and in favor of dramatic appeal. The Art Institute's *Reclining Woman with Red Hair* demonstrates the decorative qualities of van Rysselberghe's style that, nonetheless, is not without a certain sensuality and expressiveness of mood.

DHV

SUGGESTED READINGS:

Eeckhout, P. **Rétrospective Théo van Rysselberghe**. *Exhibition catalogue. Ghent: Musée des Beaux-Arts, 1962.*

Hamilton, George Heard. **Painting and Sculpture in Europe, 1880-1940**. *Baltimore: Penguin Books, 1967.*

Gaston La Touche

(1854-1913) French

LE DINER AU CASINO (DINNER AT THE CASINO), *around 1906*

Oil on canvas

39 x 37 5/8 inches

Gift of Mrs. Robert Schermer, 1975.33

The elegance and pastimes of *fin de siècle* France are portrayed with accuracy and panache in Gaston La Touche's painting, *Dinner at the Casino*. Here, gentlemen and ladies dressed in evening attire sit on the outdoor terrace of a fashionable club's restaurant exchanging pleasant conversation. In the center of composition, one man seems to be making advances to the young lady who sits with her back to him. Her smile, perhaps in response to this attention, underscores the lighthearted tenor of the scene. In the soft candlelight, one can easily imagine a string quartet playing music by Claude Debussy or Reynaldo Hahn and the balmy evening breeze wafting the scent of the flowers through the green arched trellis of the terrace. In the distant sky, fireworks crown the festive evening with shimmering gold and pink light.

Around the 1890s, La Touche's Academic style evolved towards freer, more lyrical compositions using a palette that was increasingly close to that of the Impressionist artists. Unlike many of his contemporaries, La Touche favored subjects which recalled the *fêtes champêtres et galantes* (pastoral outings) of 18th century artists such as Antoine Watteau and Jean-Honoré Fragonard. These works rarely depict specific occasions, yet, they accurately capture the mood of pre-World War I France, as the world's capital of political and artistic power, glittering parties, and elegant social gatherings. His sensitivity seems perfectly meshed with his era's predilection for richness and exaggerated beauty. Through all his paintings of nymphs, lunching ladies, and serene gardens, La Touche's masterful and harmonious use of color remains astonishing and captivating, a talent often remarked upon during his lifetime and appreciated equally well today.

DHV

SUGGESTED READINGS:

Frantz, Henri. **Gaston La Touche 1854-1913**. London, 1915.

Post-Impressionism: Cross-Currents in European Painting. Exhibition catalogue, Royal Academy of Arts. New York: Harper & Row, 1979.

Georges Rouault

(1871-1958) French

NOTRE DAME DES CHAMPS
(OUR LADY OF THE FIELDS), NO. 4, around 1920

Oil on paper, mounted on canvas

29 1/4 x 24 1/4 inches

Gift of Mr. John W. Sweeterman in memory of Jeanne F. Sweeterman, 1996.255

Although few well-known artists of the 20th century have addressed overtly Christian themes, Georges Rouault has produced some of the most successful and moving religious art of the century. As a young man, Rouault was apprenticed to a stained glass window maker, and it is not difficult to imagine the bold, outlined forms of this painting translated into glass panels. Rouault was a highly spiritual man who voiced his opinions against war, poverty, cruelty, and vice through his art. It is little wonder that his early paintings often depicted biblical stories and that he was greatly influenced by the religious paintings of Rembrandt van Rijn..

As Rouault's personal style developed in the early part of the century, his paintings became bolder, more colorful, and more intense. At the same time, he began to depict the people he encountered on the streets in his Paris neighborhood as well as circus performers, prostitutes, and an important theme, judges and lawyers. Rouault seemed especially sensitive to those individuals who, charged with administering justice, misused their authority for personal gain.

Around World War I and with the support of his art dealer Ambroise Vollard, Rouault conceived and began work on a major series of aquatints that he entitled the *Misèrere*. These 58 prints constitute a visual meditation on the themes of war, death, and salvation. One of the last images in this series, a Madonna and Child (*Our Lady of Land's End Keeps Vigil*), is clearly the same theme and composition as the Art Institute's painting. Rouault's process of exploring certain images in a variety of media demonstrates an active mind as well as his desire to immerse himself in the full intensity of his subject, in this case the healing love of the Madonna for the infant Jesus.

DHV

SUGGESTED READING:

Getlein, Frank, and Dorothy Getlein. **Georges Rouault's Misèrere**. Milwaukee: Bruce Publishing Co., 1964.

Ker-Xavier Roussel
(1867-1944) French

THE INFANCY OF JUPITER, *1923-1924*

Distemper on canvas
83 1/4 x 60 1/4 inches
Gift of Mr. Walter P. Chrysler, Jr., 1960.28

Ker-Xavier Roussel began his artistic career training with the older generation of French academic artists, including William Adolphe Bouguereau. He soon came under the influence of the Impressionists, and later of a small group of young artists who called themselves the *Nabis*, from the Hebrew word for "prophet." Among other things, the *Nabis* artists believed that a painting, drawing, or print should always be truthful to and reflect its essential structure—that is, its flatness. As a result, their paintings emphasized the nonillusionistic and decorative qualities of color, shape, and pattern.

Although painted many years after the *Nabis* had formed (1889-1899), Roussel's *The Infancy of Jupiter* reflects the influence of his earlier ties with them. The painting's highly patterned surface compresses various layers of vegetation against an intense blue sky with little suggestion of pictorial depth. Roussel often, as here, worked in distemper, an opaque medium not unlike poster paint whose appearance is somehow more solid and flat than varnished oil paint, which glistens and has a surface life unto itself. This panel was part of a series of large decorative works created especially for a private Paris apartment.

While classical and mythological subject matter had largely disappeared from many 20th century artists' work, Roussel continued to use themes from Europe's Renaissance and Baroque periods. Although the title of this refers to the childhood of Jupiter, the most important of the classical gods, the painting itself shows little that might distinguish it from any bucolic scene of a woman and child sunning and playing in a wooded glen. Traditionally, Jupiter (or the Greek god, Zeus) was born in either Arcadia in Greece or on the island of Crete. In one legend, he was nurtured as a child by the goat, Amaltheia; in another, he was tended by two nymphs, Neda and Ithome, one of whom may be suggested here.

DHV

Suggested Readings:

Hamilton, George Heard. **Painting and Sculpture in Europe, 1880-1940**. *Baltimore: Penguin Books, 1967.*

Mathieu, Pierre-Louis. **The Symbolist Generation, 1870-1910**. *New York: Skira/Rizzoli International Publications, 1990.*

Rewald, John. **Post-Impressionism from Van Gogh to Gauguin**. *New York: The Museum of Modern Art, n.d.*

Selected
Works from

PRE-COLUMBIAN ART

The Dayton Art

Institute Permanent

Collection

Maya (Yucatán, Mexico)
Late Classic period
CARVED PANEL BOWL, *A.D. 600-900*
Ceramic
H: 5 3/8 inches
Museum purchase with funds provided by Miss Anne E. Charch, 1968.114

In 1839, the American explorer John Lloyd Stephens and his companion, artist Frederick Catherwood, discovered the ruins of the "lost Maya" in the dense vine-covered jungles of the Yucatán, Mexico. Responding to a massive sculpted altar, Stephens, regarded by many as the father of American archaeology, wrote:

> The sight of this unexpected monument put at rest at once and forever, in our minds, all uncertainty in regard to the character of American antiquities, and gave us the assurance that the objects we were in search of were interesting not only as remains of an unknown people, but as works of art, proving, like newly-discovered historical records, that these people who once occupied the continent of America were not savages.

This deeply incised vessel was discovered in the Chocholá region of southwestern Yucatán. This is a fine example of Maya ceremonial pottery. The design depicts two priests or lords, their high status indicated by the elaborate clothing and the jaguar pelt–covered cushions at their backs, in a religious rite that includes autoblood sacrifice as indicated by the knotted cloth on the chest of the figure shown in this plate. The glyph on the opposite side reads "ad-?-na ah-ahaw" ([nominalized item]–he, lord).

This carved brown Late Classic period Maya vessel displays the same techniques used to carve the massive monument described by Stephens, producing a dramatic chiaroscuro effect in the bright tropical sun of the Yucatán peninsula. Later ceramics were usually mold-pressed rather than carved. This age of the Maya marked the beginning of their gradual decline. The Maya had flourished since the start of the millennium from the south of Mexico through the jungles of Belize, Guatemala, El Salvador, and Honduras and are known for their monumental architecture, astronomy, and hieroglyphic writing as well as their artistic creations including ceramics and painting.

ALN

SUGGESTED READINGS:

Fagen, Brian M. **Kingdoms of Gold, Kingdoms of Jade: The Americas Before Columbus**. *New York: Thames and Hudson, 1991.*

Schele, Linda. **The Blood of Kings: Dynasty and Ritual in Maya Art**. *New York: George Braziller in association with the Kimball Art Museum, 1986.*

Spinden, Herbert Joseph. **A Study of Maya Art, Its Subject Matter and Historical Development**. *Cambridge, MA: The Museum, 1913.*

Stephens, John Lloyd. **Incidents of Travel in Yucatan**. *New York: Harper & Brothers, 1860.*

Stephens, John Lloyd. **Incidents of Travel in Central America, Chiapas and Yucatan**. *New York: Harper & Brothers, 1863.*

Von Hagen, Victor Wolfgang. **Maya Explorer: John Lloyd Stephens and The Lost Cities of Central American and Yucatan**. *San Francisco: Chronicle Books, 1990. (University of Oklahoma Press, 1947).*

Maya (Guatemala)
Late Classic period
CYLINDRICAL VASE, *around A.D. 900*
Polychrome painted, fired earthenware
H: 6 1/2 inches; Dia: 6 1/2 inches
Museum purchase with funds provided by the Associate Board's 1967 Art Ball, 1967.78

They make of ground maize and cacao a kind of foaming drink which is very savory, and with which they celebrate their feasts and rituals.

Bishop Diego de Landa
First Bishop of Yucatán

The Mayan language refers to cylindrical vessels such as this Late Classic period example as *uch'ab* or "drinking vessel." As this 16th century account by a Spanish priest indicates, vessels such as these were used for the consumption of this common chocolate-based drink as part of their important ritualistic life.

Painted vessels are among the few media to survive from the strong Maya painting tradition. Most works-on-paper, paintings on cloth, and murals have been ruined by the less-than-favorable natural elements. Those that escaped the hot and humid environment were often destroyed by overzealous Spanish priests in their efforts to rid the indigenous people of their "pagan" images or by the Maya themselves as a result of internal turmoil.

Pottery served a role as social currency in Maya society. Often used as gifts to secure and proclaim support, painted vessels of the Late Classic period represent a myriad of styles, mirroring the complex politics of the age. Works such as this fine example often depicted imagery drawn from religious teachings and mythology as well as specific moments from Maya history and ritual.

Maya painters approached cylindrical vessels in two ways. They first divided the vase's exterior into two halves, repeating the scene on both faces. Or, as in the case of this vessel, they created a continuous painting that wraps completely around the vase. This work depicts a priest with an elaborate headdress. A fish is nibbling the lotus blossom, an image similar to work found at Copan, the great Maya ceremonial center. The priest sits between two serpents with a monkey on a third serpent, which probably refers to the god *Quetzlquatl.*

In Maya society artists were learned and literate, probably limited to the priesthood and the nobility, including royal offspring not in line for the throne. In the Mayan language the verb *ts'ib* can mean to paint, draw, and write as one, being regarded technically and conceptually as the same activity.

The activity in which they seem to excel over all other human intellects and which makes them appear unique among the nations of the earth is the craft they have perfected representing with real feathers, in all their natural colors, all the things that they and other excellent painters can paint with brushes.

Bartolomé de las Casa (1527-1550)
Apoligetica historica

SUGGESTED READINGS:

de las Casa, Bartolomé, trans. Bill B. DeGeer. **Christian Harvest or A Very Brief Account of the Destruction of the Indies.** *New York: Carlton Press, 1988.*

Reents-Budet, Dorie. **Painting the Maya Universe: Royal Ceramics of the Classic Period.** *Durham and London: Duke University Press, 1994.*

Schele, Linda. **The Blood of Kings: Dynasty and Ritual in Maya Art.** *New York: George Braziller and the Kimball Art Museum, 1986.*

ALN

Classic Mexica (Aztec)
CEREMONIAL BLOCK WITH RELIEF CARVING, *1324-1521*
Basalt stone
H: 7 1/2 inches
Museum purchase, 1960.13

The Mexica, or Aztec drew their power from a loose patchwork of alliances bound together by a network of taxes and tributes. They had migrated to the Valley of Mexico by the mid-12th century and built a civilization on the foundations, both literal and figurative, of the people of Teotihuacán, who proceeded them. According to legend, the war god Huitzilopochtli ordered a priest to search for a great eagle perched in a cactus, which, in turn, marked the region that would be their new home. This led them to the place of the prickly pear cactus, on the south end of Lake Texcoco, the site of present day Mexico City. Here they founded their great capital Tenochtitlan. In 1519, when the Spanish arrived, Montezuma ruled more than five million subjects from northern Mexico to the border of Guatemala and from the Gulf of Mexico to the Pacific Ocean.

This black volcanic rock is carved on three sides, indicating it was probably used as a foundation or cornerstone. Some traces of mortar lie in deeper recesses, but there is no trace of stucco or paint. Like the "pagan idols" described by the classic narrative of Bernal Diaz del Castillo, *The Discovery and Conquest of Mexico, 1517-1521*, this carving may have been brightly painted. On the top surface is the 17th Aztec day sign, Ollin. Accompanying the sign are four day markers, recording the date as 4-Ollin (4-Movement) in the highland Mexican calendrical system.

Obtained in 1960 from a California dealer, who had acquired the work from a Mexican collector, the stone possibly relates to the sun and heavens. The depiction of the feathered serpent probably refers to the revered Aztec deity *Quetzalcoatl*, which translated from the native Nahuatl language means "plumed serpent." This god participated in the creation of the earth, was the king who ruled the Valley of Mexico before the arrival of the Aztec, and was later banished from the valley. Legend provided he would return in the year 1519, which unfortunately and coincidentally was the year Cortez arrived—the year of "One Reed." Montezuma was convinced he was the returning Toltec god. Montezuma, as each of his predecessors, had assumed the throne upon the reading of an ancient Toltec passage:

> Remember that this is not your throne but that it is only lent to you and that one day it will be returned to Quetzalcoatl, to whom it truly belongs.

ALN

SUGGESTED READINGS:

Emmerich, Andre. **Sweat of the Sun and Tears of the Moon**. Seattle: University of Washington Press, 1965.

Kon, Michael, Clement Meighan and H.B. Nicholson. **Sculpture of Ancient West Mexico: A Catalogue of the Proctor Stafford Collection at the Los Angeles County Museum of Art. Los Angeles: Los Angeles County Museum of Art** (published in association with the University of New Mexico Press), 1989.

Nicholson, Henry B with Eloise Quiñones Keber. **Art of Aztec Mexico: Treasures of Tenochtitlan**. Washington, D.C.: National Gallery of Art, 1983.

Northern Peru

Early Chavin period

STIRRUP-SPOUT VESSEL, *around 1220-1000 B.C.*

Terra-cotta

H: 9 1/2 inches

Museum purchase, 1973.23

The Chavin united the ancient world of pre-Columbian Peru for the first time more than 3,000 years ago. Blending cultures on the coast and highlands, the Chavin shared a single religion, technology, and culture. Elements of local pottery styles were incorporated into this very distinctive art form, which excelled in the production of ceramics. The ceramics tradition was present in Peru as early as 1800 B.C. and to the north in Ecuador as early as 3500–3000 B.C.

The culture's name is derived from the archaeological site, Chavin de Huantar, in the north central highlands of Peru. Describing the site in 1616, Spaniard Vasquez de Espinosa wrote it was "an ancient oracle and pilgrimage center to which people journeyed from all parts of Peru." Even today, the massive city is an awesome sight to behold.

This vessel represents one variant of the Chavin style known as *Cupisnique*, named for the small valley located between the Chicama and Jequetepeque valleys. Characterized by a thick tubular spout defining a small arch and with large flaring lips atop the squat opening, the surface decorations are continued onto the arch of the spout. The skillful use of texture, in this case a highly abstracted organic motif, enhances the three-dimensional qualities of the decoration. The characteristic black ceramic surface is a result of smudge firing rather than oxidation firing.

The reasons for the distinctive stirrup-handle spout form, which originated with the Chavin, are unknown. It has been presumed to have had symbolic meaning for the ancient Peruvians. This form was used by numerous later cultures in Peru including the Moche, Lambayeque, and Chimú.

ALN

SUGGESTED READINGS:

Donnan, Christopher B. **Ceramics of Ancient Peru**. Los Angeles: Fowler Museum of Natural Cultural History, UCLA, 1992.

Mosley, Michael. **The Incas and their Ancestors: The Archaeology of Peru**. London: Thames and Hudson, 1992.

Peru (Paracas)
DOUBLE-SPOUT VESSEL, *around 300-100 B.C.*
Ceramic, painted resins, and pigments
7 1/4 x 9 1/2 inches
Museum purchase, 1973.49

Named for the archaeological site found in 1925 by the renowned Peruvian archaeologist Julio C. Tello on the Paracas Peninsula in southern Peru, this double-spout vessel is a classic example of this distinctive ceramic style. The surface is decorated with two stylized feline heads rendered in multicolored resin paints. This work is believed to be from the site of Chuco located south of the Paracas Peninsula.

The Paracas style dominated southern Peru from the Paracas Peninsula southward to the Ica Valley flourishing from approximately 800 to 100 B.C. These ceramics are noted for their brightly colored resin paints. This vessel is in remarkable condition considering the fragility of the resin paints, which were applied after the work was fired. Rounded bottoms and the double-spout and bridge form typify Paracas ceramics, although this unusual pot lacks a bridge. Paracas pottery was made with thin, even walls, combining modeling, combing, and paddle and anvil techniques. Designs were incised while the clay was still wet then smoothed and burnished.

Simplified feline masks are characteristic of Paracas ceramics. Throughout Peru and Meso-America the most powerful animal known, the jaguar or puma, became the focal point for a complex relationship between priests or shamans, the puma, and the people. As a result, imagery such as on the surface of this work reflected the strong influences of mythological and religious beliefs. This feline figure is closely related to the deity known as the "Occulate Being," characterized by large eyes formed by concentric circles and a jagged-tooth smile.

The Paracas practiced a complex funerary rite. Bodies of the deceased were mummified, lavishly clothed in elaborate woven textiles, for which the Paracas are best known, and accompanied by food and drink in highly decorated vessels and dishes, and weapons for use in the afterlife. Deep shaft tombs widened at the bottom to form a burial chamber were then excavated to contain the deceased and the abundant grave goods. One of the more intriguing facets of these burials has been the evidence of successful brain surgery, including the removal of brain tumors.

ALN

Suggested Readings:

Donnan, Christopher B. **Ceramics of Ancient Peru**. *Los Angeles: Fowler Museum of Natural Cultural History, UCLA, 1992.*

Morris, Craig and Adriana Von Hagen. **The Inka Empire and its Andean Origins**. *New York: Abbeville Press, 1993.*

Huari (Peru/Bolivia)
CONCH SHELL TRUMPET, *around A.D. 600-800*
Conch shell inlaid with jade, Spondylus, and other shells
H: 7 1/2 inches
Museum purchase, 1970.32

This exquisite conch shell object depicts a standing dignitary holding a bird-headed staff in each hand. Shells such as this were used as ceremonial trumpets by many pre-Columbian cultures. Few can match the power or regal quality of this example from the central coast of Peru.

The Huari (also known as Wari-Tiahuanaco) supplanted the Nazca people at the beginning of the 8th century. With a centralized capital for government and religion, unified irrigation and road systems, the Huari were able to draw the regional states of Peru's south coast into a single empire. Lasting until near A.D. 1000, it was not until the rise of the Inca that such a vast region was again unified in southern Peru.

This trumpet shell has been inlaid with what were considered by the ancient Peruvians to be extremely precious materials. The *Spondylus* shell, jade, and other shells carried trade and commerce importance for the Huari and other ancient Peruvian peoples trading up and down the vast region between the Andes and the Pacific Ocean.

The figure on the shell is seen wearing a poncho, the hallmark of the Huari weaver. Ponchos had special meaning as precious cultural artifacts and were found in all parts of the Huari empire. Woven with more weft than warp threads, the weft threads are interwoven to produce a completely weft-faced design with intricate color and detail. The iconography of the poncho has possible heraldic meaning, much like the later Inca shirts, *uchus*.

ALN

SUGGESTED READINGS:

Clifford, Paul. **Art of the Andes: Pre-Columbian Sculpted and Painted Ceramics**. Washington, D.C.: Arthur M. Sackler Foundation, 1983.

Morris, Craig and Adriana Von Hagen. **The Inca Empire and its Andean Origins**. New York: Abbeville Press, 1993.

Townsend, Richard F., ed. **The Ancient Americas: Art from Sacred Landscapes**. Chicago: The Art Institute of Chicago, 1992.

Chimú Culture (Peru)
FUNERARY MASK, *around A.D. 1100-1400*
Hammered gold, copper
10 1/2 x 16 1/2 inches
Museum purchase with funds provided by Mr. and Mrs. Ralf Kircher and
Mr. Louis Jacobs, 1967.46

For more than 500 years, this exquisite Chimú gold mask lay buried, undisturbed by Spanish conquistadors of the 16th century and generations of *huaceros*, as Peruvian grave robbers are known. Excavated in the 1960s near the ruins of Chan Chan, the ancient capital of the Chimú, this mask once adorned the mummy of a wealthy and prominent leader. It is one of the finest examples of a Chimú funerary work in the United States.

This work is exceptional for its completeness, being comprised of 35 separate pieces, its rare large size, and its elaborate execution and design. The intricate cutout anthropomorphic ornamentation on the ear flanges is notable. Although no traces of red cinnabar paint are found, the mask may very well have been painted and decorated with semiprecious stones, shells, and colorful feathers.

The Chimú empire, a highly sophisticated society that immediately proceeded the dominance of the Inca, flourished between A.D. 1100 and 1400. They occupied an area along the north coast of Peru ranging from the Ecuador border to near present-day Lima. Expanding the region of their predecessors, the Moche, they improved irrigation and drainage systems, extended networks of roads, and enlarged urban and ceremonial centers. The Chimú believed in an afterlife closely linked to their earthly world. The dead were prepared for their journey into the next life with elaborate tombs and copious amounts of goods buried alongside the departed. The carefully wrapped mummies were adorned with elaborate ornamentation, of which this mask was a part. It was probably sewn into the fabric wrappings of the mummy's head. The mask and other decorations played an important role in the intricate conveyance of the dead from this world into the next, as symbols of wealth and status and because they were believed to protect and beautify the dead.

Gold in Peruvian society, as in many cultures across the Americas, was revered as a precious commodity. Believed by the Inca to be the "sweat of the sun," gold possessed a mystical and religious quality. It was used only for ceremonial adornment of the dead, in temples and other sacred places, and in other ceremonial and status-conferring objects.

At the time of Francisco Pizarro's arrival in 1532, Peru enjoyed the richest supply of gold in the New World, mining an estimated six million ounces annually. Commenting on this abundance of wealth, the Spanish missionary and explorer Father Diego de Cordova wrote:

> "It is certain that the treasures of gold and silver and jewels that the Incas had exceeded beyond all comparison all those that all the Kings of the Earth had enjoyed."

ALN

Suggested Readings:

Fagen, Brian M. **Kingdoms of Gold, Kingdoms of Jade: The Americas Before Columbus**. *New York: Thames and Hudson, 1991.*

Kirkpatrick, S. **Lords of Sipan: A True Story of Pre-Inca Tombs, Archaeology and Crime**. *New York: Henry Halt, 1992.*

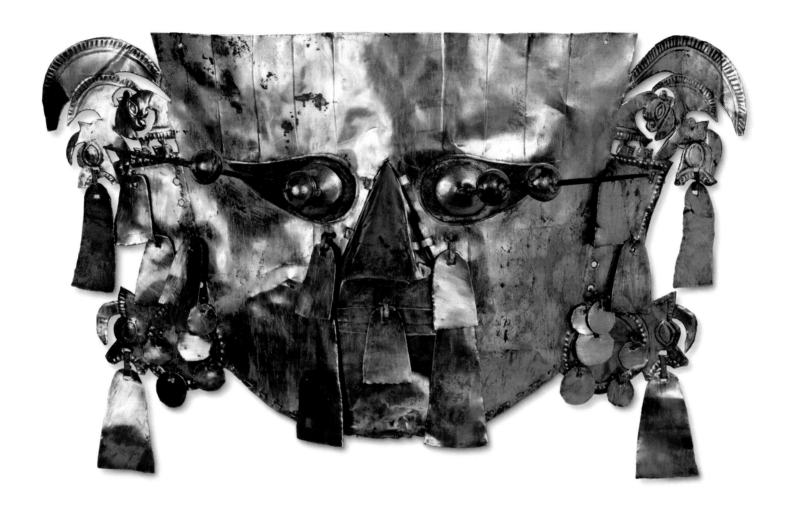

INDEX

T

V

DAI
DAI Softcover C

000332
$ 19.95

August 9-2008 Sandra, Sylvia, Donna, Rod